UNDERSTANDING PLANT BIOCHEMISTRY

By

Dr. Shubhrata R. Mishra

Deptt. of Botany
Vikram University
Ujjain (M.P.)
(India)

DISCOVERY PUBLISHING HOUSE PVT. LTD.

NEW DELHI-110 002

Published by:
Tilak Wasan
DISCOVERY PUBLISHING HOUSE PVT. LTD.
4831/24, Ansari Road, Prahlad Street
Darya Ganj, New Delhi-110002 (India)
Phone: +91-11-23279245, 43764432
Fax: +91-11-23253475
E-mail: parul.wasan@gmail.com
info@discoverypublishinggroup.com
discoverypublishinghouse@gmail.com
web: www.discoverypublishinggroup.com

First Edition: 2011
ISBN: 978-81-8356-863-0

Understanding Plant Biochemistry

Printed at:
Shree Balaji Art Press
Delhi

PREFACE

The present title "*Understanding Plant Biochemistry*" provides a structured approach to learning by covering all the important topics in a uniform, systematic format. The book has been comprehensively designed incorporating recent advances in this fast moving field. It is written to provide accessible information on plant biochemistry in compact form for undergraduate students in biology and related life sciences. It will be useful for both beginning students and those who are more advanced. In addition, busy lecturers who require a quick reference compendium will find it useful, particularly for tutional planning. Simple, yet hopefully clear figures and tables are provided throughout the book.

The over-riding goal of this book, and indeed of the whole *Understanding series,* is to present the essential information concering microbiology in a compact, readily accessible form which leads itself to student learning and revision. The convergence of various approaches has generated a rich panorama of detail, the significance of which we are still attempting to unraval. The present text has been written as an introduction to this rapidly growing field.

To make the work more comprehensive and informative, the author has consulted many authoritative books, research journals, abstracts, monographs etc., so there can be no claim to originality except in the manner of treatment.

The author expresses his thanks to his friends and colleagues whose continue inspirations have initiated him to bring out this book.

The author expresses his gratitude to Mr. Wasan and staff of M/s Discovery Publishing House Pvt. Ltd. for their whole hearted co-operation in the publication of this book.

In the mean time, the author will remain sincerely responsible for any shortcomings of the book and be grateful to the readers for their suggestions and constructive criticism for the continuous betterment of the book. He takes this opportunity to appeal to the readers to send their suggestions straightaway to his Publisher.

Author

CONTENTS

INTRODUCTION

F*riedrich Miescher* in (1868) isolated a material from pus cells by digesting them for weeks with dilute HCl and called this material as *nuelein*. *Hoppe Segler* and his co-workers confirmed the work of *Miescher* and also proved the presence of nuclein in yeast and the erythocytes of the birds and reptiles and various other tissues.

The term *nucleic acid* was introduced by *Altrnann*. *Albrecht Kassel*, *P.A. Levine and Walter Jones* described the chemical nature of nucleic acid. According to them the nucleic acid is composed of phosphoric acid, a sugar and nitrogenous bases.

Franklin W. Stahl presented first evidence that nucleic acid forms the genetic material. *Chargoff* (1951) described the occurrence of nitrogenous bases in equal proportions. *Dotty* 1961) has emphasized much on the physical properties of DNA.

In 1962 *Willkins*, *Kiatson* and *Crick* proposed *a* model to explain the d,)uble helicular structure of DNA. They also shared the Nobel Prize for the same.

DEOXYRIBONUCLEIC ACID OR DNA

DNA is found in the cells of all living organisms except plant viruses, where RNA fo rms the *genetic material* and DNA is absent. In bacteriophages and viruses there is a single molecule of DNA, which remains coiled and is enclosed in the *protein coat*. In bacteria, mitochondria and plastids of eukaryotic cells DNA is circular and lies naked in the *cytoplasm*. In the nuclei of *eukaryotic* cells DNA occurs in the forms of long *spirally* coiled and unbranched threads. The number of DNA molecules is equivalent to the number of chromosomes per cell.

In them DNA is found in combination with proteins forming nucleoproteins—the *Chromatin* material and is enclosed in the nucleus. DNA is a polymer, the monomeres of which are the deoxyribonucleoside monophosphates.

Most DNA have high molecular weight, varying from 10' to 10' or more. Chemical analysis of DNA molecules from different kinds of organisms suggest that in one kind of DNA the number of adenine (A) nucleotides was always the same as the number of *thymine* (T) *nucleotides*.

Similarly the number of guanine (G) nucleotides was always the same as the number of cytosine (C) nucleotides. This evidence suggests that nucleotides occur in pairs in the DNA molecule.

Further, quantity of A present in one organism's DNA (and it varies from species to spocies) is equal precisely to the amount of T. Similarly the amount of G present is always equal to the amount of C.

PHYSICAL STRUCTURE OF DNA

According to the model proposed by *Watson* and *Crick*, the DNA contains two polynucleotide chains running antiparallel and twisted around each other in the form of a regular double helix Figure elsewhere in this chapter. The diameter of the *helix* is about 20A and each chain makes a complete turn every 34A.

Each chain is polynucleotide in which the sugar of each nucleotide is linked by a phosphate group to the sugar of the *adjacent nucleotide*. There are 10 nucleotides on each chain in every turn of the helix. The two helices are coiled in such a way that they cannot be *separated* without *unwinding*.

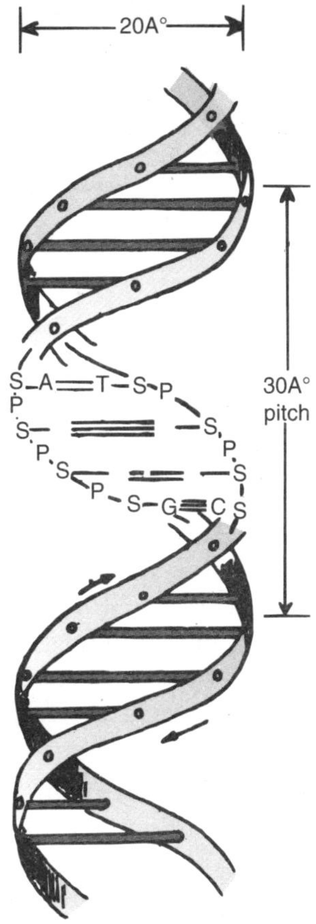

Figure 1.1: The Watson-Crick base pair in DNA,"Adenine-Thymine, and Guanine-Cyrosine.

The two chains of a *helix* are of opposite polanty. In one chain ruins in 3'-5' direction, then the other will run as 5'-3' direction. The *molecular* weight for purified DNA is found in the tsaoge 1000,000 to 120 × 10'. The amount of DNA in a mammalian cell correspounds to about 25,000 molecules of molecular weight 120 × 10^4, a total of about 10,000 million nucleotides.

MOLECULAR STRUCTURE OF DNA

The DNA molecule is a polymer consisting of several'

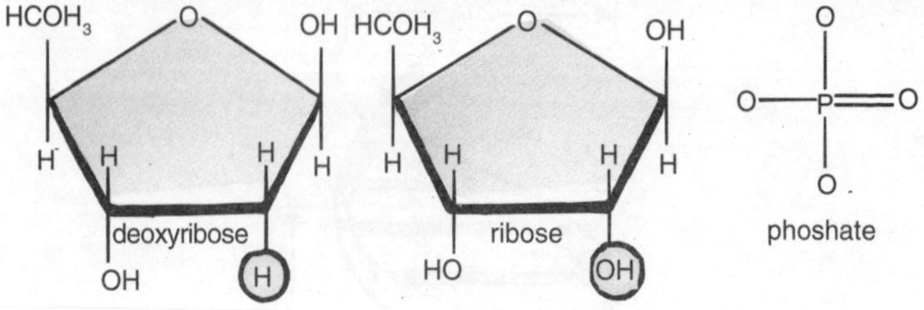

Figure 1.2: Pentose Sugar.

thousand pairs of nucleotide monomers. Each nucleotide consist of the pentose sugar, Figure. *deoxyribose, a phosphate* group and *nitrogenous base,* which may be either a *purine* or a *pyrimidine.*

Deoxyribose Sugar

Levine (1909) identified ribose sugar as a main constituent of nucleic acid structure. *Mori* (1929) isolated sugar from the uanine nucleoside and showed that it is deoxyribose sugar. It s pentose type which in DNA molecule shows the *absence* of ine oxygen molecule from carbon-2 position of ribose sugar.

Both deoxyribose and ribose (pentose sugars of nucleic acids) lave a pentagonal ring with five carbons, among which two (*i.e.* 3' and 5') are attached to phosphoric acid and three (1') to the base.

This sugar is called *deoxyribose* and it simply acts a support column to which bases are attached.

Phosphate

In the DNA strand the phosphate groups alternate with deoxyribose. Each phosphate group is joined to carbon atom 3' of one deoxyribose and to carbon atom 5' of another.

Thus each strand has a 3' end and a 5' end. The two strand are oriented in opposite directions.

The 3' end of one strand corresponds to the 5' end of the other. Consequently the oxygen atoms of deoxyribose point in opposite directions in the two strands. *Phosphodi-*

Table 1.1: Four nitrogen bases, nucleosides and nucleotides of DNA molecule.

Nitrogen base	*Base+deoxyribose =deoxyribonucleo-side*	*Deoxyribonucleoside +Phosphoric acid= Deoxyribonueleotide*	*Abbreviation for nucleotide*
1. Adenine (A)	Deoxyadenosine	Deoxyadenylic acid (Deoxyadenosine monophosphate)	3'-dAMP
2 Guanine (G)	Deoxyguanosine	Deoxyguanylic acid (Deoxyguanosine monophosphate)	3'-dGMP
3. Cytosine (C)	Deoxycytidine	Deoxycytidylic acid (Deoxycytidine monophosphate)	5'-dCMP
4. Thymine (T)	Deoxyhymidine	Thymidylic acid (Deoxythymidine monophosphate)	5'-dTMP

ester bonds are formed between the sugars of two different nucleotides and a phosphate group.

Nitrogenous Bases

The nitrogenous bases of nucleic acid are of two types '*urine* and *Pyrimidine*. Purine bases comprise mainly *adenine* (A) and *guanine* (G) which are common to both DNA and RNA while *pyrimidine* bases comprise *cytosine* (C) and *thymine* (T) in DNA and in the cases of RNA, thymine (T) is replaced by *uracil* (U).

These bases are arranged linearly as the back bones of chains which (back bones) are composed of alternating sugar and phosphate. The bases have specific way of combining, if C is found in one chain G will be opposite to it and in other if A is on one T must be on the other. Or in other words adenine (A) is always paired with thymine (T) and guanine (G) with cytosine (C).

Among bases A-T and G-C, two hydrogen bonds are formed between A and T and three hydrogen bonds are formed between C and G. This hydrogen bond formation precludes A-C or G-T pairs Table elsewhere in this chapter. Only these arrangements A-T and G-C are possible, for two purines would occupy too much space to allow a regular helix and correspondingly, two pyrimidines would occupy too little.

The stickness of these pairing rules in a complementary, relation between the sequences of bases on the two *interwined* chains. For example, if we have a sequence ATGTC on one chain, the opposite chain must have a sequence TACAG.

The hydrogen atom with its positive charge is shared between an oxygen atom and a nitrogen atom, both with slight negative charges. Although *hydrogen* bonds are weak, the fact that there are so many gives stability to the DNA molecule. The weak hydrogen bonding enables the two strands of the DNA to separate during replication.

The bases are joined to the pentoses by N-C *glycosidic bonds*. For the purine, the glycosidic bond is between the C_1 position of the pentose sugar and the N_9 position of the bases. For the pyrimidines the linkage joins the C_1 and N_3 *positions*.

Nucleosides and Nucleotides

A sugar molecule and a nitrogenous base form a *nucleoside*, and a nucleoside plus a phosphate group form a *nucleotide*. In other words a nucleoside is a base-sugar *combination* and a nucleotide is a nucleoside phosphate.

The nucleotides of RNA are called *ribonucleotides*, and those of DNA deoxyribonucleo-tides. *Ribonucleotides* contain the sugar ribose, and deoxyri bonucleotides the sugar deoxyribose. The *nucleosides* are usually abbreviated as A, T, G or C, with d-as a prefix for *deoxynucle-osides* (e.g. dG- is the abbreviation for deoxy *gnanosine*.

Structural Variation in DNA

The double helicular nature of the DNA has been proved by a number of workers using the isotope and besides this single stranded DNA and *circular* shaped DNA, having the same chemical composition have beeh observed. Thus after the discovery of such *abnormal* variety of DNA, one can placethem under the following headings:

1. Double stranded DNA
2. Single stranded DNA
3. Circular DNA

Double Stranded DNA

This is the common DNA present in all the living organisms. These contain two polynucleotide chain running *antiparallel* and twisted around each other in the form of a regular double helix. The detailed *structure* of this type of DNA has already been explained.

Table 1.2: Showing amount of various bases in different tissues.

S. No.	*Source*	*Adenine*	*Guanine*	*Cytosine*	*Thymine*	*A+T G+C*
1.	Human liver	30.3	19.5	19.9	30.3	1.53
2.	Human sperm	30.7	19.3	18.8	31.2	1.62
3.	Hen red cells	28.8	20.5	21.5	29.2	1.38
4.	Rat bone narrow	28.6	21.4	21.5	28.4	1.33
5.	Herring sperm	27.8	22.2	22.6	27.5	1.23
6.	*Paracentrotus* lividus (sea urchin) sperm	32.8	17.7	18.4	32.1	1.85
7.	Salmon	29.7	20.8	20.4	29.1	1.43
8.	Wheat germ	26.5	23.5	23.0	27.0	1.19
9.	Yeast	31.3	18.7	17.1	32.9	1.79
10.	Diplococcus pneumoniae	29.8	205	18.0	31.6	1.59
11.	K-12 Escherichla coil	26.0	24.9	25.2	23.9	1.04
12.	Mycobacterium tuberculosis	15.1	34.9	35.4	14.6	0.42
13.	Bacteriophate T_2	32.5	18.2	16.7	32.6	1.86

Single Stranded DNA

At first it was thought that all DNA molecules are double stranded except during *replication*, when small portion near the Y regions are temporarily in a *non-hydrogen bonded*, single *stranded* form.

Many people were surprised, therefore, when conclusive experiments revealed that the DNA of several groups of small bacterial viruses exists normally as single stranded *molecules*. This single stranded DNA is having the same *chemical* composition as we find in the double stranded DNA.

Circular Shaped DNA

The circular form of the DNA has been observed recently in oolvma virus. In *E. coil chromosome* (*DNA molecule*), the circular shaped DNA has also been seen. The linear molecule of the DNA can be converted into the circular form but we do not know the *chemistry* of *converting*

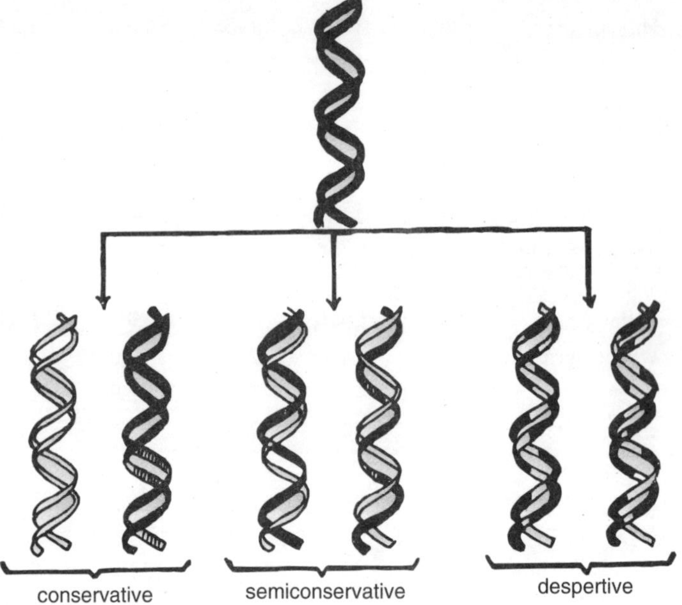

Figure 1.3: A diagram illustrating three possible modes of DNA replication.

a linear molecule of DNA into circular form. When the phage-DNA molecule is isolated from the free phage, it is linear in shape. However, by *controlled* heating and *recooling* it can be reversibly converted to a *circular* form.

Z-DNA OR LEFT HANDED DNA

On the basis of the arrangement of pentose sugar forming chains of DNA two forms of DNA have been reported. Usually the sugar chain has the pentose sugar with ascending sequence of carbon atoms.

This is the right handed DNA or B-DNA. Recently in 1979, another form of DNA having pentose sugar with descending arrangement of *carbon atom* has been reported and named Z-DNA or left handed DNA.

BIOLOGICAL REPLICATION OF DNA

Study of replication of DNA is one of the interesting aspect of molecular control of heredity. Various study of the duplication of genetic material was presented from time to time in different organisms. But most of them are discarded because no concrete ideas have been proposed till *Watson* and *Crick* proposed a detailed scheme for the molecular structure of DNA.

Later on, *Korenberg*, *Stahl* and *Taylor* have confirmed the Watson-Crick hypothesis. They also made a suggestion for its mode of replication which follows in a natural and attractive fashion from the proposed structure. During the *replication*, the DNA duplicates exactly into two chains. In the beginning both the strands of double stranded DNA, apart from each other by the *disolution* of *hydrogen* bonds and thus *uncoiling* of the chains occur.

And then new chains "the *complementary chains*" are built on them so that the newly formed daughter chains are the mirror images of each other Figure elsewhere in this chapter.

Mechanism of DNA Replication

The entire process of DNA replication involves following steps in *E. coli:*

Recognition of the Initiation Point

Replication of DNA begins at a specific point; called initiation point. Specific initiator proteins are required to recognise the *initiation* point on DNA.

The initiator protein along with DNA directed RNA polymerase initiates the synthesis of RNA primer for the formation of new DNA chain.

Unwinding of DNA

The unwinding prote id to the nicked strand of the *duplex* and open up a lobuble, separating the two strands or DNA duplex.

RNA priming

The DNA directed RNA polymerase now synthesizes the primer strands of RNA (*RNA primer*). The priming RNA strands are complementary to the two strands of DNA and are formed of 50 to 100 nucleotides.

Formation of DNA on RNA primers

The new strands of DNA are formed in the 5'-3' direction -om the 3'-5' template DNA by the addition of deoxyribouclеotides to the 3' end of RNA primer.

The addition is Tected by DNA polymerase III in the presence of ATP. The *awinding* proteins separate the duplex strands ahead of the application fork. The leading strand of DNA synthesized in 5'-3' direction.

The following strand of DNA is formed in its opposite direction to DNA strands are synthesized in short segments, consisting of 1,000 to 2,000 nucleotides. These segments are called *Okazaki fragments*.

Excision of RNA primers

Once a small segment of an Okazaki fragment has been ned, the nucleotides of RNA primer are removed from the nd one by one by the action of 5'-3' exonuclease activity of A polymerase-I.

Joining of Okazaki fragments

The gaps left between Okazaki fragments are filled with

complementary deoxyribonucleotide residues by DNA polynierase I. Finally the adjacent 5' and 3' ends are joined by DNA ligase.

In eukaryotic cells the mechanism of DNA replication is expected to be more complex than in *prokaryotes*. The replication of eukaryotic DNA begins at multiple points of origin. Their RNA primer is formed of about 10 nucleotides and the *Okazaki fragments* are much shorter (about 1000 to 150 *nucleotides*).

Enzymes for DNA synthesis

Different prokaryotic and eukaryotic cells have been formed to contain three kinds of enzymes that act on DNA namely nucleases, *polymerases* and *ligases*.

Nuclease enzymes

These enzymes attack on the *DNA molecules* directly. There are two type of nuclease enzyme

(*a*) *Exonuclease enzyme*. The exonuclease begins its activity either at a free 3'-OH end of a *polynucleotide* and *progressively* cleave the bands as the 3'-OH side of the phosphodiester back bone or it begins at a free 5'-P end and digests the polynucleotides in a 5'-3', direction. In both the cases the enzyme travels along the chain in a stepwise manner.

(*b*) *Endonuclease enzyme*. Endonuclease enzyme also attacks one of the two sides of phosphodiester linkages, but they react only with those bonds that occur within the interior of a polynucleotide chain.

If the polynucleotide chain in single stranded (e.g., viral DNA) such an attack will *obviously* cut the chain into two piecies. If however, the polynucleotide strand is a member of a DNA helix (e.g., *prokaryotic* and eukaryotic DNA), a single endonucleolytic cut will create a nick in the *helix*; the *helix* remain in one piece but it now *possesses* a gap that contains two free ends, which can serve as substrates for exonucleases.

A nicked double helix suffers a localized disruption of its secondary structure. The molecules becomes free to bend or rotate around its intact strand and the two broken ends are free to *dangle*. The increased molecular motion in the region of the nick will very likely *interrupt* hydrogen bonding between bases in the vicinity of the nick, thus effecting a limited "*unraveling*" of the helix.

DNA Polymerase

For many years, *Korenberg polymerase* was believed to be the enzyme responsible for the replication of the *E. coli* chromosome. But recently *Delucla* and *Cairus* isolated a true *replicase* from *E. coli* and named as *DNA polymerase*.

The polymerase catalyses the formation of a polymer. The synthesis of a new complementary chain becomes possible in the presence of *polymerase* enzyme. There are three *categories* of DNA *nolvmerase* enzymes.

DNA polymerase I

Discovered by *Korenberg* in 1955 and has been studied in *E. coli*. It is believed to take part in the repair of DNA. DNA polymerase I is a single polypeptide chain with a molecular weight of about 109,000. There may be as many as 400 molecule of DNA polymerase I in *E. coli*.

DNA polymerase II

It is also made up of a single polypeptide chain having a molecular weight of about 90,000. The number of DNA polymerase II molecule is about 40 in *E. coli*. This enzyme can elongate Okazaki segments even in the absence of poly merase I.

DNA polymerase III

It is considered to be a true replicase of *E. coli*. It consists. of two polypeptide chains with molecular weight of 140,000 and 40,000. It is most effective and can polymersize about 15000 nucleotides per minute in *E. coli*.

DNA Ligases

DNA ligase enzymes are capable of *catalyzing phosphodiester* bond formation between free 3'-OH and free 5'-P groups of a nick of DNA which is created by endonuclease enzyme, thereby restoring an intact DNA duplex. Many DNA ligases have already been discovered.

The ligase enzyme from *E. coli* requires the presence of oxidized nicotinamide adenine dinucleotide (NAD*) a cofactor, whereas, the ligase enzyme specified by *T. bacteriophage* requires ATP to bring about the joining reaction.

RNA primers in DNA replication

Short segments of RNA are first synthesized before actual DNA replication starts. These RNA segments are later excised and filled with DNA with the help of enzyme DNA polymerase I.

It was found that if RNA synthesis is stopped by a drug rifampicin, DNA replication stops thus proving the role of RNA primers in DNA replication. There are several other evidences which established this point.

Types of replication

Three different types of replication of DNA have been discovered:

(1) Semiconservative

(2) Conservative

(3) Dispersive

Semiconservative

Here the replication of DNA involves the unwinding of the double helix, but no rupture of the separated *polynuclotide* strands. Thus the primary DNA is causevned during the replication process.

According to this mechanism, the unwinding of the original strands would be accompanied or followed by the guided synthesis of the complementary strands of each of the two separated polynucleotide strands.

The linearly *assembly*, *catalyzed* by *enzymes*, of the *nucleotides* of the complementary sequence would be guided by their paining with the Watson-crick partners on the *original* strands. In this manner the proper nucleotide sequence would be automatically assumed. The DNA helix would thereby regenerated each of the strand of the original helical duplex uniting with its freshly synthesized complement to form a total of two new double stranded structures.

The *semi-convervative* model thus predicts that entire polynucleotide strands of the parental DNA will be passed on to the progeny in intact form. Each molecule of *progeny* DNA will receive either one half or none of its nucleotides from the parental DNA.

Conservative

According to this *mechanism* both the primary and secondary structure of the parental DNA are conserved. Thus the *replication* process would involve neither the rupture of the individual strands nor the unwinding of the helical *duplex*.

The details of these propose that the sequences of hydrogen bonded base pairs, rather than individual bases, serves the *genetic determinant*. According to this picture, particular base pairs might preferentially bind specific nucleotides and determine their sequential position in the daughter *polynucleotide*. The convervative model allows for no redistribution of parental DNA among the progeny. The original DNA is transferred as an intact unit or not at all.

Dispersive

Into this class fall all mechanisms which postulate a

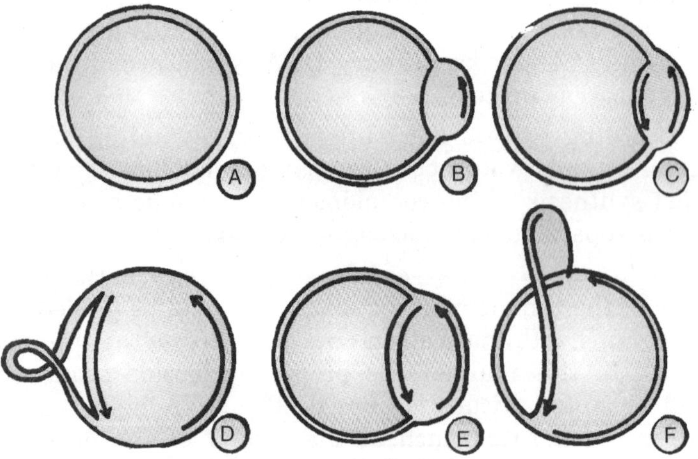

Figure 1.4: Cairn's model for circular DNA replication.

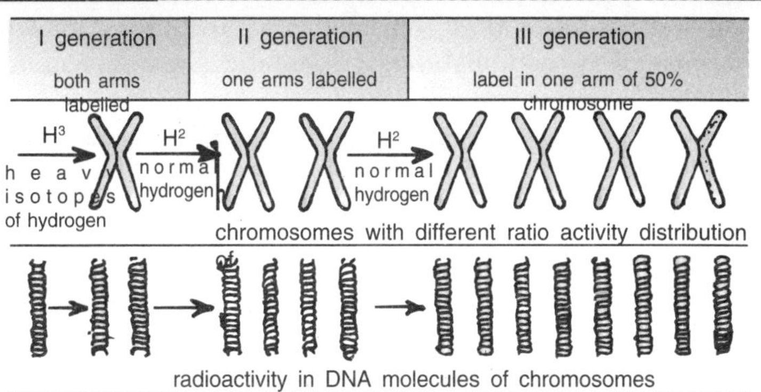

Figure 1.5: Taylor's experiment on Vicia faba.

general break up of the parental DNA and its more or less uniform distribution among the progeny.

It is difficult to propose a model of this type which can possibly allow the preservation of nucleotide sequence. Moreover, the existing experimental evidence is uniformly *inconsistent* with this kind of scheme.

Hybrid DNA

When double helical DNA molecules are heated above physiological temperature (to near 100°C), their hydrogen bonds break and the complementary strands often separate from each other (*DNA denaturation or melting*).

If cooled slowly, the two complementary strands can meet and reform the normal double helix. This process of reunion is called *denaturation* or *annealing*. This ability to renature DNA molecules permits as to show that artificial hyrid DNA molecules can be formed by slowly cooling mixture of denatured DNA from two species.

For example, hybrid molecules can be formed containing one strand from man and one from a mouse. Only a fraction (25%) of the DNA strands from a man can form hybrids with mouse DNA.

This is, of course not surprising since it merely means that some genes of a man are very similar to those of a mouse, whereas others have quite different nucleotide sequences.

It now appears that this molecular technique may be quite useful in establishing the genetic similerity of the various taxonomic groups.

EVIDENCE IN SUPPORT OF SEMICONSERVATIVE REPLICATION OF DNA

Meselson and Stahl's Experiment

(*i*) *Meselson* and *Sthal* 1958) cultured a species of bacteria (*Escherichia cola*) in a culture medium containing N^{15} isotopes of nitrogen. After these had replicated for a few generations in that medium both the strands of their DNA contained N^{15} as constituent of purines and pyrimidines.

When these bacteria with N^{15} were transferred in cultural medium containing N^{14}, it was found that DNA separated from fresh generation of bacteria possesses one strand heavier than the other.

The heavier strand represents the parental strand and lighter one is the new one synthesized from the culture indicating semiconservative method of DNA replication.

(*ii*) Density determination experiments were also conducted. The DNA of parental generation (labelled with N'^{5}) was found to be heaviest. In first generation it was lighter than the first one. In second generation two bands

Table 1.3: Genetic RNA in Different Viruses.

Type of Viruses	*Name of Viruses*	*Type of RNA*
1. Plant viruses	1. TMV	1. Single stranded
	2. Wound tumour	2. Double stranded
2. Animal viruses	3. Influenza virus	3. Single stranded
	4. Poliomyelitis	4. Single stranded
	5. Reo virus	5. Double stranded
3 Bacteriophages	6. MS_2	6. Single stranded
	7. F_2	7. Single stranded
	8. r_{17}	8. Single stranded

were observed indicating the presence of DNA with two different densities, as is expected according to semiconservative method of DNA replication.

These two bands were of equal intensity in the second generation. In the subsequent generations the intensity of light density bands gradually increased and the intensity of hybrid density band gradually decreased.

Cairn's Autoradiography Experiment

J. Cairns demonstrated the semiconservative type of replication by using a technique of autoradiograpby as given in the following lines:

In autoradiography technique, the material is first supplied with a suitable radioactive material like tritiated thymidine (H'-TdR ; H^3 is heavy isotope of hydrogen and it replaces normal hydrogen in thymidine to give rise to tritiated thymidine).

Tritiated thymidine is used since this will selectively label only DNA and will not label RNA, since thymine base is absent in RNA. The tritiated thymidine gets incorporated into DNA and replaces ordinary thymidine.

The material is then sectioned or else the cells may be broken down to release the intact bacterial chromosome on slides. These slides are then covered by photographic emulsion and stored in the dark.

During this storage the particles emitted by tritiated thymidine will expose the film, which can be developed. This photograph will then show the regions of the presence of tritium and thus. indirectly the presence of labelled DNA. Using this above technique, the replication of DNA could be easily followed by *J. Cairns* and the results were reported in 1963.

During incorporation of tritiated thymidine, autoradio graphs could be prepared at regular known intervals. Autoradiographs from this replicating material prepared at regular known intervals demonstrated semi-conservative mode of replication.

It would be expected that in regions, where one cycle of replication of DNA has been completed, the density of dots will be higher than in the region where the replication has not taken place.

The lighter density of dots is considered to indicate that only one of the two strands is labelled, while a heavier density of dots will indicate that both strands are labelled. Such a situation was actually observed.

The rate at which the replication proceeds could also be worked out by measuring the length of DNA undergoing replication in a known interval of time. The generation time was worked out by *Cairns* as 30 minutes in *E. coli*.

The length of the chromosome was worked out to be about 1 mm. The rate of replication as obvious would be approximately 30μ to 40μ per minute. (1 mm =l000μ).

Figure elsewhere in this chapter indicates that after replication, one of the two rands in the daughter DNA molecules is derived from the trent molecule and the other is synthesized afresh.

In θ shaped figure, which is obtained in the second cycle of repliition in presence of label, the two arcs in the split region ould never be equally labelled.

For instance, one arc would be twice as heavily labelled as the other arc. This is what was actually observed by *Cairns*. Thus the observation support the semi-conservative type of replication of DNA.

Taylor's Experiment on Vicia Tabs Root Tips

J.H. Taylor (1957) and his coworkers also demonstrated the semiconservative method of DNA duplication in the root tip cells of *Vicia faba* by autoradiography.

The roots were grown in a medium containing radioactive thymidine, so that the radioactivity is incorporated in the DNA of these cells. The outline of this labelled chromosome on a photographic film appears in the form of scattered black dots of silver grains.

When these root tips with labelled chromosomes were

transferred to the unlabelled medium containing colchicine and studied for radioactivity, the following observations were made:

1. In the chromosomes of first generation the radioactivity was found to be uniformly distributed in both the on romatids, because in them the original strand of DNA double helix was labelled with radioactivity and the new one was nonlabelled.
2. In the chromosomes of second generation only one of the two chromatids in each chromosome was radioactive.

This experiment demonstrates the semiconservative method of chromosome replication. But as it is known that each chromatid is composed of only one double helical molecule of DNA, it is the replication of DNA.

BIOLOGICAL SIGNIFICANCE OF DNA

There are four general requirements that genetic material can be expected to fulfil

(*i*) That it replicates itself accurately during cell growth and duplication.

(*ii*) That its structure be sufficiently stable so that heritable changes, mutation occur only very rarely.

(*iii*)That it has the potentiality to carry all kinds of necessary biological information.

(*iv*) That it transmits the informations to the cell.

RIBONUCLEIC ACID (RNA)

Ribonucleic acid usually occurs in nature as long unbranched polymeric molecule formed of single chain. RNA is generally present in the cytoplasm as well as in nucleolus. *Casperson* 1950 and *Brachet* in 1955 suggested that there is an association between RNA and protein synthesis.

A large number of studies have been undertaken to characterise physically the nature and structure of RNA and their biochemical properties and by now we have acquired a lot of knowledge about the various types of RNA and their molecular structures but still there are various gaps to be filled to make a complete picture.

Some plant viruses (e.g., TMV, turnip yellow mosaic viruses, wound tumour viruses, etc.,), animal viruses (e.g., influenza viruses, foot and mouth viruses; rous sarcoma viruses, poliomyelitis viruses reoviruses etc.) and bacteriophages (e.g., MS2, etc.) contain ribonucleic acid (RNA) as their genetic material. That is why in these cases it is called the *Genetic RNA*.

PRIMARY STRUCTURE OF RNA

RNA usually occur in nature as long unbranched polymeric molecule made up of single chain of helix of polynucleotide strand Ribnucleic acid is composed of pentose sugars, phosphoric acid and nitrogenous bases. The pentose sugar of RNA is ribose sugar.

The sugar forms the back bone along with the phosphoric acid just in a manner studied in DNA. Phosphoric acid is also one of the constituent of the RNA which along with the pentose sugar forms the back bone, or which the nitrogenous bases are linearly arranged, as shown in the Figure elsewhere in this chapter.

On the basis of phosphate or phosphoric acid, the chemical constituents of RNA can be written in two ways:

Nitrogenous Base+ Ribose Sugar+Phosphate = Nucleotides

Nitrogenous Base+Ribose Sugar=Nucleoside

The nitrogenous bases of ribonucleic acid are of two types

(*i*) Purine

(*ii*) Pyrimidine.

Purine bases comprise mainly adenine (A) and guanine (G) while pyrimidine bases comprise cytosine (C) and Uracil (U). These bases are joined to the pentoses by N-C *glycosidic bonds*.

For the purine bases the glycosidic bond is between the

C_1 position of the pentose sugar and the N_9 position of the base. For the pyrimidines, the linkage joins the C_1 and N_1 positions as shown in figure elsewhere in this chapter.

The bases are arranged on the back bone of the chain which is composed of alternating sugar and phosphate. The bases are attached to the ribose sugar in the same way, the bases in DNA are attached.

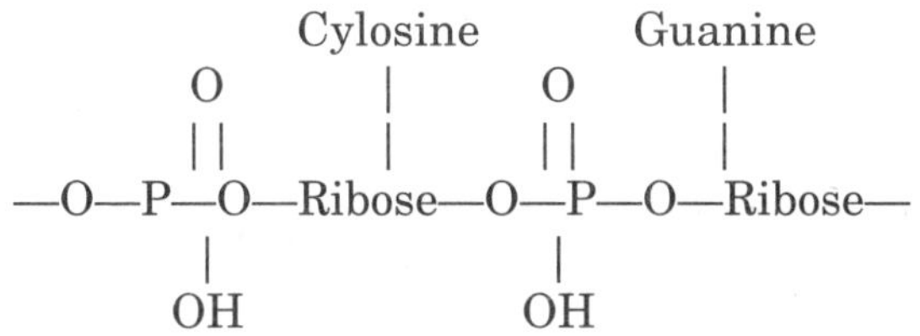

The arrangement of the bases on the back bone is shown in Figure elsewhere in this chapter.

SECONDARY STRUCTURE OF RIBONUCLEIC ACID

Generalization as to the secondary structure of RNA is probably less justified than in the case of DNA, as the available information is much less extensive. The available information does permit the following conclusions:

(*i*) There is no evidence for the existence of more than one polyribonucleotide strand in the natural RNA's

(*ii*) Hence the helical regions of natural RNA arise from the hair pin like bending of the single strand back upon itself.

(*iii*) The helical regions are stabilized by A-U and C-G interactions similar to those which stabilize the confirmation of DNA. However, the irregular base composition of RNA roes not allow the incorporation of the entire molecule into Jouble perfect belie of this type, and the helical zone co-exist .vith the random segments.

(*iv*) Two alternative models for the structure of RNA may be postulated:

(*a*) The non-helical fraction of RNA may take the

form of extended amorphous zones separating segments of nearly perfect helical organization. This model pre-suppose that extensive complementary sequences exist within the single strand. These tend to seek each other out to form perfect or nearly perfect, helical regions.

(*b*) Alternatively, nucleotides which do not participate in the helical organization may occur largely as numerous small loops external to the helically paired structure.

TYPES OF RIBONUCLEIC ACIDS

Four types of robonucleic acids have been studied and they -are as follows:

(*i*) mRNA

(*ii*) tRNA

(*iii*)rRNA

(*iv*) vRNA

Messenger (mRNA)

Studies by *Huxley* and later by *Volkin* and *Astrachan* with T_2 bacteriophage infected (bacterial virus, *E. coli*) in 1956 led to the first existence for the unique kind of the RNA, later called messenger RNA.

Jacob and *Monod* (1961) who first proposed this name, believed "*messenger*" to be necessary to convey the message of the genetic code from the DNA of the nucleus to the cytoplasm. This messenger is know as mRNA and it acts as a template for the translation of the DNA code into a specific protein.

Thus it helps in determining the structure of protein. mRNA molecules exist in a large variety of lengths, depending on the length of the polypeptide chain for which they code. Its molecular weight and sedimention value vary considerably.

Generally the life span of mRNA is relatively short, although in some eukaryotic cells there is evidence of some degree of stability. Further mRNA is always complementary to a portion of strand of DNA, with the exception that uracil replaces thymine.

It should therefore hybridize with the DNA from -which it was transcribed. It is now an established fact that when the code has been transcribed from DNA on to mRNA, the later leaves the nucleus passes through the nuclear membrane into the cytoplasm.

Here it moves to the ribosomes, the site of protein synthesis. mRNA molecules attaches reversibly to the surface of ribosome always binding to the smaller sub-units. The magnesium cation, Mg^{++} is involved in the formation of a complex between mRNA and ribosomes.

Types of mRNA

On the basis of size and the coding two types of mRNA has been described:

Monocistronic mRNA

Mostly the mRNA carries the codons of single cistron (i.e., codes for one complete protein molecule) of the DNA. Such mRNA molecule is called monocistronic mRNA. For example, for the synthesis of a polypeptide chain of 300 to 500 amino acid residues, a monocistronic mRNA of *E. coli* contains 900 to 1500 nucleotides in its molecule.

Polygenic or polycistronic mRNA

Sometimes a mRNA molecule carries the codes from several adjacent DNA cistrons and become much longer in size. This type of mRNA is called polygenic or polycistronic mRNA.

For example, for the metabolism of the histidine protein the cell synthesizes about 10 specific enzymatic proteins and a mRNA in this case may carry codons for all the 10 enzymes.

INFORMOSOMES

In eukaryons mRNA is associated with protein forming ribonucleo-protein complexes. Some of these complexes remain free in the cytoplasm without being attached to the poly ribosomes.

These are named as informosomes by *Spirin*. These are very stable and can remain in the cell cytoplasm for several days. The stability is attributed by the presence of protein sheath around mRNA molecule.

In informosomes proteins and mRNA are found in the ratio of 4 : 1. These occur in the form of particles of 80S or less. Since informosomes are very stable, these are used by the cell in protein synthesis only when there is delay in translation.

In embryonic cells, genetic apparatus starts functioning only late during organogenesis. Therefore, in early stages of cleavage when there is no rRNA, informosomes govern the process of protein synthesis.

Stability

The cell does not contain large quantities of mRNA. This is because mRNA, unlike other RNAs is constantly undergoing breakdown. It is broken down to its constituent ribonucleotides by ribonucleases.

In bacteria, mRNA may be so shortlived that while one end is translating protein the other end may be undergoing breakdown. In *E. coli* the average halflife of some mRNA is about two minutes. Eukaryotic cells, on the other hand, contain metabolically stable mRNA.

Mammalian reticulocytes are immature RBC which have lost their nuclei but have retained ribosomes. These cells can synthesize haemoglobin for many hours and even days by utilizing the mRNA transcribed by the nuclei when they were present.

Transfer Ribonucleic **Acid**

In the literature, tRNA molecules have been variously termed tRNA, sRNA for soluble RNA, or adaptor RNA. It forms about 10-15% of the total RNA in most of the existence. Each tRNA contains approximate 80 nucleotides.

The soluble **or tRNA** forms large varieties of different

Table 1.4: Comparison of the different types of RNA.

	Ribosomala RNA (rRNA)	*Messenger RNA (mRNA)*	*Transfer RNA (rRNA)*
Percentage or total RNA of cell	80%	3 to 5%	10 to 20%
Sedimentation Coefficient	28S, 18S, 5.8S, 5S 23S, 16S. 5S	8S	3.8S
Number of nucleotides	5S RNA : 120 nucleotides 16-18S RNA : 1,600 to 2,500 nucleotides. 23-28S RNA : 3,200 to 5,500 nucleotide	*E. coli* : 900 to 1,500 nucleotides.	73 to 93 nucleotides.
Molecular weight	23S RNA : 1.1×10^6 30S RNA : 0.55×10^6	500,000	25,000-30,00
Unusual bases bases	Small amount of methylated bases.	Small amount of unusual bases,	High content unusual (*E. coli* : 1 per

	Ribosomala RNA (rRNA)	***Messenger RNA (mRNA)***	***Transfer RNA (rRNA)***
		1 per 30-40	100-150 nucleotides).
Site of synthesis	Derived from nucleolar DNA	Synthesized in nucleus on DNA template.	Synthesized in nucleus on DNA template.
Beginning of Synthesis	Synthesis begins at gastrulation, and increases as development proceeds.	Some mRNA is found in the ovum. New mRNA is synthesized during	tRNA synthesis occurs at the end of cleavage stages.
	Ribosomala RNA (rRNA)	***Messenger RNA (mRNA)***	***Transfer RNA (rRNA)***
Base of relationship DNA	No obvious base relationship to rDNA, rRNA is from only small section of DNA.	mRNA shows base relationship to DNA. It is formed from all sections of DNA	Same as in rRNA.
Function	Unpaired bases may bind mRNA and tRNA to ribosomes.	Conveys genetic information from DNA of chromosomes where it takes part in protein synthesis	Adaptor for attaching amino acids to mRNA template.

Table 1.5: Comparison between DNA and RNA.

Deoxyribonucleic acid	*Ribonucleic acid*
1. DNA is the usual genetic material	1. RNA is the genetic material of some viruses.
2. RNA is usually double-stranded, (In certain viruses DNA is single stranded, $\phi\chi$ 74).	2. Most cellar RNA is single stranded. (Some viruses e.g., reovirus, have double stranded RNA).
3. The pentose sugar is deoxyribose	3. The pentose sugar is ribose.
4. The common organic bases are adenine, guanine, cytosine and thymine.	4. The common organic bases are adenine, guanine, cytosine and uracil.
5. Base pairing: adenine pairs with thymine and guanine with cytosine	5. Adenine pairs with uracil and guanine with cytosine.
6. Pairing of bases is throughout the length of the molecule.	6. Pairing of bases is only in the helical region.
7. There are fewer uncommon bases.	7. There are more uncommon bases.
8. DNA is only of one type.	8. There are three types of RNA, messenger RNA, ribosomal and RNA transfer RNA.
9. Most of the DNA is found in the chromosome. Some DNA is also found in the cytoplasm e.g., in mitochondria and chloroplasts.	9. Messenger RNA is formed on the chromosomes, and is found in the nucleolus and cytoplasm. rRNA and tRNA are also formed on the chromosomes, and are found in cytoplasm.
10. Denaturation (melting) is partially reversible only under certain conditions of slow cooling (renaturation)	10. Complete and practically in stantaneous reversibility of the process of melting.
11. Sharp, narrow temperature interval of transition in melting	11. Board temperature interval of transition in melting.
12. DNA on replication forms DNA, and on transcription forms RNA.	12. Usually RNA does not replicate or transcribe. (In certain viruses RNA can synthesize an RNA chain)
13. Genetic messages are usually encoded in DNA.	13. The usual function of RNA is translating messages encoded in DNA into proteins.
14. DNA consists of a large number of nucleotides, up to 4,3 million.	14. RNA consists of fewer nucleotides, up to 12,000.

cells, is homogenous in its molecular size having a molecular weight of about. 25000. The nucleotide sequence of tRNA was first worked out by *Hollay et al* (1965) for yeast alanine tRNA.

Since then the sequence of about 75 different tRNAs has been establi.,bed. According to the Holley's leaf model the tRNA is a polynucleotide chain which is folded upon itself to form 5 arms. As a result of the folding the 3' and 5' ends of the chain come near each other.

An arm consists of a stem and a loop. Bases are arranged in pairs in arms. There is no base pairing in the loops. The 3' end of the polynucleotide chain ends in CCA base sequence. This represents site for the attachment of activated amino acid.

The end of the chain terminates with guanine base. The bent in the chain of each tRNA molecule contains a definite sequence of three nitrogenous bases which constitute the anticodon. It recognizes the codon on mRNA.

Four different regions or special sites can be recognized in the molecule of tRNA. These are:

Amino acid attachment site

It occurs at the 3' end of the tRNA chain and has OH group of ribose molecule free to pair. This—OH group combines with the specific amino acid in the presence of ATP forming amino-acyl tRNA. It is common to all the tRNA molecules.

Recognition site

It contains a specific base sequence which dictates the attachment of correct amino acid to the tRNA molecule. It matches with the amino acid activating enzyme through which attachment of amino acid to tRNA takes place.

Anticodon or codon recognition site

This site has three unpaired bases (triplet of base) whose sequence is complementary with a codon (triplet) in mRNA. Therefore, it determines the pairing of tRNA with the specific codon (triplet) of mRNA. It is, therefore, the most specific region of tRNA molecule.

Ribosome recognition site

This helps in the attachment of tRNA to the ribosome. This site is common to all the molecules of tRNA.

Three dimensional structure of tRNA

In order to understand the structure-function relationship of tRNA, its three dimensional structure (TDS) should be known. With the availability of tRNA in crystalline form in 1968, TDS of tRNA could be studied through X-ray crystallography as was done for DNA double helix.

About a dozen models for TDS were proposed, but the latest and most acceptable model was proposed in 1973 by *S.H. Kim*. He suggested that TDS of tRNA takes the shape of letter L with a thickness 22 Å.

This can be easily derived from two dimensional clover leaf model. The extra arm which varies in different tRNA molecules can be extended without distorting TDS conformation. The CCA stem projects out and can take different orientations.

Unusual bases

In addition to the usual bases A, U, G and C, tRNA contain a number of unusual bases, and in this respect differs from mRNA and rRNA. The unusual bases of tRNA account for 15-20% of the total RNA of the cell.

Most of the unusual bases are formed by methylation (addition of $-CH_3$ or methyl group to the usual bases), e.g., cytosine and guanine on methylation yield methylcytosine and methylguanine, respectively. Precursor tRNA molecules transcribed on the DNA template contain the usual bases.

These are then modified to unusual bases. The unusual bases are important because they protect the tRNA molecule against degradation *by* RNAse. This protection is necessary because RNA is found floating freely in the cell.

Some of the unusual bases of tRNA are methylguanine (GMe), dimethylguanine (GMe_2), methylcytosine (Me), ribothymine (T) pseudouridine (ψ), dihydrouridine (DHU_2, H_2U, UH_2), inosine (I) and methylinosine (IMe, Mel).

Ribsomal Ribonucleic acid rRNA

Ribosomes are small particles of about 200 Å to 250 Å in diameter, and are generally present in the cytoplasm either lying free in the cytoplasm or attached to the outer membrane of endoplasmic reticulum or "*nuclear membrane*".

These particles are ribosomes containing about 60% *ribonucleic* acid or RNA which is ribosomal RNA or rRNA and 40% protein. It is generally agreed that *cytoplasmic* ribosomes or their subunits are made in the nucleus and are subsequently transferred to the cytoplasm. However, the mode of their passages across the nuclear membrane is still a matter of controversy.

Even from the morphological evidence, it would appear t the reticular or microvesicular spheres of the nucleus could be engaged in either the synthesis of rRNA, or its assembly or both. The finding that hybridization of rRNA takes place with the chromatin associated with the nucleolar region suggests that rRNA is synthesized on the part of the chromosome traversing the nucleolus (the nucleolar organizer) or, in some cases, on DNA detached from the chromosome and associated with the nucleolus.

Ribosomal RNA differs in size and base contents from RNA and from other RNA classes of most cells. r-RNA from ost organims is relatively rich in guanine and cytosine, and lacks many of the rare bases found in tRNA, although some ethylated bases are present.

The function of rRNA in protein synthesis is not yet cometely clear. The unpaired bases in the molecule may bind RNA and tRNA to ribosomes possibly by Mgt linkages between phosphate groups on the two molecules.

Ribosomal RNA also gives some evidence for developing the double helical structure.

Virual RNA (vRNA)

Viruses may contain either DNA or RNA. However, each particular virus generally contains nucleic acid of only one type. Some examples of RNA viruses are influenza, turnip yellow mosaic, tomato bushy stunt, tobacco necrosis, and the. particularly well studied tobacco mosaic virus (TMV).

REPLICATION OF RIBONUCLEIC ACID

At first it was difficult to apply the rules of DNA replicationto RNA replication, because less is known about the macromolecular structure of DNA, but with the basic principles of the template theory laid down, the synthesis of RNA became accessible to further investigation.

As discussed above the four various kinds of RNAs, which are structurally alike, but differ considerably in molecular weight and are distributed in different parts of the cell, are replicated or biosynthesized as follows:

Biosynthesis of rRNA

rRNA although present in ribosomes is formed inside the nucleus. DNA associated with the nucleolus is responsible for coding rRNA. This part of DNA is known as nucleolar organizer.

In bacteria about 10-200 cistrons are concerned with the rRNA synthesis, whereas in higher organisms 200-2000 tightly clustered rDNA cistrons are involved in rRNA synthesis. The two types of rRNA (28S and 18S) are transcribed from the nucleolar DNA as a single elongated unit of 45S.

Inside the nucleus, the 45S RNA is methylated and complexed with protein. Finally, via a number steps of it is cleaved into 32S and 18S segments. The 18S RNA gets associated with basic proteins to form the small subunit of ribosome.

The 32S segment is further severed and finally change to 28S RNA. This 28S RNA also gets associated with proteins and forms the large subunit of ribosome. These units then come out into the cytoplasm.

The 5S RNA has a extranucleolar origin, transcribed from geneslocated outside the nucleolar organizer. It gets associated with each large ribsomal subunit. The function of 5S RNA is unknown.

Biosynthesis of mRNA

The existence of a short lived type of RNA was predicted on theoretical grounds by *F. Jacob*, *J. Monod*, and associates. The name messenger RNA was used to describe a form of RNA that would be made in the cell nucleus, but would be transferred to the cytoplasm during protein synthesis.

During protein synthesis, the amino acid sequence was determined by DNA which is mainly in the nucleus. The information from DNA in the form of a specific sequence of bases had to be transferred some how to the cytoplasm.

The notion of a mRNA demanded that DNA acts as template for RNA synthesis. The principle of base pairs still applies here, because uracil in RNA has the same dimension as thymine in DNA, and one can substitute for the other. In this manner a DNA strand could function as template for RNA synthesis.

```
A—T—T—G—A—C DNA
|  |  |  |  |  |
U—A—A—C—U—G mRNA
```

Biosynthesis of Transfer RNA

It is of low molecular weight. The structure of tRNA has been explained already. Although the details of its synthesis are not known. It is known that tRNA is synthesized on DNA templates by steps similar to those of the other types of RNA. Several aspects of tRNA merit some comment. One is that all tRNA types so far isolated contain the same sequence of bases at one end of the molecule, cytosine-cytosine-adenine (C-C-A).

Another irteresting observation is that in tRNA one invariably finds nucleotides not yet described: Seudo-uridylic acid and subothymidylic acid. The presence of the two bases present a problem.

If synthesis of tRNA proceeds by the same mechanism as other types of RNA, the enzymes involved in tRNA synthesis must be assumed to have unique specificity for the two new nucleotides.

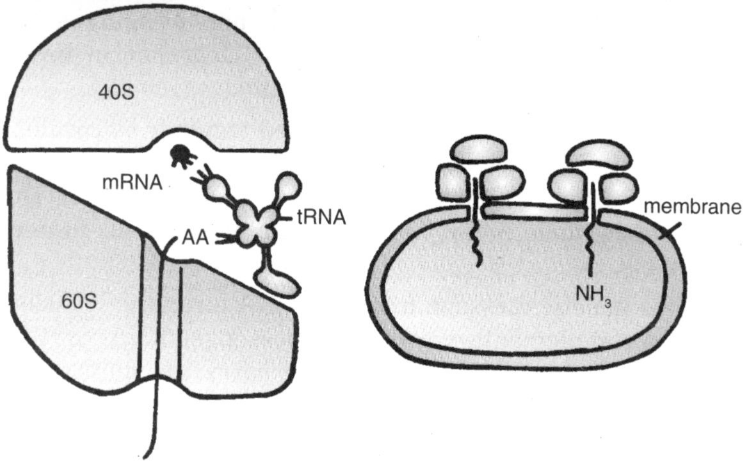

Figure 1.6: Diagram of ribosome showing the two sub-units and the probable position of mRNA and tRNA.

A more attractive idea is that tRNA is formed from the familiar four nucleotides, and by enzymatic modification of selected uridylic acid units in the tRNA, the new nucleotides, are formed.

Pseudouridylic acid could be the product of an isomerization reaction of tRNA. Ribothymidylic acid is known to be formed by methylation of uridylic acid present in tRNA. The characteristic terminal-C-C-A sequence is believed to be added enzymatically after tRNA is already made.

PROTEIN SYNTHESIS

The proteins are highly organized and complex structures. The proteins have significant role in the structural and functional organisation of the cell. The structural proteins constitute various cellular components and some extracellular parts such as cuticle and fibres, etc.

The functional (e.g., enzymatic and hormonal) proteins control almost all metabolic, biosynthetic, bioenergetic, growth regulating, sensory and reproductive activities of the cell.

All the proteins which are required by the cell for its different purposes are synthesized by the cell itself intracellularly. Chemically, proteins are polymers of amino acids. The amino acids molecules are linked together in linear fashion forming long polypeptide chain.

The adjacent amino acid are joined together by covalent peptide bond between the carboxy group of one amino acid and the amino group of the other. DNA initiates the mechanism since it carrys the genetic message for protein synthesis.

This genetic message from one DNA strand is transferred to a complementary strand of messenger RNA ; mRNA then passes out of the nucleus and carry the message to the ribosomes where it is used to synthesize the particular type of protein molecule.

The first step is called *transcription* because it involves copying of the genetic information from DNA into mRNA which transmits the coded information from DNA to ribosomes, the site of protein synthesis. The second step is termed as *translation* as it involves the translation of the information encoded on mRNA with newly synthesized protein molecule.

CENTRAL DOGMA AND REVERSE CENTRRAL DOGMA

It is a sort of relationship between DNA, RNA and protein. It details with the flow of genetic information and can be studied under the following heads:

One way flow of informations

Crick (1958) suggested that DNA transmits the genetic informations for protein synthesis by transcribing mRNA (transcription) and other types of RNAs. These RNAs then translate the nucleotide sequence into the sequence of amino acids (translation). This is known as one way flow of information or central dogma.

Circular flow of information

Barry Commoner (1968) suggested circular flow of information. The DNA transcribes RNA (mRNA, tRNA etc), RNA translates the information into protein, protein then directs the synthesis of RNA and RNA dictates the synthesis of DNA.

Inverse flow of information

Temin (1970) has described the presence of an enzyme-RNA *dependent DNA polymerase*, which controls the synthesis of DNA from a single strand of RNA. *D. Baltimore* (1970) has described the presence of this enzyme in certain RNA tumour viruses.

In tumour viruses the RNA is genetic RNA but in certain cases the nongenetic RNA synthesized under the control **of** DNA may also control the synthesis of DNA by inverse flow of information. This is known as central dogma reverse.

Role of amino acids

Amino acids are the units from which the protein molecules are made. In the cytoplasm of every cell a number of amino acids are present. Out of these 20 amino acids stake the important part in protein synthesis.

The amino acids are distributed through out the cytoplasm, which are collected by specific tRNAs. tRNAs bring the amino acids to the actual site of protein synthesis i.e., to ribosomes where the synthesis of protein takes place.

ROLE OF MRNA DURING SYNTHESIS OF PROTEIN

According to *Jacob* and *Monod* (1961) mRNA conveys necessary message of genetic code from the DNA of the nucleus to the cytoplasm. It acts as template for the translation of he DNA code into specific protein. It is formed from DNA luring repliciation with similar base composition.

The evidence that DNA is the main source from which RNA is synthesized can be received by using deoxyribonuclease, which eases protein synthesis.

The inhibition of protein synthesis is due to a fact, that mRNA is not formed in the absence of DNA as it is digested by the enzyme. *Hall* (1961) further gave imilar evidence regarding the formation of mRNA from DNA. Messenger RNA molecules necessarily exist in a large variety of lengths, depending upon the length of the polypeptide chain for which they code. There are very few polypeptide chains which contain less than 100 amino acids, and so very few molecules which contain less than 300 nucleotide units, the length of mRNA which carries information necessary to determine the complete polypeptide chain of a protein molecule is called *a cistron*, as postulated by *Benzer*.

Some mRNA molecules are able to carry information for the synthesis of more than one protein molecule. Such types are known as polycistronic. The average life time of mRNA molecules is variable. In bacterial cell mRNA molecules exist for few minutes at 37°C, after which they are broken down into its components by enzymes.

In the case of mammalian reticulocytes the mRNA are long lived. There is then considerable variation in average lifetimes of mRNA molecules. While studying the impact of radioactive substances on the incubated cells, it has been observed that the labelled material is first incorporated into the nuclear RNA and then appears in the cytoplasmic RNA.

This indicates that when the code has been transcribed from DNA into mRNA, the latter leaves the nucleus. In the cytoplasm it reaches to the site of protein synthesis, the ribosome. The mRNA molecule attaches reversibly to the surface of the ribosome.

The attachment is manifested by Mg^{++} (magnesium cation) and finally a complex is formed, between mRNA and the ribosome.

Role of tRNA

It is also called as soluble RNA. This particular nucleic acid is present in the cytoplasm in sufficient amount and the main role of tRNA is to pick up the amino acid from cytoplasm and bring to the site of protein synthesis on the ribosome.

As already stated that a number of amino acids (20) are present in the cytoplasm and for every specific amino acid there is one specific tRNA, so there are different specific tRNA molecules.

A specific adopter enzyme (an-aminoacyl tRNA synthetase) is required to couple each amino acid to its specific tRNA. The part of tRNA which becomes attached to its particular amino acid appears to be same for all sorts of tRNAs.

This limb is the 3' end of the molecule, terminating in the sequence of three bases-Cytosine-Cytosine-Adenine. Another 5' end of ·the molecule terminates in the base guanine. This sequence only enables amino acid to bt attached at particular site. The process by which the amino acids become attached to the tKNA is quite complicated.

ATP provides energy which is required during the process. The link formed between the amino acid and transfer RNA is a covalent bond between the carboxyl group of the amino acid, and the ribosome of the terminal adenine nucleotide of the tRNA.

Thus there are three components necessary for the reaction:

(*i*) a specific amino acid

(*ii*) a specific enzyme, and

(*iii*) a specific tRNA.

The reaction can be shown by the following equations

(*i*) Amino acid + ATP + Amino acyladenylate → Enzyme bond Amino acid adenylate+2P

(*ii*) Enzyme bound Amino acid adenylate+uncharged tRNA → charged-RNA+Enzyme+amino acid complex.

POLYRIBOSOMES AND THEIR ROLE IN PROTEIN SYNTHESIS

The 70S free ribosomes are the active units in protein synthesis in a normall cell. The most active units are aggregates containing a mRNA molecule to which a number of 70S ribosomes are attached. The name polyribosome is designated to this assembly line of ribosomes.

Before the study of structure of polyribosomes let us know the history and the conception by which the idea of polyribosomes appeared. *Alexander Rich* studied and expressed in his words "consider for a moment the problem of synthesizing one of the polyeptide chain of, haemoglobin, which contains about 150 nino acid sub-units.

If each sub-unit is specified by a tripletide, the mRNA must contain 450 bases merely to specify the Auence of sub units in one chain. In most RNA molecules e bases are stacked on top of one another more or less like a pilo of pennie.

Since the bases have a thickness of 3.4Å units, the mRNA strand for the haemoglobin polypeptide chains ould have a molecular length of at least 1,500Å. In other possible arrangements of the RNA molecule the length might almost twice. By comparison, the individual ribosome has Diameter of only about 230Å, and so we wondered how the sig messenger molecule interacted with such a small particle manufacture a polypeptide chain".

Some investigators rough that the RNA chain might be wrapped around the out is of the ribosome, but it was hard to visualize how intimate ntact between the two should be maintained. The wrapping able would be still more difficult for RNA chain 20,000Å ag, which are found in many viruses.

Alternative suggestions at the mRNA might come how be coiled inside the ribosomes °med to present even more formidable topographical proems. It occured to us that proteins might actually be made n groups of ribosomes lined together some how by mRNA. here was already a little evidence pointing in this direction. *alter Gilbert* of Havard University, as well as other investiators, had found that when a synthetic RNA was added to a it free system of bacterial ribosomes, the ribosomes would end to clump together.

Probably the first polyribosomes were studied in mammalian (rabbit) reticulocytes that predominantly synthesize the blood protein haemoglobin contains ribosomes. The negative staining procedure of *Slayter shows* that ribosomes in a polyribosome are separated by gaps of 10 to 140M while positive staining with uranyl acetate reveals that the ribosomes are connected by a thin thread 10 to 15Å in diameter which is about the thickness of a single strand of RNA.

From these studies,. it is concluded that the over all length covered by a five unit polyribosomes is about 1,500A°. The space covered by the polyribosome is nearly the same which is needed for mRNA strand in the synthesis of haemoglobin in reticuloytes.

POLYRIBOSOME CYCLE AND ASSOCIATION AND DISSOCIATION OF SUBUNITS

Few years ago it was thought that the various molecules involved in the protein synthesis were bound on the complete ribosome. However, *Mangiarotti* and *Sclesslnger* (1966) have shown that the two sub-units of the ribosome may exist freely and that they associate during the protein synthesis and may dissociate again at the end of the process.

Kalmpfer (1965) and his associates have shown the essential features of ribosomal cycle as indicated in the figure elsewhere in this chapter. In this figure, the two different subunits (30S and 50S in *E. coli* or 40S and 60S in reticulocytes) enter in the process at the initiator end and separate at the terminator end after the completion of the cycle.

Thus, according to this concept the subunits of different ribosomes could be exchanged during the ribosomal cycle.

The factors which are responsible for the initiation of the 30S particles in the ribosomal cycle, are identified as Fl, F2, F3+ATP. The separation factor is, however, tentatively identified as F2.

ROLE OF SUBUNITS IN PROTEIN SYNTHESIS

These subunits (30S and 50S or 40S and 60S) perform different types of functions in the process of protein synthesis. In *E. coli*, mRNA binds to the 30S Subunit for the reading of genetic message. In first step small 30S subunit binds with the first codon of the mRNA to form the so called initiator complex.

The successive steps would be the binding of the first amino acyl-tRNA and then the coupling of the other subunit (50S) as shown in the figure elsewhere in this chapter. In *E. coli* it has been demonstrated that the first aminoacyl tRNA which initiates the synthesis of protein is quite specific because it contains a formyl (-CHO) derivative of methionine which is coded by AUG codon.

This codon is alway present at the beginning of all the mRNA molecules. In the protein synthesis the peptide chain always grows from the free terminal end of -NH_2 group towards the -COOH end.

Therefore, the function of formyl methionine-tRNA (F-met-tRNA of the figure) is to ensure that proteins are synthesized in that direction. In F-met-tRNA, the NH_2 group is blocked by the formyl ,group leaving only the -COOH available to react with the-NH_2 of the second amino acid.

Thus, in this way the synthesis .follows in only correct direction and sequence. The SOS subunit contains the enzyme peptidyl transferase or peptide synthetase, which is essential in the formation of peptide bond. The other function of the 50S subunit is to provide two binding sites for the two tRNA molecules.

These two sites should be next to each other in order to permit the formation of the peptide bond. However, it is possible to envision process of protein synthesis as a continu;il entrance of aminoacyl tRNA on 30S unit to the ribosome and exist of the tRNA molecules from the 50S sub unit after giving their amino acids to the developing polypeptide chain.

MECHANISM OF PROTEIN SYNTHESIS

The mechanism of protein synthesis has been investigated most throughly in bacteria (usually *E. coli*), therefore, the process of protein synthesis of *E. coli* which contains 70S ribosomei will be described in more detail and then this will be discussed in relation to our present knowledge of protein synthesis on 80S ribosomes of plants and animals.

Protein synthesis consists of two main events:

(*i*) Transcription

(*ii*) Translation

Transcription.

The formation of mRNA is called transcription. During the process an enzyme-RNA polymerase is needed. The enzyme is then attached to the DNA at the initiation site, where a short segment of the DNA molecule is opened up. The complementary nucleotides developed from

one of the DNA strands, form mRNA.

The RNA polymerase moves along the DNA strands, and the growing mRNA strand is peeled off till a termination site is reached.

The enzyme RNA polymerase consists of five different polypeptide chains, of which four collectively form the core enzyme while the fifth is called the sigma (σ) chain. They are given below.

(1) Core enzyme.

(*a*) β^1 having mol. weight 1,60,000

(*b*) β having mol. weight 1,50,000

(*c*) α having mol. weight 40,000

(*d*) ω having mol. weight 10,000

(2) Sigma factor (σ) having mol. wt. 90,000.

The sima gchain recognizes start signals along the DNA molecules. A specific protein called the rho (P) factor (mol. wt. 60,000) stops the formation of the RNA chain. Once RNA synthesis is initiated, the sigma factors dissociate and core enzymes bring about elongation of mRNA.

The mRNA makes its way through the pores in the nuclear membrane to the cytoplasm to start the next stage which is translation.

Translation

It involves the translation of the language of DNA into the language of protein i.e., the formation of protein takes place under the control of mRNA. This process can be studied under the following heads

Activation of Amino acids

The first step in protein synthesis is the activation of amino acids with ATP (Adenosine triphosphate). The reaction is catalysed by a specific enzyme *amino acyl synthetase* and by this the first product is formed which is the *amino acid adenylate* in which the energy is consumed for the requirement of the next step. The reaction can be shown by equation as follow

Amino acid+ATP+Amino acyl synthetase →

Enzyme bound amino acid adenylate+2P.

or

$$AA + ATP \underset{Synthetase}{\overset{\text{Amino acyl}}{\rightleftharpoons}} AA \sim AMP + 2P$$

Attachment of activated amino acid with tRNA

Here is this step the activated amino acids are attached with the tRNA. The adenylate remains bounded to the enzyme until it is transformed to the tRNA and this transfer is again catalysed by the same enzyme. The link formed between the amino acid and tRNA is a covalent bond between the carboxyl group of the amino acid and the ribose of the terminal adenine nucleotide of tRNA. The reaction is as shown below:

$$AA \sim AMP + tRNA \underset{\text{Amino acyl}}{\overset{\text{Synthetase}}{\rightleftharpoons}} AA \sim tRNA + AMP$$

Here

AA~AMP=Amino acyle adenylate

AA~tRNA=Amino acid tRNA complex

AMP=Adenosine monophosphate

Initiation of protein synthesis

Initiation of protein synthesis in the ribosome is a

complex step involving mRNA, formyl methionine tRNA (F-met-tRNA), the initiator factors, GTP and the small subunit.

The small subunit recognizes the initiation codon on mRNA which is always AUG in both prokaryotes and eukaryotes. F-met-tRNA attaches to the small subunit-mRNA complex. Now the larger subunit combines with this complex to form the complete ribosome.

There are three initiator factors, Fl, F2, and F3 which are loosely associated with the small ribosomal subunit. FI and F2 along with GTP are required to bind F-met-tRNA to the small subunit in response to the codon AUG. F3 factor stimulates the binding of mRNA to the initiation site of the small subunit.

In eukaryotes, met-tRNA is involved instead F-met-tRNA. Secondly in them the initiation factors are Ml, M2, and M3 which are homologous to Fl, F2, and F3 of prokaryotes.

Chain elongation

It involves the following four subphases:

Elongation factors

Elongation of the polypeptide chain requires elongation factors (EF). These are EF-Tu, EF-Ts and EF-G in prokaryotes and EF-1 and dEF-2 in eukarvotes.

Binding of aminoacyl tRNA to the a site

The second amino acid-tRNA complex (ala-tRNA) now occupies the acceptor site (A site) of the 50S subunit of the ribosome.

Peptide bond formation

The next step include the formation of a peptide bond between the amino acid and the rowing polypeptide of F-met-tRNA, if the initiation has just been completed. The polypeptide chain is transferred from its osition at the P site to the aminoacyl tRNA, located at the A site. In the reaction, the polypeptide is first cleaved from the LRNA at the P site and becomes attached to the aminoacyltRNA at the A site.

In the process, the bond formation is rnediated by an enzyme *peptidyl transferase* which is located in the 50S subunit between P and A sites. GTP is hydrolyzed to GDP+inorganic phosphate.

The energy released during hydrolysis may have a warping effect on the ribosome so that peptidyl tRNA can be aligned for bond formation between the polypeptide and the amino acid.

Translocation of polypeptide

The next step comprise the discharge of the unloaded tRNA from the P site. This translocation of the polypeptide from the A site to the P site requires the supernatant G factor, which is a ribosome-dependent GTPase. GTP is also required.

As translocation occurs, the peptidyl-tRNA is moved from the A site to the P site, and the mRNA moves one codon. The uncharged tRNA from the P site is discharged. The role played by the G factor is that by reacting with GTP to produce energy which might be converted to mechanical energy, resulting in translocation and movement of mRNA.

Chain Termination

The polypeptide chain elongates, until a termination codon on mRNA is reached. This may be UAA, UAG or UGA. The termination codon provides signals to the ribosomes for the attachment of release factors. In prokaryotes there are three release factors, RF- l , RF-2 and RF-3. RF-1 recognizes the termination codons UAA and UAG. RF-2 recognizes UAA and UGA.

RF-4 (stimulatory factor) stimulates the binding and release of RF-1 and RF-2 from the ribosome. In eukaryotes a single release factor (RF) recognizes all three termination codons. The release factors interact with peptidyl transferase, and cause hydrolysis of the polypeptide chain at the site thus the chain is released from the tRNA molecule. The residual tRNA is discharged from the P site. The ribosome dissociates into 30S and 50S subunits. The polypeptide chain may undergo further processing, like cleavage of the formyl residue and internal cleavage.

Secretory polypeptides pass tbrougb a tunnel between the two ribosomal subunits into the endoplasmic cisterna. Structural proteins are incorporated into the cell membrane.

Inhibitor of protein synthesis

Antibiotic, *chloramphenicol*, have long been known to be the inhibitor of protein synthesis. They appear to function in the transfer reaction at the step of peptide-bond synthesis. Attachment of mRNA to ribosomes seems to occur normally, synthesis seldom proceeds past the di-or tripeptide stage.

The inhibitor is probably bound to a specific site on the ribosomes. The another important inhibitor of protein synthesis, is *cycloheximide* not effective in bacteria but seems to function in mammals and further in a similar way' as does *chloramphenicol*.

Chapter 2

CHLOROPLAST

The plastids are characteristic large cytoplasmic bodies of the cell intimately related to the metabolic processes and which impart colour to the tissues. They are found mostly in plants with possible exception of the very lowest group of plants. However, plastids are also found in few animals, especially the protozoan flagellates.

They are not found in bacteria, certain algae, myxomycetes and fungi. On the basis of presence of the plastids, the living world has been distinguished into plant and animal kingdoms. Old literature indicates that *Pringshetn* first investigated the plastids.

The terra plastid was used in 1 X85 by *A.F.W. Schimper* to include the cell organelles which are primarily involved in the formation and storage of soluble and insoluble carbohydrates. *A. Meyer* in 1883, *F. Schmitz* in 1884 and *A.F.W. Schimper* in 1885 made detailed cytological studies of these cell organelles and showed that green plastids known as chloroplasts could not be formed from cytoplasm, but only from existing chloroplasts.

The plastids vary in size, number, shape and chemical organization with the particular tissue and organism concerned. In contrast to the smaller cytoplasmic granules such as the mitochondria, important physical and chemical differences in the plastids can be easily recognized, such as changes in size or shape, the presence or absence of the

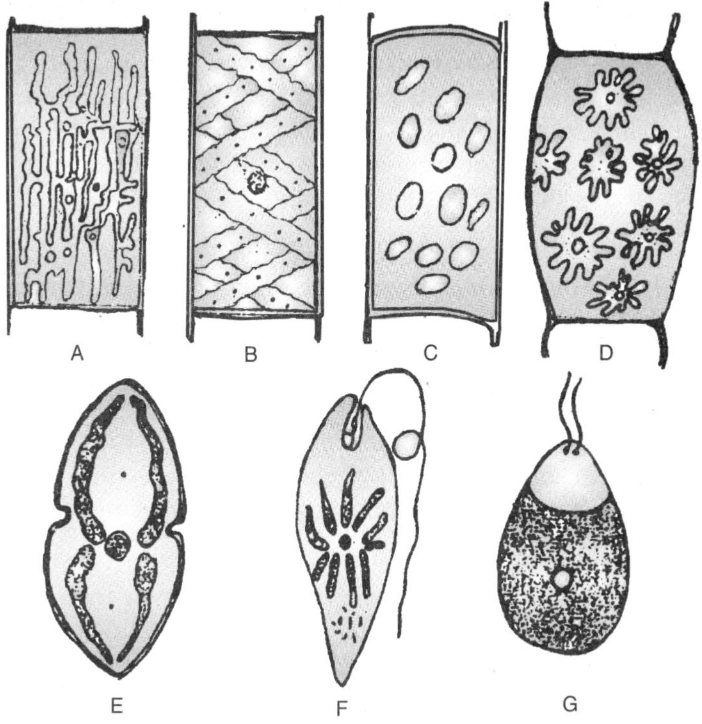

Figure 2.1: Various types of chloroplasts. A-Oedogonium, B-Spirogyra, C-Phyloiella, D-Rhodochlorton, E-Euastrun, F-Euglena, O-Chlamydomons.

chloroplastid, carotenoids and starch. Mature plastids can be shown to arise from more or less undifferen-tiated plastid primordia which occur in the meristematic cells, or hose of the developing embryo.

The plastids are self-duplicating bodies and their life history, especially of the chloroplast, may be divided into three phases. In the first phase, self duplication and enzymatic activities with some concern to RNA takes place.

The second phase is mainly concerned with differentiation to form the enzymes required for photosynthesis. In the third phase the activities of the enzymes that predominates are those concerned with photosynthesis.

VARIOUS TYPES OF PLASTIDS

Plastids may be divided into two general groups; the *chromoplasts* (coloured plastids); and the *leucoplasts* (colourless plastids). The chromoplasts may be further divided into two subgroups; those that are photosynthetically active and those that are not.

Photosynthetically Active Chromoplasts

The photosynthetically active chromoplasts are chloroplasts, phacoplasts, rhodoplasts, blue-green chromoplasts and chromatophores of photosynthetic bacteria.

Chloroplasts

These are green plastids of green algae and higher plants and contain chlorophyll A and B in the ratio of 2.3 : 1. These have different appearance and varying sizes.

Pheoplasts (Brown or yellow plastids)

This type of plastid is commonly present in the brown algae, diatoms and dinoflagellates. **In** these pheoplasts, brown carotenoids mask the chlorophyll.

As reported by *Strain* (1951) the yellow or brown colour of the pheoplasts appears to result from the physical state or condition of the pigment from their geometrical arrangement in the plastids. Brown algae contain fucoxanthin which can absorb light and transfer energy to chlorophyll.

Rhodoplasts

Various members of Rhodophyceae con tain red coloured plastids. The red colour is due to a pigment phycobilin and protein phycoerythrin. The colour of plastids may be the result of light absorption. There may be phycotcyanin too in traces. *Haxo, Blink* and *Young (1952)* found that light is absorbed by phycobilin and is transmitted to chlorophyll *a*.

Blue-green Chromatophore

Two accessory protein phycocyanin and phycoerythrin impart bluetgreen colour to algae. These pigments and chlorophyll a alongwith carotenoid form lamellar structure, the *chromatophore.*

Wilson and *Morrison* (1967) mention that all the organisms, capable of performing photosynthesis do not necessarily contain plastid structures; for example, bluetgreen algae and.

photosynthetic bacteria. In blue-greens, the light-sensitive pigments are chlorophyll and phycobilin pigments. These pigments are associated with a system of membranes and lamellae in the cytoplasm of the cell. In photosynthetic bacteria also wide diversity of structures are associated with the photosynthesis. These structures are as follows

(1) Lamellae in some purple bacteria ; for example, *Rhodomicrobium,* (2) Vesicular membrane-bound structures, known as chromatophores found in non-sulphuric and purple sulphur bacteria ; for example, *Rhodospirillium, Chromatium,* and (3) Ribosome like granules found in green sulphur bacterium, *Chlorobiumthio sultatophilum.* All these photosynthetic bacteria possess a pigment system consisting of a specialized form of chlorophyll, known as bacteriochlorophyll and various carotenoid pigments.

Chromoplasts Without Photosynthetic Activity

These types of chromoplasts contain carotenoids only. They are red to yellow in colour and are much more variable in shape. They impart specific colour to various plant tissues, fruits and flowers.

The new colour that arise often due to the formation of special carotenoids, for example, the *leucopene* of tomato fruits, *prolycopene* of berries, and *capsanthin* of red pepper.

Xanthophyll is also present in adequate proportions. Coloured carotenoids are also important constituents of the coloured parts of plant.

These may be found in fungi and bacteria. Acidic carotenoids of fungi are similar to astaxanthin. *Haxo (1949)* isolated a mixture of carotenoids from the *Neurospora crassa* which includes lycopene, carotene, and spiriloxanthines as the main components.

The growth of carotenoid becomes double in presence of light. These chromoplasts are supposed to develop from the leucoplasts that contain starch.

As the carotene increase in concentration the starch disappears. The older chromoplasts appear thin plates as needles with typical crystalline appearance. They are direfringen and dichroic.

Leucoplasts

The noncoloured plastids are called leucoplasts. They do not contain pigments and the membranous structures are absent. They are found mainly in the embryonic and sexual cells. They are also found in meristematic cells and in those regions of the plants which do not receive light.

They serve mainly for the storage of starch, oils and proteins. Plastids located in cotyledons and the primordium of stem are first colourless but eventually become filled with pigments and become coloured plastids. Leucoplasts are further categorized into following three types:

Amyloplasts

These are mature plastids with predominant starch contents and generally found in storage tubers, cotyldons and endosprem. Starch is characteristic of the coloured and the colourless plastids of green algae and the higher plants.

The deposition of other carbohydrates may not necessarily be with the plastids. For example, in red algae starch is formed at the surface of the plastids. In *Euglena,* paramylum grains are considered to be produced outside the plastids. The starch grains may be of two types : assimilative starch and reserve starch.

The former is characteristic of actively photosynthesizing chloroplasts and the latter is most familiar in storage organs. The starch grains are made of a series of concentric layers successively deposited about a centre, the *hilum.*

As starch continues to be deposited, the walls of the amyloplast become greatly distended. *Frey Wysslfng (1953)* observed that the formation of a new concentric layer begins as a dense region of high refractive index, then it becomes a dense layer due to more hydration.

Chemically starch contains two components : mainly a-amylose (which stain red with iodine) and minorly β-amylose (only 20-30 per cent forming helical chain structure and stains blue with iodine).

Elaioplasts

The plastids which store oils are known as elaioplasts. In most monocotyledons, the chloroplasts after losing their chlophyll start storing oil in epidermal cells (exp. Orchidaceae and Liliaceae).

The disorganised plastids fuse to form oil droplets. In brown algae, the reserve storage is oil and this oil appears to be formed in the pheoplasts.

Aleuroneplasts

These are the plastids that contain much protein and often termed as the *proteinoplasts.* Protein crystals and granules are produced in the seeds of numerous plants specially in those seeds that also form large amount of oil, *e.g. the* Brazi Neof and seeds of *Ricinus.*

Mottier (1921) referred at protein and oil formation involves the activity of permanent plastid primordia. Protein crystals may develop independently in the cytoplasm without any aid of the aleuroneplasts, for example, in peripheral layers of potato the cells are poor F starch.

Protein crystals in epidermal cells may also represent material or may be the result of virus action. Amyloplasts are the most important of all the different types of leucoplasts.

The amyloplasts resemble proplastids and differ from them only in size. They contain fewer lamellae, but in presence of light they can build up a thylacoid structure found in chloroplasts. However, chloroplasts can also synthesize starch and store it in stromal region.

The starch in chloroplasts disappears quickly and is, therefore, known as transitory starch. The starch present

Table 2.1. Showing occurrence, functions and pigments of various plastids.

Kinds of Plastids	*Occurrence*	*Functions*	*Pigment*
I. Chromoplasts			
A. Photosynthetically active chromoplasts.			
1. *Chloroplasts*	Higher plants and green algae	Photosynthesis	Chlorophyll-a and Chloro phyll-b
2. *Pheoplasts*	Brown algae, diatoms and dinoflagellates	Light absorp-tion	Fucoxanthin
3. *Rhodoplasts*	Red algae (Rho-dophyceac)	Light absorp-tion	Phycoerythrin
4. *Blue-green*	Blue-green algae	Photosynthesis	Phycocyanin Phycoerythrin Chlorophyll-a and Carote noids
5. *Chromoplasts of Photosyn-thetic bacteria*	Purple and non-Bacteria purple sulphur bacteria	Absorption of infra red por-tion of light	chlorophyll
B. Chromoplasts devoid of photosynthetic activity			
6. *Carotenoids*	Tomato, red peppar, flower parts, fungi, ornamental bacteria and fruits		Lycopene & Capsanthia
II Leucoplasts			
7. *Amyloplasts*	Storage tubers. cotyledons and endosperm	Starch-storage	None
8. *Elaioplasts*	Epidermal cells of Orchidaceae and Liliaceae	Oil-storage	None

(Table 2.1 contd.)

Kinds of Plastids	Occurrence	Functions	Pigment
9. *Aleuronplasts*	Epidermal cells of Helleborus and seeds of *Ricinus* and Brazil nut	Protein-storage	None

in leucoplasts, on the ether hand, can be stored for monger periods and is, therefore, known as reserve starch. The starch development begins with the formation of a particle in the stroma.

This particle has several tubuli and thylcoids and is surrounded by additional rings of starch. It grows till the amyloplasts is filled with starch. As a result, the tubuli are pressed against the wall and ultimately starch granule exceeds the size of amyloplast.

The wall of the plastid then ruptures and finally withers away so that only the starch granules can be seen.

Chloroplasts

Chloroplasts are the plastids that are most common and of greatest biological importance, since by *otosynthesis* they produce most of the chemical energy used living organisms. Without chloroplasts there would be no imams, because animals feed on the food stuffs produced by ants.

Distribution and Orientation

Chloroplasts are sometimes distributed homogeneously within the cytoplasm, but are frequently packed near the nucleus, or close to the cell wall.

The distribution and orientation of the chmoroplasts within the cell may vary with the amount of light energy. Chloroplasts apparently multiply by division-elongation of the plastid and constriction of the central portion.

They have a higher density than the cytoplasm and migrate to the centrifugal pole of the cell when submitted to the action of centrifugal force.

MORPHOLOGY

Shape

Higher plant chloroplasts are generally biconvex or planoconvex. However, in different plants cells, chloroplast may have various shapes, viz., *filamentous, saucer-shaped, spheroid, ovoid* or *discoid shaped.*

They are vesicular and have .a colourless centre. Some chioroplasts are *club shaped,* having a thin middle zone and bulging ends filled with chlorophyll. Algae often possess a single huge chloroplast that appears as a network, *a spiral band,* or a *stellate plate.*

Size

The size of chloroplast varies from species to species 'but is constant for a given cell type. The average size of chloroplasts in higher plants measure 4-6,u in diameter and l

3μ in thickness. The chloroplasts of polyploid plant cells are larger than those in the corresponding diploid cells. In general, chloroplasts of plants grown in the shade are larger and contain more chlorophyll than of those plants grown in sunlight.

Number

The number of chloroplasts is relatively constant in the different plants. In higher plants there are 20 to 40 chloroplasts per cell. It has been calculated that the leaf of *Ricinus communis* contains about 400,000 chloroplasts per square millimeter of surface area.

When the number of chloroplasts is insufficient, it is increased by division; when excessive, it is reduced by degeneration.

Conformational Changes and Ion Movements

Chloroplasts undergo striking conformational changes which are dependent on the action of light. In the dark they undergo swelling and separation of the membranes of the thylakoid.

This phenomenon is reversible ; in the presence of light the membranes again return to close apposition. Mitochondira eject H+ ions during the electron transport and that the interior becomes more alkaline.

In the case of chloroplasts the opposite reactions occur. Under the action of light H^+ ions which are absorbed, the interior becomes acidified. At the same time K^+ and Mg^{++} are ejected into the medium.

In the dark, H^+ is ejected and K^+ and Mg^{++} are reabsorbed by the chloroplasts. Thus, the chloroplast membrane has a vectorial organization that is the reverse of the mitochondiral membrane.

In physical terms it is understood that dark reactions, being of a thermochemical nature, do not need an ordered structural arrangement (i.e. they are carried out by soluble enzymes).

On the contrary, photophosphorylation requires the separation of positive and negative charges into specific pathways of electron flow.

Chemical Composition

Chloroplasts of spinach leaf cells contain about 56% protein, 32% lipid and 8% chlorophyll. The lipids include xantbophylls, carotenoids, triglycerides, steroids, waxes and phospholipids. Chloroplasts of higher plants contain approximately 35-55% proteins, 20-30% lipids, 9% chlorophyll, 4-5% carotenoids and 2-3% nucleic acids. In cytoplasm the protein-lipid ratio is generally 90 : 1.

In plastids this ratio is about 40 : 30. Thus the grana have a high concentration of lipid. The nucleic acid DNA and RNA have been demonstrated in the chloroplasts of higher plants.

Chlorophyll has a tetrapyrrole structure and consists of a hydrophilic head and a hydrophobic tail. The head is made up of a magnesium atom surrounded by four pyrrolic nuclei (tetrapyrrole structure).

The long tail consists of a phytol china. Green plants

have two types of chlorophyll, *chlorophyll a* and *chlorophyll b*. In chlorophyll *b* one of the methyl (-CH=) groups of chlorophyll a is replaced by a formyl (-CHO) group.

Structure

Plastids are dynamic organelles whose structure changes in response to changes in environment. A mature plastid is having the following parts

(1) Limiting membrane

(2) Stroma

(3) Grana

Limiting Membrane

Each mature plastid is covered by a double membrane as in mitochondira, each unit is about 40 to 60A in thickness. The limiting membrane functions as a semipermeable membrane as well as a boundary.

Stroma

The inner space which is formed by a limiting membrane is filled with a proteinaceous matrix called the 'stroma'. A number of starch grains and sometimes osmiophilic droplets are embedded in the stroma. When the plastid be comes inactive or ages, the number of osmiophilic droplets may increase.

Grana or lamellar system

These are flat bodies shaped like platelets or discs, which in a lateral view appear as dense bands perpendicular to the limiting membrane of plastid. A number of grana are embedded in the stroma or matrix of plastid.

The size of the grana varies between 0.3-l.7μ depending on the species. Each granum consists of a stack of double membrane or lamellae. The lamellar membranes are composed of lipids and proteins. Protein contents are about 45% while lipids contents are 55% in amount. Each lamella is 30-35Å thick and the space between two such lamellae is of' 65-70Å. The lamellae can be placed under two groups

(*a*) Stroma lamellae

(*b*) Grana lamellae

Those lamellae, extending through the entire length of the plastids are called the stroma lamellae. These are not directly connected with the cell wall.

The grana lamellae are alwayss densely packed. Any way, the system of lamellae represents a closed unit, and thus both stroma and grana lamellae are closely related to one another, i.e., each granum lamella represents a local adhesion of two or more stroma lamellae.

Both stroma and grana lamellae may stay coupled for a long distance and then separate again from each other. Another term *thylakoid (reek ;* sac like) has been used for the double membranous lamellae already explained.

The stroma lamellae are larger thylakoids while the smaller, stacked thylakoids are the grana lamellae. One more term has been added by *Weler* and others, which is *fret* to discribe stroma lamellae as a flattened tubular channel connecting adjacent grana.

Recel studies have provided evidence that the membranes within ti chloroplasts form a continum and the cavities of the thy, lakoids (loculi) communicate via fret work connection.

The total number of grana in plastids of certain plants have been calculated. There is a considerable variation in the number of grana in a single plastid, depending upon the species. In *Euglena* only one granum is present in one plastid while in Spinach, where about 40-60 grana are present in each plastid.

In *Chlamydomonas,* the plastid envelope is sometimes continuous with elements of the endoplasmic reticulum. In *Ochromonas* as well as in *Chlamydomonas,* connection with other cytoplasmic membranes with single plastid have also been traced.

QUANTOSOME CONCEPT

The membranes of thylakoids are composed of many paracrystalline spheroid particles known as the quantosomes. The quantosomes are about 160A° by 180A° and about 100A^3 thick. *Sauer* and *Calvin (1962)* have shown that 3 to 6 quantosomes many aggregate together to form a large particle of 500 × 100A°.

Park and *Beggins* (1964) have reported that each quantosome is composed of four subunits. According to *Honwell- and Moundrianakis* (1967) these quantosomes are the smallest units capable of carrying out the photochemical reaction and each of them contains about 200 chlorophyll molecules.

According to the size, nature and arrangement of quantosomes in the membrane of thylakoids and stromal lamellae, *Branton* and *Park* (1967) have recognised three types of membranes which are as follows

1. Membrane with quantosomes.
2. Membrane with smaller particles (110A°).
3. Membrane with rough surface and with a few or no particles.

The chloroplasts, thus, act as elaborate biochemical machines and transform the energy at the molecular level.

FUNCTIONS OF THE CHLOROPLAST

Photosynthesis

Photosynthesis involves two major sets of reactions, each set consisting of many steps. One set, the *light reactions,* transform ("transduce") energy acquired through the absorption of light into usable chemical forms, namely ATP and the reduced form (NADPH) of the coenzyme NADP.

This is accomplished via oxidation-reduction sequences that include the removal of electrons from water, releasing oxygen and protons (H+). These protons and others transferred across the thylakoid membranes during the oxidation-reduction reactions contribute to an ATP-producing proton gradient like the one described for mitochondria.

The other reactions in photosynthesis, the *dark reactions,* occur both in the light and in the dark. They use the

ATP and NADPH to build carbohydrates from CO_2. The most common pathway by which this is done is the "carbon reduction cycle" (the *Calvin cycle),* which starts with the reaction of CO_2 with the 5-carbon sugar ribulose 1,5-diphosphate. This generates two 3-carbon molecules that undergo the cycle schematized.

This initial CO_2 fixation is catalyzed by the enzyme ribulose I,5-diphosphate ("bisphosphate") carboxylase, often called RuDP carboxylase or carboxydismutase.

The Light Reactions

The green colour of chlorophyll is due to its selective

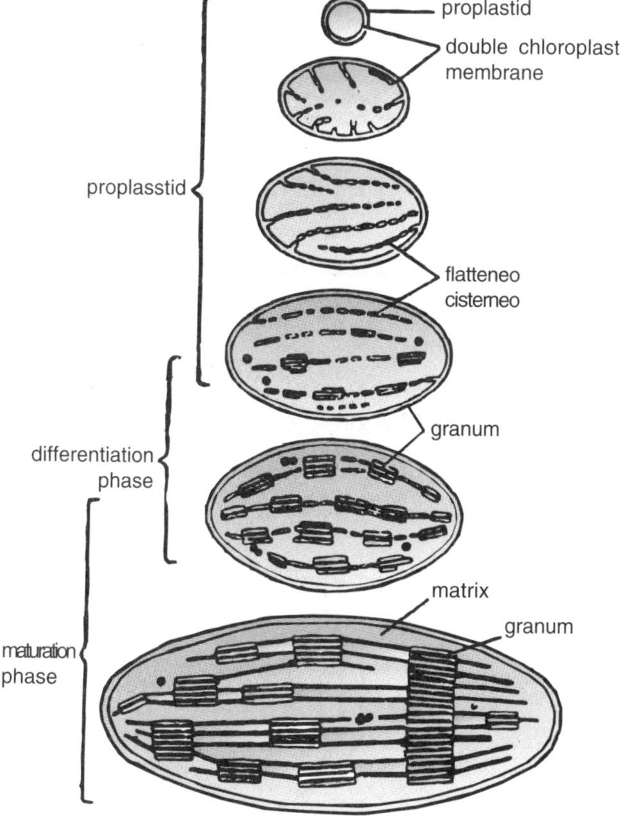

Figure 2.2: Development of a chloroplast in sun light.

absorption of light with wavelenghts of 650 to 700nm. (Light of these wave-lengths appears to the eye as red; when red light is removed from white light, as by absorption, what is left appears green.)

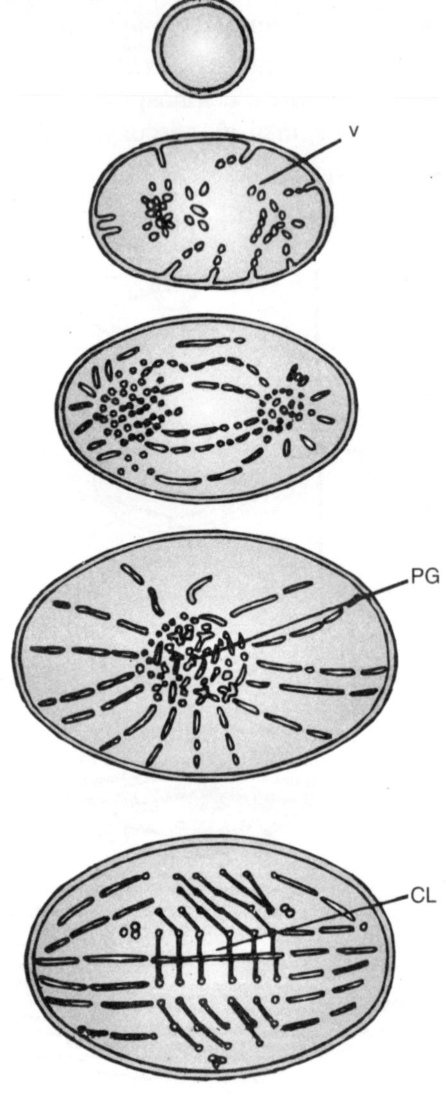

Figure 2.3: Developed of a chloroplast in dark.

Chlorophyll also absorbs light at shorter wavelenghts (4C0 to 475nm, corresponding to the violet-blue region of the spectrum). Two major chlorophyll types are present in eukaryotic plastids Chlorophyll a shows absorption maxima (peak absorption) at about 670 nm and at about 490 nm, Chlorophyll b absorbs maximally at about 650 and 470 nm.

Wavelength is an indicator of the energy carried by packets *(photons)* of light. The shorter the wavelength, the greater the energy. The absorption maxima of the chlorophylls and other photosynthetic, pigments indicate the portion of the spectrum of sunlight that can be captured for energizing photosynthesis.

When a chlorophyll molecule absorbs a photon, an electron of the chlorophyll's porphyrin ring acquires the photon's energy and thereby is excited. This is the basis of the chloroplast's ability to transduce light energy to chemical energy.

The excited electron can enter a series of electron transport reactions involving iron-containing proteins (ferrodexins, cytochromes), a copper-containing protein (plastocyanin), lipid-soluble molecules (plastoquinones) resembling coenzyme Q and other participants, some yet to be identified.

Two distinguishable "*photochemical units*", *photosystems,* cooperate in photosynthesis. This cooperation as currently envisaged by a majority of investigators. The functional heart of each unit is a reaction center (action center) that carries out the essential processes by which energy derived from light is made available to the electron transport sequences and other phenomena of the light reactions.

Each photosystem is characterized by a particular form of pigment molecule associated with the reaction center ; the pigments almost certainly are chlorophylls. In photosystem I (PSI), the reaction center pigment absorbs light maximally at 700 urn and hence, is called P 700. Excited electrons from P 700 pass from the PSI reaction center to the electron transport sequence that reduced NADP.

The electrons "lost" from P 700 in this process are replaced through electron transport from photosystern II (PSII) ; the cyclic pathway diagrammed represents an alternative replenishment mechanism, which some investigators believe is actually the predominant one, at least under some physiological circumstances.

The reaction center pigment of PSII, P 680, absorbs light preferent-ially at 680 nm. The PSII reaction center transfers electrons from this pigment to an electron transport chain that links PSII to PSI. The "loss" of electrons from P 680 is made up by the removal of electrons from water molecules; it is this PSI· mediated oxidation ("splitting") of water that generates O_2.

In net effect the two photosystems collaborate via electron transport to transfer electrons from water to NADPH. Accomnanvintt this transfer is the establishment of an electro-chemical H^+ gradient across the thylakoid membranes : The thylakoid interior is maintained at low pH relative to the stroma.

The H^+ ions freed in the "splitting" of water also contribute to this gradient. The proton gradient is used to generate ATP (photosynthetic phosphorylation).

As with mitochondira, vesicles formed from fragmented thylakoids are capable of both electron transport and phosphorylation but can no longer phosphorylate if broken open or otherwise treated to disrupt the permeability barrier inherent in the membrane.

Moreover, chloroplast vesicles can produce ATP for a brief period if simply soaked for a time in a medium of low pH, until their interior equilibrates with the medium, and then transferred into a medium of high pH, establishing a transient H+ gradient across the vesicles' membranes.

Experiments of this sort were crucial in verifying the plausibility, in general of chemiosmotic mechanisms for production of ATP.

ORIGIN OF THE PLASTIDS

Plastids are generated only by other preexisting plastids or proplastid body. They are self reproducing cell organelles like the chromosomes and the centrioles. The proplastid may be regarded as the "stem" plastid, giving rise to metabolically active leucoplasts or chloroplasts which may later develop into other types of chromoplasts through a kind of degeneration.

Plastids are transmitted directly to daughter cells during division, providing a genetic continuity in plastid lineage. Although the origin of initials that develop into proplastids is not entirely clear, some observations in fern suggest the nuclear envelope as a possible source.

In Lower Plants

In algae and lower plants, the plastids are quite large and often of different shapes and the process of their division is easy to follow. Here the division begins with an infolding of the inner membrane of the limiting chloroplast envelope. Later on the outer membrane invaginates until the plastid is divided into two. The daughter plastids thus formed, may or may not be equal in size.

In Higher or superior Plants

In higher plants the process of formation of plastids is more complicated. The process **can** be effected even by sun light, as the formation of plastids

In sun light and in dark, show vast differences in either case.

In sun light

During the development the proplastids increase in size. Protoplastids are limited by a double memo brane. In the presence of light the inner limiting boundary invaginates at several places, producing small vesicle like structures.

These vesicles later on pinch off as free units, which then aggregate in several arrangements to form the lemellae of the mature plastid.

In dark

If the proplastids are left in dark, the process of mation upto vesicle stage is the same, as in presence of light. But the arrangement of vesicles is different. In dark. the clusters of vesicles or discs constitute the lamellar system or a series of concentric rings are developed.

Formation of leucoplasts, chromoplasts and chloroplasts from proplastids. The non-lamellated proplastids can also transform themselves into leucoplasts. These, in turn, can develop into immature lamellar plastids or by a reversible process, into starch containing amyloplasts.

The mature proplastids then grow to become either mature chloroplasts or other chromoplasts or even, by storing proteins, aleurone plastids. Mature chloroplasts can become chlorophyll free chromoplasts or, by absorption of many lipids elaioplasts.

Nuclear origin

A large number of initials around the nucleus have been observed under special conditions, where the cell organelles are breaking down. This suggested that the initials originated due to evaginatin of the double nuclear membrane and gave rise to mitochondria and proplastids.

Symbiotic Origin

To much surprise, resemblance has been observed between mitocho-ndria and bacteria on the one hand and chloroplast and blue-green algae on the other hand. They are not only some what similar in shape and structure but also in function.

All possess DNA, much smaller than nuclear *DNA* and circular, not organised in chromosomes ; their ribosomes are all about the same size, smaller than the cytoplasmic matrix ribosomes of animal and plant cells. In bacteria the respiratory chain is localised in the membrane comparable to inner membrane of mitochondria.

Further comparable to cristae of mitochondria, infoldings of plasma membrane (mesosomes) have been reported in certain bacteria. In mitochondria and bacteria both, the protein synthesis is inhibited by chioramphenicol, whereas the exracellular protein synthesis of higher cells is not effected.

These similarities have led some to consider the mitochondria and chloroplasts of today as generally modified descendents of an ancestral free living bacteria and blue green-algae respectively (autotrophic microorganisms) which at one time came together with the ancestral eukaryotic cell (heterotrophic host cell) to form a symbiotic relationship.

This hypothesis is no doubt highly attractive, but still it is evident that the electron transport system in chloroplasts and the enzymes required for making the photosynthetic pigments are controlled by the nuclear genes.

Chapter 3

CHLOROPHYLL

Green is the predominant colour of the plant kingdom. With only a few exceptions all leaves are green in colour as are also many other plant organs such as herbaceous and young woody stems, young fruits, and sepals of flowers. The green colouring of plants is often termed chlorophyll, although actually a number of kinds of chlorophyll occur in plants.

Less evident is the fact that the leaves and many other organs of plants also contain yellow pigments. These are seldom apparent except in leaves in which the chlorophyll fails to develop, or in which it is destroyed as a result of senescence or other physiological changes.

Corn plants that have grown from seed in the dark, for example, do not synthesize chlorophyll, but are usually yellow in colour because of the presence of yellow pigments. In the autumn disintegration of the .chlorophyll in the leaves of many woody species results in unmasking the yellow pigments which are also present in the leaves.

The yellow chloroplast pigments of leaves belong to the group of compounds called *carotenoids.* Except in blue-green algae and the photosynthetic bacteria, chlorophylls occur only in the chloroplasts.

The carotenoids of leaves are also restricted to the. chloroplasts, and this also appears to be true of the carotenoids in the cells of most algae. All of these pigments appear to be present only in the grana of the chloroplasts. In certain other plant organs, such as flower petals, the yellow pigments occur in chlomoplasts.

The chlorophylls and associated carotenoids are often called the chloroplast pigments. In some kinds of algae pigments of another group, called the phycobilins, also occur in the chloroplasts.

The best known of these are the phycoerythrin of most Ted and some blue-green algae, and the phycocyanin of most blue-green and some red algae. These two pigments are -closely related chemically. Both are colloidal proteinaceous pigments and can be extracted from the cells with hot water.

The Chlorophylis

A number of different kinds of chlorophyll occur in the plant kingdom. Of these, chlorophyll a is most nearly of universal occurrence being present, as far as is known, in all photosyn-thetic organisms except the green and purple bacteria.

Chlorophyll *b* is found in all higher plants and in the green algae, but is not present in algae of most other phyla. Chlorophyll *c* is found in the brown algae and diatoms, which do not contain chlorophyll *b*.

Similarly red algae contain chlorophyll *d* but no chlorophyll *b*. In the purple bacteria still another kind of chlorophyll called *bocteriochlorophyll* is present, whereas the green bacteria contain another apparently similar pigment called *bacteriovlridln.*

All of these chlorophylls are very similar in chemical composition, and all of them are compounds which contain magnesium.

Chlorophylls *a* and *b* are the characteristic chlorophylls of the higher plants. Neither is water soluble, but both are soluble in a number of organic reagents.

Chlorophyll *a* is readily soluble in absolute-ethyl alcohol, ethyl ether, acetone, chloroform, and carbon bisulfide.

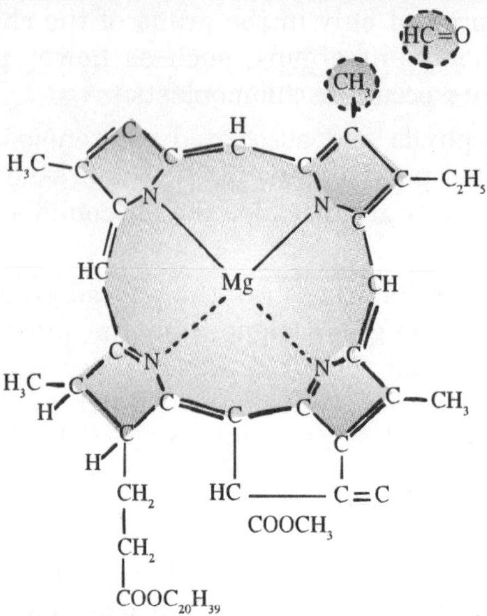

Figure 3.1: Structural formula of chlorophyll a, Another arrangement of the double bonds in this formula is possible. The formula for chlorophyll b is the same, except that a HC=O group occurs in place of the CH_3 group enclosed in the dotted circle.

Chlorophyll *b* is soluble in the same reagents, although generally less so.

Chlorophyll *a* is blue-green in solution, and blue-black in the solid state; chlorophyll *b* is almost pore green in solution, and grnenish black in the solid state.

All of the chlorophylls possess the property of *fluorescence*. This term refers to the peculiar property possessed by certain substances when illuminated of re-radiating light of wavelengths other than those absorbed by the substance.

Usually the radiated light (fluorescent light) is longer in wave length than the incident light. Chlorophyll *a* in ethyl alcoholic solution exhibits a deep blood red fluorescence, best seen by viewing the solution in reflected light.

Similar solutions of chlorophyll *b* exhibit a brownish-red fluorescence. Chlorophyll in living cells also exhibits fluorescence.

The Chemistry of the Chlorophylls

Willstatter and his associates have isolated chlorophylls *a* and *b* in pure form from over two hundred different species of higher plants and found them to be identical in chemical composition.

They also succeeded in determining the molecular formulas of these two chlorophylls. For chlorophyll *a* this is $C_{55}H_{72}O_6N_4Mg$; for chlorophyll *b* it is $C_{b6}H_{70}O_6N_4Mg$. Each chlorophyll yields a separate series of degradation products, but one of the products derived from both after mild hydrolysis is an unsaturated primary alcohol which is, called *phytol* ($C_{20}H_{39}OH$).

Splitting of the phytol group from the chlorophyll molecule can also be accomplished by the enzyme *chlorophyllase,* which occurs in leaves. Phytol makes up about one-third of the chlorophyll molecule. It has a strong affinity for oxygen and may be responsible for the reducing action of chlorophyll.

When ashed pure chlorophyll leaves a residue composed solely of magnesium oxide. Although iron and other minerals seem essential for the formation of chlorophyll in living cells magnesium' is the only metallic constituent of the chlorophyll molecule.

From the results of the intensive study of the chemistry of the degradation. products of chlorophyll the probable structural formulas of both chlorophyll *a* and chlorophyll *b* have been determined.

As shown in Figure elsewhere in this chapter the nucleus of a molecule of chlorophyll a consists of a complex ring structure composed principally of four pyrrol nuclei linked together by intermediate atomic groupings. Each such ring bears side chains, the most prominent of which is the phytyl ($C_{20}H_{29}O$—) grouping which upon hydrolysis gives rise to phytol.

Absorption Spectra of the Chlorophylls

When a coloured solution such as an ether solution of

a chlorophyll is interposed between a source of "white light" and a spectroscope, it can readily be shown that certain wave lengths of light are much more completely absorbed than others.

The regions of the spectrum in which complete or nearly complete absorption takes place appear as dark bands. Chlorophylls *a* and *b* both show a definite and characteristic absorption spectrum when in solution.

The exact appearance of such absorption spectra will vary, however, depending upon the kind of solvent and the concentration and thickness of the layer of solution which is examined.

Absorption curves for chlorophyll a and *b* in ether solution as determined by photoelectric measurements we shot in Figure elsehwhere in this chapter. Both chlorophylls exhibit maximum absorption in the blue-violet region and a secondary maximum in the short red.

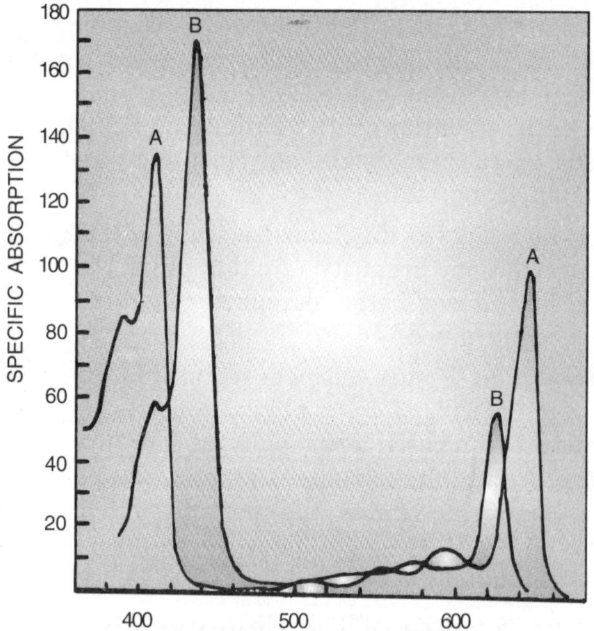

Figure 3.2: Absorption spectra of chloropbylls a and b in ether solution.

As a rule the absorption spectrum of a leaf does not correspond very closely with the spectrum of a solution of the pigments from that same leaf.

In general there is relatively more absorption of light by leaves in those spectral regions where absorption by solutions is low, and a relatively less absorption of light by leaves in those spectral regions where absorption by solutions is high. Some of the principal reasons for this are :

(1) the pigment in the leaf is not continuous, but located only in the plastids; hence some light may pass. through the leaf without traversing any pigment;
(2) actual or apparent absorption, the latter a result of scattering of light within the leaf, by the nonpigmented parts of cells affects the overall absorption of light by the leaf; and
(3) the concentrationof thepigment in the leaf is usually different from its concentration in extracts; as a result, specific absorption values of pigments in the leaf are different from those in a solution.

Physicochemical State of the Chlorophylls in the Chloroplasts

Although the extensive investigations of extracts of chlorophylls in organic solvents have advanced our knowledge of their physical and chemical properties, it should be rememberd that these are only *extracts* and the physicochemical state of the chlorophylls in them bears little or no relation to its conditions in the chloroplasts.

One necessary step in learning how the chloropbylls of living cells operate will be to discover how they are related physically and chemically to the other constituents of the chloroplasts.

Any acceptable picture of the physicochemical relationships of the chlorophylls within the chloroplasts must also be reconcilable with the known structural arrangement of the chlorophylls in the grana of the chloroplasts.

A number of investigators have shown that green, opalescent, aqueous extracts can be prepared from the leaves of many species by grinding them with sand in water or solutions and clarifying by filtration, precipitation, or centrifugation. These extracts possess many of the properties of protein sols or suspensions and the chlorophyll molecules seem to be definitely associated with the protein micelles or particles.

These results have led to the postulation of the existence of *a* chlorophyll-protein compound of constant composition in plants, analogous to the hemoglobin (hemin plus globin, a protein) of the blood.

Although results of these experiments indicate that some sort of an association of chlorophylls with proteins in the chloroplasts is highly probable, there are strong reasons for doubting that this association takes the form of a protein-chlorophyll compound in the strictly chemical sense.

Actual chemical analyses of the chloroplast substance have been made by Chibnall (1939), Menke (1940), Granick (1938), Comar (1942), and others.

The protein content of the chloroplast material from several species has been found to lie within a range of 35 to 55 per cent, and the lipid content within a range of 18 to 32 per cent on the dry weight basis (chloroplasts are probably about 50 per cent water).

In the leaf cells of g oh most of the lipids present are constituents of the chloroplasts. In such chemical analyses the chlorophylls and carotenoids constitute a part of the lipid fraction, about 5-10 per cent of which is chlorophylls and 2-4 per cent carotenoids.

The relatively large quantity of lipids in the chloroplasts suggests that the pigments commonly present in tome manner may be associated with lipids as well as with proteins. The physicochemical properties of the lipids are such that it seems more probable that any association between them and the chlorophylls or carotenoids is of a physical rather than a chemical nature.

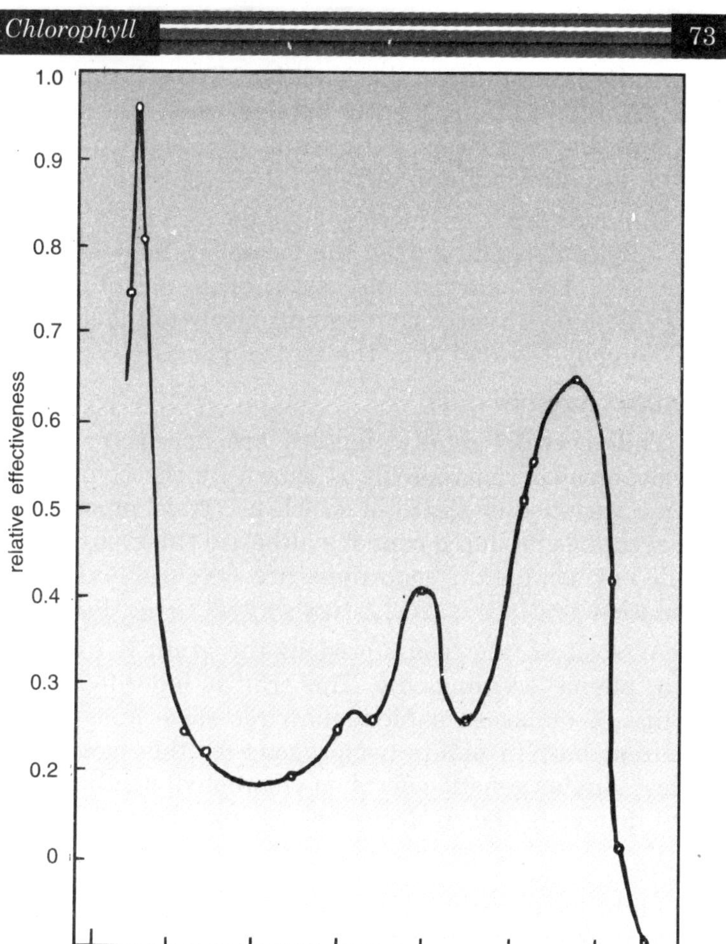

Figure 3.3: Relative effectiveness of different wave lengths in the formation of chlorophyll.

Chlorophyll Synthesis

Chlorophylls, in common with practically all the other organic substances which occur in plants, are products of the synthetic activities of the plant. A number of conditions are known to be necessary for or at least to influence greatly, the synthesis of chlorophylls in plants.

Absence of any one of these factors will inhibit chlorophyll synthesis resulting in the condition often called *chlorosis.* This term is most frequently applied when the failure of chlorophylls to develop is the result of a deficiency of one of the essential mineral elements.

Different types of chlorosis may develop in to leaves of any species depending upon the factor limiting chlorophyll formation. The following discussion of the factors influencing chlorophyll synthesis refers primarily to the formation of chlorophyll; *a* and *b* in the higher plants.

Genetic Factors

That certain genetic factors are necessary for the development of chlorophylls is shown by the behaviour of so· me varieties of maize in which a certain proportion of the seedlings produced cannot synthesize chlorophylls, even if all environmental conditions are favourable 'for their formation.

As soon as the food stored in the grain is exhausted such "albino" seedlings die. This trait is inherited in such strains of maize as a Mendelian recessive and hence is apparent only in plants homozygous for this factor. More or less similar genetic effects on chlorophyll synthesis have been demonstrated in a number of other species.

Light

Light is usually necessary for the development of chlorophyll in the angiosperms. In the algae, mosses, ferns, and conifers, however, chlorophyll synthesis can occur in the dark as well as in the light, although the quantity produced is often less in the absence of light than in its presence.

In a few angiosperms such as seedlings of the water lotus *(Nelumbo),* and in the cotyledons of citrus embryos chlorophylls can also develop in the absence of light. Relatively low intensities of light are generally effective in inducing chlorophyll synthesis in those species in which light is required for this process.

All wave lengths of the visible spectrum will, if their

energy value is adequate, cause chlorophyll development in etiolated seedlings (chlorophyll-free seedlings which have been grown in the dark) except those longer than 680 mμ.

For equal irradiances, a narrow band of wave lengths in the blue at about 445 mμ is most effective in inducing chlorophyll formation in oat seedlings, a broader wave band in the orange red (about 620-660 mμ) being next most effective. Like other complex compounds synthesized in plants, chlorophyll undoubtedly represents the terminal product of a long chain of reactions.

Cost of the steps in this sequence of 'reactions are unknown, but the evidence regarding the final step in chlorophyll synthesis seems clear. Dark-grown seedlings of higher plants are usually yellow in colour, but .actually contain traces of a green pigment, called *protochlorophyll.*

Chemically this compound is closely related to the other chlorophylls, differing from chlorophyll a only in having 'two less hydrogen atoms in the molecule. There is good evidence that protochlorophyll is the immediate precursor of chlorophyll a. Reduction of protochlorophyll to chlorophyll a appears to be the last step in the synthesis of this latter compounds.

In the higher plants, at least, this reaction occurs only in the light, and the protochlorophyll is the light-absorbing agent for its own transformation to chlorophyll *a*.

If a solution of chlorophyll in an organic solvent is exposed to bright light its colour soon fades because of a destructive effect of light upon the chlorophyll. This is in all probability a photo-oxidation process, since it is accomplished by the absorption of oxygen.

Strong light also brings about the disintegration of the chlorophylls in leaves, although at a less rapid rate than in chlorophyll solutions. In leaves exposed to intense light, therefore, synthesis and decomposition of chlorophylls are probably going on simultaneously.

In accord with this concept are the results of Shirley (1929) who found in a number of species of plants that the, chlorophyll content per unit leaf weight or per unit leaf area increased with decreasing light intensity until a relatively low intensity was reached. Further decrease in light intensity below this value caused a decrease in chlorophyll content.

Oxygen

In the absence of oxygen etrolated seedlings fail to develop chlorophylls even when illuminated underconditions otherwise favorable for chlorophyll formation. Oxygen must therefore be required in some of the steps in the sequence of reactions whereby chlorophyll is synthesized.

Carbohydrates

Etiolated leaves which have been depleted of soluble carbohydrates fail to turn green even when all of the other conditions to which they are exposed favourchlorophyll synthesis. When such leaves are floated on a sugar solution, sugar is absorbed and *chlorophyll* formation occurs rapidly. A supply of carbohydrate foods is therefore essential for the formation of chlorophyll.

Nitrogen

Since nitrogen is a part of chlorophyll molecules it is not surprising to find that a deficiency of this element in the plant retards chlorophyll formation. Failure ofchlorophylls to develop is one of the commonly recognized symptoms of nitrogen deficiency in plants.

Magnesium

Like nitrogen this element is also a part of chlorophyll molecules. Deficiency of magnesium in plants results in the development of a characteristic mottled chlorosis of the older, leaves.

Iron

In the absence of iron in an available form green. plants are unable to synthesize chlorophylls and the leaves soon become blanched or yellow in colour. While not a constituent

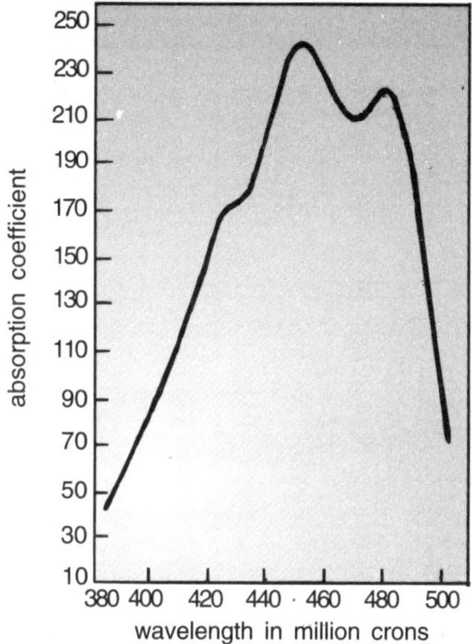

Figure 3.4: Absorption spectrum of β-carotene in ether-alcohol solution.

of chlorophyll molecules, iron is essential for its synthesis.

Other Mineral Elements

In the absence of manganese, copper, or zinc, more or less characteristic chloroses develop in plants. These substances apparently play at least indirect roles in the synthesis of chlorophyll.

Temperature

In general, chlorophyll synthesis can cur over a wide range of temperatures. In etiolated wheat plants synthesis of chlorophylls occurs at any temperature within the range 3°-48°C, but is most rapid between 26° and 30°C.

Somewhat similar results have been obtained on chlorophyll synthesis in potato tubers except that synthesis appears to be most rapid in the approximate range 11°-19°C. The range off temperatures over which chlorophyll synthesis occurs as well as the temperature of most rapid synthesis undoubtedly varies considerably from one species to another.

Table 3.1. Molecular proportions of the chioroplast pigments present in leaves at different seasons.

Species	*Date*	*Appearance of leaves*	*Molecular propartions*		
			Chlorophyll a Chlorophyll b	*Carotene Xmuhophylls*	*Chlorephyll a and b Carotens and Xanthophylls*
European Elder	July	Green	2.74	0.59	3.33
(Sambucusnigra)	Oct. 21	Green	2.61	0.60	3.15
Sunflower	Oct. 7	Green	2.86	0.54	3.66
Helionthus	Nov. 5	Yellow green	4.01	0.26	1.27
annuus	Nov. 5	Yellow	.95	0.17	0.32
Horse Chestnut	Oct. 24	Green	4.23	0.47	3.06
(Aesculus hlp-pocastanum)	Oct. 24	Yellow green	4.23	0.20	0.81

Water

Desiccation of leaf tissues not only inhibits synthesis of chlorophylls but seems to accelerate disintegration of the chlorophylls already present. A familiar example of this effect is the browning of grass during droughts.

The mechanism of chlorophyll synthesis is very sensitive to any type of physiological disturbance within the plant. Many other conditions besides those already discussed, such as lack of certain other mineral elements, deficient aeration of the roots, infestations of insects, or infection with bacterial fungous or viral diseases, may induce, directly or indirectly, partial or complete chlorosis of the leaves.

The failure of chlorophyll synthesis to take place normally is often one of -the first observable symptoms of almost any derangement in the metabolic conditions within a plant.

The Carotenoids

This group of orange, red, yellow, and brownish pigments includes a number of chloroplast pigments. At least sixty different carotenoids are known to be present in plants. Best known of the pigments in this group is the - orange-yellow *carotene.*

This is a hydrocarbon with the formula $C_{40}H_{54}$ and exists in three isomeric forms. β-carotene is the most abundant of these in plants, and appears to be invariably present in the chloroplasts.

This compound is the precursor of vitamin A which is formed in the animal body by a simple hydrolytic splitting of the molecules of n-carotene, as follows:

$$C_{40}H_{51}+2H_2O \rightarrow 2C_{20}H_{29}OH$$

Lycopene, a red pigment found in the fruits of tomato, red peppers, roses, and other species, is also isomeric with carotene.

The xanthophylls or carotenols are mostly yellow or brownish pigments, many, but not all, of which have molecular formula $C_{40}H_{65}O_2$. Chemically the carotenols are closely related to carotene, and undoubtedly transformations from one kind of carotenoid to another occur readily in plants.

Luteol is by far the most abundant carotenol is leaves other leaf xanthophylls include zeaxanthol, violaxanthol, cryptoxanthol, flavoxanthol, and neoxanthin.

Numerous other xanthophylls occur in the various *phyla* of *algae*. Among the most abundant of these pigments art the fucoxanthins which impart to brown algae their distinctive colour.

Several brownish carotenols are also present in the diatoms, including fucoxanthins, diatoxanthin, and diadinoxanthin. The carotenoids are not water soluble, but they can be extracted from plant tissues by use of suitable organic solvents.

Carotene, for example, is soluble in ethyl ether, chloroform, and carbon bisulfide. Leaf xanthophylls are soluble in chloroform and ethyl alcohol, but only slightly soluble in carbon, bisulfide.

All of the carotenoids are highly unsaturated compounds and hence readily oxidizable. Loss of a considerable proportion of the carotenoids present in a plant tissue may be occasioned by oxidation during extraction procedures.

As shown by its absorption spectrum, β-carotene absorbs only wave lengths in the blue-violet portion of the visible spectrum. The absorption spectra of other carotenoidse are similar to that of carotene.

Most, if not all, of the carotenoid pigments can be synthesized by plants in the absence of light.

Relative Quantities of the Chloroplast Pigments Present fn ,Green Leaves. Data regarding the molecular proportions of the chloroplast pigments in the leaves of several species are presented in Table elsewhere in this chapter.

The leaves listed in this table contain about three molecules of the chlorophylls to one molecule of 'the carotenoids, about three molecules of chlorophyll a to each molecule of chlorophyll *b*, and about two molecules of xanthophylls to each molecule of carotene.

Although these values can be taken as representative, considerable variation in the proportions of the chloroplast pigments occurs as a result of differences in genetic factors, environmental conditions, and the age of the Leaf.

As shown in Table elsewhere in this chapter, with senescence of leaves in the autumn there is a marked increase in the proportion of carotenoids to chlorophylls as a result of the disintegration of the chlorophylls.

The proportion of chlorophyll a to b in leaves may vary considerably depending upon the light intensity to which the leaves have been exposed. Will Matter and Stoll (1928) and others, for example, have shown that the proportion of chlorophyll b to a is higher in shade leaves of many species than in sun leaves of the same species.

As an example of genetic differences in the pigment content of leaves, results obtained with dark and burley varieties of tobacco may be taken as illustrative.

Although the ratio of chlorophyll *a* to *b* was virtually the same in all varieties studied the total chlorophyll content per gram of dry weight was, on the average, more than 50 per cent greater in the dark varieties than in the burley varieties. Carotene content of the dark varieties was also appreciably higher than in the burley varieties.

THE ROLE OF CHLOROPHYLL IN PHOTOSYNTHESIS

Any effort to understand the basis of life on this planet must always come back to photosynthesis : the process that enables plants to grow by utilizing carbon dioxide (CO_2), water (H_2O) and a tiny amount of minerals.

Photosynthesis is the one large-scale process that converts simple, stable, inorganic. compounds into the energy-rich combination of organic matter and oxygen and thereby makes abundant life on earth possible. photosynthesis is the source of all living matter on earth, and of all biological energy.

The overall reaction of photosynthesis can be summarized in the following equation : CO_2+H_2O+light "' (CH_2O)+O_2 → 12,000 calories of energy permole. (CH_2O) stands for a carbbhydrate ; for example, glucose : $(CH_2O)_6$. "Mole" is short !hr' "*gram molecule*": one gram multiplied by the molecular weight of the substances in question-in this case carbohydrate and oxygen.

The state of knowledge of photosynthesis was first summarized 30 years ago. The whole process was, heavily shrouded in fog.

Rabinowitch; Scientific American Offprint 34]. Later investigation had penetrated the mists sufficiently to disclose some of the main features of the process [see "Progress in, Photosynthesis," by Eugene I. Rabinowitch ; Scientific American, November, 1953].

Since then much new knowledge has been accumulated in particular the sequence of chemical ,steps that convert carbon dioxide into carbohydrate is now understood in considerable detail [see "The Path of Carbon ins Photosynthesis," by J.A. Bassham ; Scientific American .Offprint 122].

The fog has thinned out in other areas, and, the day when the entire sequence of physical and chemical events in photosynthesis will be well understood seems much, closer.

The photosynthetic process apparently consists of three main stages:

(1) the removal of hydrogen atoms from water and the production of oxygen molecules;

(2) the transfer of the hydrogen atoms from an intermediate compound in the first stage to one in the third stage, and

(3) the use of the hydrogen atoms to convert carbon dioxide into a carbohydrate.

The least understood of these three stages is the first : the removal of hydrogen atoms from water with the release of oxygen. All that is known is that it entails a series of steps probably requiring several enzymes, one of which contains manganese.

The third stage-the production of carbohydrates from carbon dioxide-is the best understood, thanks largely to the work of Melvin Calvin and his co-workers at the University of California at Berkeley. The subject of our article is the second. stage : the transfer of hydrogen atoms from the first stage to the third.

This is the energy-storing part of photosynthesis ; in it, to use the words of Robert Mayer, a discoverer of the law of the conservation of energy, "the fleeting sun rays are fixed and skillfully stored for future use."

The light energy to be converted into chemical energy by photosynthesis is first taken up by plant pigments, primarily the green pigment chlorophyll. In photosynthesis chlorophyll functions as a photocatalyst; when it is in its energized state,. which results from the absorption of light it catalyzes an energy-storing chemical reaction.

This reaction is the primary photochemical process ; it is followed by a sequence of secondary "dark"—that is, non photo-chemical-reactions in which no further energy is stored. Once it was thought that in photosynthesis the primary photochemical process is the decomposition of carbon dioxide into carbon and oxygen, followed by the combination of carbon and water.

More recently it has been suggested that the energy of light serves primarily to dissociate water, presumably into hydroxyl radicals (OH) and hydrogen atoms; the hydroxyl radicals would then react to form oxygen molecules.

It is better than either of these two formulations to say that the primary photochemical process in photosynthesis is the boosting of hydrogen atoms from a stable association with oxygen in water molecules to a much less stable one with carbon in organic matter.

The oxygen atoms *"left behind"* combine into oxygen molecules, an association also much less stable than the one between oxygen and hydrogen in water. The replacement of stable bonds (between oxygen and hydrogen) by looser bonds (between oxygen and oxygen and between hydrogen and carbon) obviously requires a supply of energy, and it explains why energy is stored in photosynthesis.

The transfer of hydrogen atoms from one *molecule* to another is called *oxidation-reduction*. The *hydrogen atom* is transferred from a donor molecule (a "*reductant*") to an acceptor molecule (an "*oxidant*"); after the reaction the donor is said to be oxidized and the acceptor to be reduced.

The transfer of an electron can often substitute for the transfer of a hydrogen atom: in an aqueous system (such as the interior of the living cell) there are always hydrogen ions (H+), and if such an ion combines with the electron acceptor, the acquisition of an electron becomes equivalent to the acquisition of a hydrogen atom (electron + H^+ ion $\rightarrow$ H^+ atom).

The chain of oxidation-reduction reactions in photosynthesis has some links that involve electron transfers and others, that involve hydrogen-atom transfers. For the sake of simplicity we shalls speak of electron transfers, with the understanding that in some cases what is actually transferred is a hydrogen atom. Indeed, the end result of the reactions undoubtedly is the transfer of hydrogen atoms.

In the oxidation-reduction reactions of photosynthesis the electrons must be pumped "*uphill*", that is why energy must be supplied to make the reaction go.

The tiny chlorophyll containing chloroplasts of the photosynthesizing plant cell act au chemical pumps; they obtain the necessary power from the absorption of light by chlorophyll (and to some extent from absorption by other pigments in the chloroplast).

It is important to realize that the energy is stored in the two products organic matter and free oxygen and not in either of them separately. To release the energy by the combustion of the organic matter (or by respiration, which is slow, enzyme-catalyzed combustion) the two products must be brought together again.

How much energy is stored in the transfer of electrons from water to carbon dioxide, converting the carbon dioxide to -carbohydrate and forming a proportionate amount of oxygen?

Oxidation-reduction energy can conveniently be measured an terms of electrochemical potential. Between a given donor of electrons and a given acceptor there is a certain difference of oxidation-reduction potentials.

This difference depends not only on the nature of the two reacting substances but also on the nature of the products of the reaction ; it is characteristic of the two oxidation-reduction "couples." For example, when oxygen is reduced to water (H_2O) its potential is +.81 volt, 'but when it is reduced to hydrogen peroxide (H_2O_2) the potential is +.27 volt.

The more positive the potential, the stronger is the oxidative power of the couple; the more negative the potential, the stronger is its reducing power.

When two oxidation-reduction couples are brought together, the one containing the stronger oxidant tends to oxidize the one containing the stronger reductant. In photosynthesis, however, a weak oxidant (CO_2) must oxidize a weak reductant (H_2O), producing a strong oxidant (O_2) and a strong reductant (a *carbohydrate*).

This calls for a massive investment of energy. The specific amount needed is given by the difference "between the oxidation-reduction potentials of the two couples involved in the reaction:oxygen-water and carbon-dioxidec-arbohydrate.

The oxygen-water potential is about -h.8 volt ; the carbon-dioxide-carbohydrate potential, about -.4 volt. The transfer of a single electron from water to carbon dioxide thus requires +.8 minus-.4, or 1.2, electron volts of energy.

For a molecule of carbon dioxide to be reduced to

CH_2O—the elementary molecular group of a carbohydrate *four* electrons (or hydrogen atoms) must be transferred ; hence the total energy needed is 4.8 electron volts.

This works out to 112,000 calories per mole of carbon dioxide reduced and of oxygen liberated. In short, the pumping of electrons in the second stage of photosynthesis entails the storage of 112,000 calories of energy per mole for each set of four electrons transferred.

We know the identity of the primary electron donor in photosynthesis (water) and of the ultimate electron acceptor (carbon dioxide), but what are the intermediates involved in the transfer of electrons from the first stage to the third?

This has become the focal problem in recent studies of the photosynthetic process. As a matter of fact, it is not yet definitely known what compound releases electrons from the first stage, and what compound receives them in the third; that is why these compounds are respectively labeled ZH and X in the illustration at the left. About the donor, ZH, we have almost no information ; the following considerations suggest the possible nature of the primary acceptor, X.

From the study of the mechanism of respiration we are familiar with an important oxidation-reduction catalyst : nicotinamide adenine dinucleotide phosphate, or NADP (formerly known as triphosphopyridine nucleotide, or TPN). NADP has an oxidation reduction potential of about-.32 volt, thus in itself it is not a strong enough reductant to provide the -.4-electron volt potential needed to reduce carbon dioxide to carbohydrate.

NADP can achieve this feat, however, if it is supplied with additional energy in the form of the high-energy compound adenosine triphosphate, or ATP. A molecule of ATP supplies about 10,000 calories per mole when its terminal phosphate group is split off, and this is enough to provide the needed boost to the reducing power of NADP.

Furthermore, we know that NADP is reduced when cell-free preparations of chloroplasts are illuminated. Put together, these two facts led to the now widely accepted hypothesis that the second stage of photosynthesis manufactures both ATP and reduced NADP and feeds them into the third stage.

At first it was assumed that NADP is identical with X, the primary acceptor in our scheme. Subsequent experiments by various workers-notably Anthony San Pietro at Johns Hopkins University and Daniel. Arnon and his colleagues at the University of California at Berkeley-suggested, however, that NADP is preceded in the "*bucket brigade*" of electron transfer by ferredoxin, a protein that contains iron.

This compound has an oxidation-reduction potential of about -.42 volt ; therefore if it is reduced in light it can bring about the reduction of NADP by a "dark" reaction requiring no additional energy supply. More recently Bessel Kok of the Research Institute for Advanced Studies in Baltimore has found evidence suggesting that compound X may be a still stronger reductant, with a potential of about -.6 volt.

If this is so, plants have the alternatives of either applying this stronger reductant directly to the reduction of carbon dioxide or letting it reduce first ferredoxin and then NADP and using reduced NADP to reduce carbon dioxide.

It seems a roundabout procedure to create a reductant sufficiently strong for the task at hand, then to sacrifice a part of its reducing power and finally to use ATP to compensate for the loss. It is not unknown, however, for nature to resort to devious ways in order to achieve its aims.

For photosynthesis to be a self-contained process the required high-energy phosphate ATP must be itself manufactured by photosynthesis. The formation of ATP has in fact been detected in illuminated fragments of bacteria by Albert W. Frenkel of the University of Minnesota and in chloroplast fragments by Arnon and his co-workers.

As a matter of fact, November, 1960. As a matter of fact, ATP is needed not only to act as a booster in the reduction of an intermediate in the carbon cycle by reduced NADP but also for another step in the third stage of photosynthesis.

According to a sequence of reactions worked out in 1951 by Andrew A. Benson and his colleagues at the University of California at Berkeley, carbon dioxide enters photosynthesis by first reacting with a "*carbon dioxide acceptor*," a special sugar phosphate called rebulose diphosphate.

It turns out that the production of this compound from its precursorribulose monophosphate-cells for a molecule of ATP. ATP is produced both in chloroplasts and in mitochondria, the tiny intracellular bodies that are the site of the energyliberating stage of respiration in animals as well as plants.

The mitochondria produce ATP as their main function, exporting it as packaged energy for many life processes. The chloroplasts, on the other band, make ATP only as an auxiliary source of energy for certain internal purposes.

The energy of the light falling on the chloroplasts is stored mostly as oxidation-reduction energy by the uphill transfer of electrons. Only a relatively small fraction is diverted to the formation of ATP, and this fraction too ultimately becomes part of the oxidation reduction energy of the final products of photosynthesis : oxygen and carbohydrate.

Let us now consider the uphill transport of electrons in greater detail. Recent investigations have yielded considerable information about this stage. Apparently the pumping of the etectrons is a two-step affair, and among the most important intermediates in it are the catalysts called cytochromes.

The idea of a two-step electron transfer process grew from a consideration of the energy economy of photosynthesis. Precise measurements, particularly those made by the late-Robert Emerson and his co-workers at the University of Illinois, showed that the reduction of one molecule of carbon dioxide to carbohydrate, and the liberation of one molecule of oxygen, requires a minimum of eight quanta of light energy.

The maximum quantum yield of photosynthesis, defined as,, the number of oxygen molecules that can be released for each quantum of light absorbed by the plant cell, is thus 1/8, or 12 per cent. Since the transfer of four electrons is involved in the reduction of one carbon dioxide molecule, it was suggested that it takes two light quanta to move each electron.

Emerson and his colleagues went on to determine the *quantum* yield of *photosynthesis* in *maximicronatic right* of different *wavelengths* throughout the visible spetrum. They found that the yield, although is remained constant at about 12 per cent in most of the spectrum, dropped sharply near thespectrum's far-red end.

This decline in quantum yield, called the "red drop," begins at a wavelength of 680 millimicrons in green plants and at 650 millimicrons in red algae. These are two chlorophylls present in green plants; chlorophyll *a* and chlorophyll *b*.

Only chlorophyll *a* absorbs light at wavelengths longer than 680 millimicrons; the absorptionn of chlorophyll b rises to a peak at 650 millimicrons and becomes negligible at about 680 millimicrons.

Emerson found that the quantum yield of photosynthesis at the farred end of the spectrum beyond 680 millimicrons can be brought -to the full efficiency of 12 per cent by simultaneously exposing the plant to a second beam of light with a wavelength of 650 milli microns.

In other words, when light primarily absorbed by chlorophyll a was supplemented by light primarily absorbed by chlorophyll *b*. both beams gave rise to oxygen at the full rate.

This relative excess in photosynthesis when a plant is exposed to two beams of light simultaneously, as compared with the yield produced by the same two beams separately, is known as the Emerson effect, or enhancement.

On the basis of his discovery Emerson concluded that photosynthesis involves two photochemical processes: one using energy supplied by chlorophyll a, the other using energy supplied by chlorophyll *b* or some other *"accessory"* pigment.

Experimenting with various combinations of a constant far-red beam with beams of shorter wavelength. and using four different types of algae (green, red, blue-green and brown), Emerson's group found that the strongest enhancement always occurred when the second beam was absorbed mainly by the most important accessory pigment (the green pigment chlorophyll *b* in green cells, the red pigment phycoerytbrin in red algae, the blue pigment phycocyanin in blue-green, algae and the reddish pigment fucoxanthol in brown algae).

Such results suggested that these other pigments are not mere accessories of chlorophyll a but have an important function of their own in photosynthesis.

Certain findings concerning the behaviour of pigments in living plant cells, however, seemed to make this conclusion untenable, illuminated plant cells fluoresce; that is pigment molecules energized by the absorption of light quanta reemit some of the absorbed energy as fluorescent light. The source of fluorescence can be identified, because each substance has its own characteristic fluorescence spectrum.

The main fluorescing pigment in plants always proves to be chlorophyll a, even when the light is absorbed by another pigment. This had first been shown for brown algae in a study conducted in 1943 by H. 7. Dutton, W. H. Manning and B. B. Duggar at the University of Wisconsin; later the finding was extended to other organisms by L. N. M. Duysens of the University of Leiden.

Known as sensitized fluorescence, the phenomenon indicates that the initial absorber has transferred its energy of excitation to chlorophyll *a*; the transfer is effected by a kind of resonance process.

Careful measurements have shown that pertain accessory pigments-chloropbyll *b*, phycoerythrin, phycocyanin and facoxanthol—pass on to chlorophyll a between 80 and 100 percent of the light quanta they absorb.

For some other accessory pigments-for example carotene—the transfer is less efficient. This puts accessory pigments back 'n the role of being mere adjuncts to chlorophyll a. True, they can contribute, by means of resonance transfer, light energy to photosynthesis, thereby improving the supply of energy in regions of the spectrum where chlorophyll *a* is a poor absorber.

Chlorophyll *a,* however, collects all this energy before it is used in the primary *photochemical* process. Why, then, the enhancement effect ? .Why should chlorophyll a need, in order to give rise to fullrate photosynthesis, one "*secondhand*" quantum obtained by resonance transfer from another absorber in addition to the one quantum it had absorbed itself?

A better understanding of this paradox resulted from the discovery that there apparently exist in the cell not *only* chlorophyll *a* and chlorophyll *b* but also two forms of chlorophyll *a*. These two forms have different light-absorption characteristics, and they probably also have different photochemical functions.

In the living cell chlorophyll a absorbs light most strongly in abroad band with its peak between 670 and 680 millimicrons. In our laboratory at the University of Illinois we ,undertook to plot the Emerson effect more carefully than before as a function of the wavelength of the enhancing light.

We found that for green and brown cells the resulting curve showed, in addition to peaks corresponding to strong absorption by the accessory pigments, a peak at 670 millimicrons that most be due to chlorophyll a itself. It was this finding that suggested the existence of two forms of chlorophyll *a*.

The form that absorbs light at the longer wavelengths-mainly above 680 millimicrons—seemed to belong to one pigment system, now often called System I.

The form that absorbs at 670 millimicrons seemed to belong to another pigment system ; System II. In the second system the form of chlorophyll a that absorbs at 670 millimicrons is strongly assisted by accessory pigments, probably by resonance transfer of their excitation energy.

Careful analysis of the absorption band of chlorophyll a by C. Stacy French of the Carnegie Institution of Washington's Department of Plant Biology, and also in our laboratory, confirmed that the band is double, with one peak near 670 millimicrons (at 668 millimicrons) and another band at 683 millimicrons.

If chlorophyll a is extracted from living plants, there is only one product; we must therefore assume that in the living cell the two forms differ in the way malecules of chlorophyll a are clumped together, or in the way they are associated with different chemical partners (proteins lipids or other substances).

Be this as it may, the important implication of the new finding is that photosynthesizing cells possess two light-absorbing systems, one containing a form of chlorophyll a absorbing around 683 millimicrons and the other a form , absorbing around 670.

The latter system includes chlorophyll *b* (in green-plant cells) or other accessory pigments (in brown, red and blue-green algae). Further investigation-particularly of red algae-has suggested however that the distribution of these two components in the two systems may be less clear-cut.

In red algae a large fraction of the chlorophyll a absorbing at 670 millimicrons seems to belong to System I rather than System II. In all likelihood the two systems provide energy for two different photochemical reactions, and efficiency in photosynthesis requires that the rates of the two reactions be equal.

What are these reactions? This question brings us to

another significant finding, which suggested the participation of *cytochromes* in *photosynthesis*.

Cytochromes are proteins that carry an iron atom in a& attached chemical group. They are found in all mitochondria, where they serve to catalyze the reactions of respiration. Robert Hill and his co-workers at the University of Cambridge—first found that chloroplasts also contain cytochromes-two kinds of them. One, which they named cytochrome f, has a positive oxidation-reduction potential of about 4 volt.

The other, which they named cytochrome b_6, has a potential of about 0 volt. In 1960 Hill, together with Fay Bendall, proposed an ingenious hypothesis as to how the two cytochromes. might act as intermediate carriers of electrons and connect the two photochemical systems.

They suggested that cytochrome b_6 receives an electron by a photochemical reaction from the electron donor ZH ; the electron is then passed on to cytochrome f by a "downhill" reaction requiring, no light energy. (The oxidation-reduction potential of cytochrome *f* is much more positive than that of cytochrome b_6).

A second photochemical reaction moves the electron uphill again, from cytochrome *f* to the electron-acceptor X in the third stage of photosynthesis. In this sequence the photochemical reactions store energy and the reaction between the two cytochromes releases energy.

Some of the released energy, however, can be salvaged by the formation of an ATP molecule; this occurs in, the transfer of electrons among cytochromes in respiration. In this way ATP is obtained without spending extra light quanta on its formation, which the tight energy economy of photosynthesis does not allow.

Experiments by Duysens and his associates confirmed this, hypothesis, by showing that the absorption of light by System 1 causes the oxidation of a cytochrome, whereas the absorptionn of light by System II causes its reduction.

This is exactly what we would expect. The illustration

on the opposite page shows that the light reaction of System II should flood the intermediates between the two photochemical reactions with electrons taken from ZH; the light reaction of System I should drain these electrons away, sending them up to the acceptor X and into the third stage of photosynthesis.

This, then, describes in a general way the oxidation-reduction process by which the chloroplasts store the energy of light in photosynthesis. Several other investigators havecontributed evidence for the two-step mechanism; notable among them are French, Kok, Arnon, Horst Witt of the MaxVollmer Institute in Berlin and their colleagues.

In detail the process probably is much more complex than our scheme suggests. Its "*downhill*" central part seems to include, in addition to the two cytochromes, certain compounds of the group known as quinones and also plastocyanin, a protein that contains copper. What is known of the submicroscopic structure in which the reactions of the second stage of photosynthesis take place?

There is, much evidence that the *photosynthetic* apparatus consists of "*units*" within the chloroplasts, each unit containing about 300 *chlorophyll molecules*. This picture first emerged. from experiments conducted in 1932 by Emerson and William Arnold on photosynthesis during flashes of light; it was later supported by various other observations.

The pigment molecules are packed so closely in the unit that when one of them is excited by light it readily transfers its excitation to a neighbor by resonance. The energy goes on traveling through the unit, rather as the steel ball in a pinball machine bounces around among the pins and turns on one light after another.

Eventually the migrating energy quantum arrives at the entrance to an enzymatic "conveyor belt," where it is trapped' and utilized either to load an electron onto the belt or to unload one from it. (The steel-ball analogy should not betaken litorally the migration of energy is a quantum-mechanical phenomenon, and the quantum's location can only be defined in terms of probability; its entrapment depends on the probability of finding it at the entrance to the conveyor belt).

How is the quantum trapped ? The trap must be a pigment molecule with what is called a lower excited state; the migrating quantum can stumble into such a molecule but cannot come out of it. Kok has found evidence that System I contains a small amount of a special form of chlorophyll called pigment 700 because it absorbs light at a wavelength of 700 millimicrons; this pigment could serve as a trap for the quantum bouncing around in System I.

There seems to be a proper amount of pigment 700: about one molecule per unit. Furthermore, experiments suggest that pigment 700 is oxidized by light absorbed in System I and reduced by light absorbed in System II.

It has an oxidation reduction potential of about +.4 volt. All these properties fit the role we have assigned pigment 700 in our scheme: collecting energy from a 300-molecule unit in System I, using it to transfer an electron to the acceptor X and recovering the electron from cytochrome *f*.

One suspects that there should be a counterpart of pigment 700 in System II, but so far none has been convincingly demonstrated. We believe, however, that a pigment we have tentatively named pigment 680-from the anticipated position of its absorption band-does serve as an energy trap in System II.

Its existence is supported by the discovery of a new fluorescent emission band of chlorophyll at 693 millimicrons, which is compatible with absorption at 680 millimicrons. This band is emitted by certain algae when they are exposed to strong light of the wavelengths absorbed by System II.

What is the spatial organization of the pigment systems in the electron-boosting mechanism of the second stage of photosynthesis ? It seems that the two systems may be arranged in two monomolecular layers, with a protein layer between them containing the enzymatic conveyor belt. Chloroplasts are known from electron microscope studies to consist of a set of lamellae thin alternating layers of protein and fatty material piled one atop the other. Each layer appears to consist of particles arrayed rather like cobblestones in a pavement.

The particles were first observed in electron micrographs made by E. Steinmann of the Technische Hochschule in Zurich ; subsequently Roderio B. Park and John Biggins of the University of California at Berkeley made clearer micrographs of the particles and named them quantasomes.

The units comprising Sytems I and II may operate independently or they may be sufficiently close together to exchange energy by resonance, when such exchange is needed to maintain a balanced rate of operation by the two systems.

The picture of the energy-storing second stage of photosynthesis presented in this article is, of course, still only a working hypothesis. Alternative hypotheses are possible, one of which we shall briefly describe.

For many years the late James Franck, who shared the Nobel prize in physics for 1925, tried to develop a plausible *physio-chemical* mechanism of photosynthesis. In 1963 he proposed, together with Jerome L. Rosenberg of the University of Pittsburgh, a concept according to which the two consecutive photochemical steps occur in one and the same energy trap.

In other words, according to Franck, the same *chlorophyll molecule* that takes the electron away from the initial donor ZH and transfers it to a cytochrome then supplies energy for the transfer of the electron from the cytochrome to the acceptor X. In the first transfer, Franck suggested, the chlorophyll a molecule functions in the short-lived "*singlet*" excited state (in which the valence electrons have opposite spins) ; in the second transfer it functions in the long-lived "*triplet*" state (in which the valence electrons have parallel spins).

Franck's hypothesis avoids certain difficulties of the "two trap" theory, but new difficulties arise in their place. On balance the two-trap picture seems to us the more plausible one at present.

No doubt this picture will change as more information emerges. It is merely a first effort to penetrate the inner sanctum of photosynthesis, the photocatalytic laboratory in which the energy of sunlight is converted into the chemical energy of life.

Chapter 4 STRUCTURAL PROTEINS

Any discussion of chloroplast and mitochondrial structural proteins (SP) raises the questions just what feature of a protein species distinguishes it as a *structural* protein; and does a class of proteins exist in such membrane systems which either has an exclusive structural role or which is central to the *membrane* structure while possibly being involved in some *additional* function?

In such *comparatively* simple units as the spherical plant viruses, one can readily obtain a structural protein fraction which has no other known function. In bacterial viruses, this fraction, with an equally well-defined role as *structural* or coat protein, in some cases also has a *demonstrable enzymic* function.

Mitochondrial and *chloroplast* membranes, on the other hand, with their large array of components have no such obvious species to assign a structural role. In the *simplest* sense, all the membrane *proteins* are structural proteins as all *contribute* in some way to the structure.

Further analysis makes it apparent that not all of these proteins are equally tightly associated with the membrane and that some *obviously* contribute much more to the *structure* than others.

While this type of approach may be need to rule out weakly associating components as candidates for the key element of membrane structure, it offers no means of selecting a unique protein component and stating that this is a *structural* protein.

The claim for the existence of a unique structural protein class in mitochondria and chloroplasts was based mainly on the preparation of a protein fraction, accounting for nearly 50 per cent of the *membrane* protein, for which no other function could be detected and on analogy with other membrane systems which have structural protein. *Subsequent* work on this membrane fraction has been *largely* aimed at investigation of its chemical and physical properties and at the study of any property which might define its *structural role*.

It will be this work that is reviewed here. It will become evident to the reader that much of this review will deal with evidence that a class of structural proteins does exist and with a discussion of the properties of these proteins.

While this may seem a somewhat one-sided approach to the question, it must be kept in mind that it is very difficult to establish a structural role for a protein from such complex organelles, and even more difficult to rule out the existence of such a specific structural protein. The requirement for proof lies with the proponents of the structural protein, and it is this information which is assembled.

Methods of Isolation of structural protein

Structural protein (SP) was first isolated from mitochondria by ammonium sulphate fractionation of the mitochondrial preparation "*solubilized*" by a combination of the *detergents cholate*, *deoxycholate*, and *sodium dodecyl sulphate*.

From such detergent solubilized preparation, SP is generally precipitated at 12 to 14 per cent saturation with ammonium sulphate. After washing with buffer and removal of *lipid*, this material is essentially free of coloured *components* and accounts for near 40 per cent of the *mitochondrial* protein.

Several subsequent methods of preparation have been proposed to obtain a product with different binding properties or with a higher degree of purity. *Richardson et al.* eliminated the use of sodium *dodecyl sulphate* in their isolation procedure to obtain a preparation which had greater capacity to bind *phospholipid*.

This preparation also would serve as Factor 4 in the partial reconstitution of the phosphorylating system of the electron transport chain. A modification of this procedure has subsequently been worked out by Allman *et al.* Other preparations of MSP (mitochondrial structural protein) fractions include *potassium hydroxide solubilization* and *neutralization* to precipitate SP extraction of SP from mitochondria with 10 mM HCl solubilization of the protein by succinylation and solubilization of a protein fraction with 1.4 per cent *acetic acid*.

Pinna and Wadkins solubilized the mitochondrial fraction with 8 M urea and 0.2 M mercaptoethanol and *precipitated* out SP by dialysis against dilutebuffer. Some further fractionation of *components* isolated in these preparations by extraction with urea solutions has been reported by Lenaz *et al.* The "*Factor 4*" studied by Racker and co-workers, which may have as a major protein component the same species *isolated* as SP, is isolated by *extraction* with 1.2 M *ammonium hydroxide* followed by *ammonium sulfate: fractionation*.

Structural protein has been isolated from mitochondria with altered respiratory capacity prepared from petite yeast cells and also from the *promitochondrial* fraction of *anaerobically* grown *yeast cells*. In both of these cases, a SP fraction with the same general amino acid composition or with the same pattern of *electrophoretic mobilities* on *discgel* observed, in wild type cells was found.

Thus, even though major components of the *electron transport* chain are absent or at very low *concentration* in these *mitochondria* the pattern of SP is the same.

The yield of structural protein from all of these preparation procedures is in the range of 40 per cent of the total mitochondrial protein. The degree of *homogeneity* of the products. from each *procedure* varies *greatly* and will be discussed below.

Fewer *preparations* of chloroplast structural proteins have been *reported* and correspondingly less work has been done in characterization of this material. *Menke* and *Jordan* described the extraction of soluble or readily solubilized protein from chloroplasts with dilute *buffers* to leave what was termed an *insoluble membrane* structural protein *fraction*.

Solubilization of *chloroplast lamellae* with various detergents and organic solvents has led to the description of a number of protein or *protein-chlorophyll fractions*. The fractions obtained are heterogeneous in nature and have been reported to have average molecular weights from approximately 20,000 to over one million.

Bailey *et al.* have described a *fractionation* of *lamellae proteins* with *acetic acid* extractions and have investigated the homogeneity of their preparation with disc gel electrophoresis.

Criddle & Park carried out a fractionation of washed *chloroplast lamellae* using essentially the same *procedures* employed for isolation of the mitochondrial protein. This led to a preparation of a low molecular weight protein, with solubility properties resembling *preparations* of MSP.

SP from non-mitochondrial sources

A structural protein fraction has been isolated from a large number of membrane sources. As several recent reviews in this area have been published these proteins will not be considered here. Of particular interest, however, is the report by Munkres & Woodward of the isolation of the same structural protein from mitochondrial, microsomal, and nuclear membranes, as well as from the soluble fraction from *Neurospora*.

The evidence for the identity of the protein isolated from each of these fractions is based upon amino acid analyses, peptide mapping, similar solubility properties, and *immunological* cross *reaction*.

While this may still leave the question of exact identity open, the marked similarities are of great interest. It has been clearly established that mutations resulting in changes in SP amino acid composition from the mitochondrial source appear as identical changes in the protein from each of these sources.

The recent observations of Attardi and Attardi that an RNA produced in the mitochondria of Hela cells may be exported to other membrane structures may account for the appearance of similar proteins in these different membranes.

The question of how an insoluble membrane protein can appear in the soluble phase following cell fractionation has puzzled many, but may be accounted for by the formation of SP complexes with other cell components.

The ability to form such soluble complexes with other proteins or lipids has been noted. Just what role these soluble complexes may be playing and just what is the necessity of structural protein in such complexes is still unknown.

PROPERTIES OF SP PREPARATIONS

Molecular weight. The molecular weight of MSP from beef heart was first measured by Criddle *et al.* to be 22,000 by means of *sedimentation equilibrium* in solutions containing 0.05 per cent sodium *dodecylsulphate*.

As was pointed out, these solution conditions gave rise to some experimental *uncertainty* in the exact value of this molecular weight, but other sources of *information* have yielded additional, *evidence supporting* this value.

This includes molecular weight measurements of SP complexes with *cytochromes* with *myoglobin*, and combining weights of SP with these same components.

NADH .has been reported to bind in a ratio of one molecule per 20,000 to 25,000 mol wt *structural proteins*, and ATP is also bound stoichiometrically under appropriate conditions to give a minimal combining weight of 23,000.

Table 4.1: Amino acid composition of structural proteins moles AA per mole protein (22,500 G/M).

Amino acid	*Beef heart*	*Yeast*	*Neurospora*
Ala	17.8	13.3	18.9
Arg	9.5	7.4	9.9
Asp	14.6	16.7	16.5
1/2 Cys	4.5	9.0	3.5
dlu	20.1	17.4	18.5
sly	16.2	9.2	16.0
His	2.5	3.1	4.3
lieu	9.7	9.7	9.8
Leu	17.1	15.3	16.0
Lys	119	13.1	11.7
Met	4.0	2.9	3.8
Phe	8.5	7.7	7.2
Pro	8.3	7.4	7.7
Ser	10.4	10.7	10.7
Thr	9.2	9.0	9.8
Tryp	1.8	1.8	2.5
Tyr	5.8	5.4	5.2
Val	12.9	10.3	13.1

Structural protein from other *mitochondrial* sources yielded similar *molecular weight* values.

Neurospora MSP, for example, has a molecular weight of 22,000 to 25,000 based on sedimentation equilibrium and binds one mole of the *mitochondrial* enzyme *malic dehydrogenase*, one molecule of NADH, or one molecule of ATP per mole of SP. The molecular weight of CSP (*chloroplast structural protein*) has also been measured at near 25,000.

Again the *uncertainties* of measurements on a marginally soluble material in a detergent-containing solution are apparent. In this instance, there is less direct supporting *evidence* available to *establish* the *accuracy* of this value.

Secondary information does, however, come from the X-ray studies of Menke, which indicate a *chloroplast* membrame *matrix* made up of *repeating* units of this size.

It is interesting to note that SP from many other sources, I.e., virus coat proteins bacterial membranes, and *microsomal membranes* have molecular weight which fall in this general size range of 20,000 to 30,000 mol wt. Recent studies on beef heart MSP in the *laboratory* of D. E. Green have suggested that the molecular weight of this *protein* is much higher than the *previously* reported values would *indicate*.

These values, based on centrifugation studies in quanidinium *hydrochloride solutions*, indicate molecular weights in the range of 55,000 to 70,000.

It is apparent that a gross heterogeneity of molecular sizes was present in the solutions analyzed in these studies, as the plot of mass distribution in the cell used for their calculations deviated from the ideal straight line such that: "In many of these experiments this plot resulted in a straight line for data points from the meniscus to about the midpoint of the solution".

The high values obtained certainly reflect in part this *heterogeneity*. When one notes that a molecular weight of 22,000 was obtained for *lysozyme* in these same studies [actual *molecular* weight 14,000], the accuracy of the high values reported becomes even more *questionable*.

Amino Acid Composition

The amino acid compositions of structural proteins from a large number of sources have been investigated. The similarities among the various preparations have been noted. Table elsewhere in this chapter indicates the *amino acid* composition of some SP *preparations*.

While at one time a high percentage of nonpolar side chain amino acids relative to other known proteins was suggested as a characteristic of this material as more membrane bound or *slightly* soluble proteins have been investigated for comparison, this value no longer appears *exceptionally* high. The MSP amino acid composition of the cytoplasmic "*pokey*" mutants mi-1 and mi-3 from *Neurospora* have been shown to differ in amino acid composition by a single amino acid change from the wild type.

Similar studies carried out on SP from cytoplasmic petite and wild type yeast cells, however, have shown no differences *detectable* within the experimental method of investigators.

The *techniques* employed in this case, however, were not sufficiently sensitive to detect small differences in numbers of certain of the amino acids, so that one cannot *conclude* that no change exists.

Other workers have indicated differences in SP from petite yeast in binding ATP and in gel electrophoretic pattern.

N-terminal Amino Acids

Investigation of the N-terminal amino acids of beef heart structural protein initially indicated that no significant quantities of N-terminal DNP-amino acid could be detected.

Analysis of this preparation did, however, show that acetyl serine could be isolated from the SP fraction with one mole of acetyl group per 22,000 to 26,000 grams of protein. It was postulated than an N-acetyl derivative could account for the absence of free amino terminal residues in the protein.

The only other amino acid appearing in these analyses was alanine, which was estimated to be present at less than 5 per cent of the *concentration* of the *peptide chains.* The free N-terminal amino acids of beef heart SP preparations have recently been restudied by Lenaz *et al.* *following application* of a number of their *fractionation* procedures to the preparation.

Determination of *acetyl groups* showed that a great variability in number of these groups was noted, depending upon the sample and means of *isolation*. This makes somewhat questionable the suggestion that the N-acetyl residues observed in previous studies are attached to the free amino end of the SP *polypeptide*.

These workers, in addition, searched further for free N-terminal amino acids. Two major DNP derivatives, identified as DNP-alanine and DNP-aspartate were detected, and it was concluded that these were N-terminal residues of the major polypeptide chains of their different fractions.

Careful analysis of the data reported, however, shows that even after application of a factor based on, recovery of standard amino acids, to correct for recovery losses, a yield of only 0.02 to 0.05 moles of N-terminal amino acid were obtained per mole of structural protein.

With a recovery level this low, one must conclude-as was done for previous studies with similar results-that there has as yet been no clear demonstration of free N-terminal amino acids for MSP.

Both glutamic acid and valine have been noted as N-terminal amino acids in *preparations* of yeast SP, and aspartic acid has been detected as the major free N-terminal amino acid of CSP from *spinach*.

Table 4.2: Michaelis constants of wild-type and mutant malic dehydrogenases with wild-type and mutant mitochondrial structural proteins.

MSP added	Michaelis constant for malate (K_m, mM)				
	Wild type	Mutant number			
		24	10	20	7
None	0.72	1.1	2.1	2.9	1.4
Wild type Mutant	0.72	3.3*	7*	10*	33*
Mi-I	500*	6*	3	3	1.4
Mi-3	40*	4*	1.7	1.2	4.5

*Significantly different from the value measured in the absence of MSP.

Table 4.3: Summary of binding studies of structural proteins.

Structural protein completed with	*Stoichlometry*	*Comments*
[1]Cytochrome c_1	1:1	Monomerizes c_1
[1]Cytochrome *b*	1:1	Solubilizes *b*
[1]Cytochrome oxidase		
[1]Cytochrome *c*	1:1	Dissociated by salt Kd = 3×10^{-7}
[1,2]Myoglobin	1:1	Kd = 5×10^{-7}
[1]Phospholipid	~2 µg/mg protein	Amount bound depends upon solubilization procedure
‘Desaspidin	50% inhibition at 5×10^{-7} M	^{32}Pi-ATP exchange
[3]Malic dehydrogenase	1:1	Kd=9×10^{-7}
[1.2]DPNH	1:1	Kd=6×10^{-7}
[1.2]ATP	~1:1	
[3,4]Atractyloside		Inhibits ATP binding

Other components associated with SP

During the process of isolation of SP, the protein is removed from a *membrane* containing many other *chemical entities*. Without some measurable criterion of activity related to its function in the mitochon-drion, it is difficult to ascertain whether any of these *components* are an intrinsic part of *functional* structural protein.

The final preparations of SP which are isolated are devoid of *lipid*, *carbohydrate* and nucleic acid. Pinna and Wadkins reported the presence of *phosphate* bound *covalently* as serine *phosphate* in SP from beef heart *mitochondria*.

This is consistent with the observation by *Zalkin* and *Racker* of a phosphate associated with his F_4 preparation. Structural protein is often isolated with free amino acids tightly bound, but these may be removed by repeated washing.

Binding Properties of SP

One of the basic factors in the initial postulate of a structural role for the SP fraction was the observed *interaction* of this protein with other components of the mitochondrion. *Structural protein* has been observed to combine *stoichiometrically* with the *cytochromes a, b* and *c* and with *cytochrome oxidase.*

It will also combine 1 : 1 with myoglobin but not with *hemoglobin*. A large number of non-mitochondrial proteins do not *combine* with the SP. Some of the *binding* studies are of particular interest in determining the functional role for SP and whether SP as *isolated* has any *properties* in common with the protein ins the intact *membrane*.

The first suggestion of a functional role came from the studies of *Goldberger*, which showed that complex formation between isolated cytochrome *b* and structural protein resulted in a change of the oxidation-reduction potential of the *enzyme* in such a fashion that the complex resembled + the intact *mitochondrion* in this property.

The most direct evidence for the influence of SP on the catalytic activity of mitochondrial proteins comes from the recent studies on the mitochondrial malic *dehydrogenase* activity of wild type and respiratory deficient strains of *Neurospora.*

It was found that mutants of malic *dehydrogenase* fell into two classes: one in which the enzyme itself was altered and the other in which another component of the mitochondrial structure was altered in such a fashion as to *affect* the kinetic properties of the enzyme.

Two of the mutants studied in detail. mi-1 and mi-3, showing a cytoplasmic *inheritance* pattern, were found to have no. alteration of the *in vitro* structure of malic dehydrogenase (MDH). Thus mutated MDH activity was observed only in the intact mitochondria or when MDH was associated with the membrane structure.

In these two cases, the structural protein was mutated, mi-1 being characterized by a change in *tryptophane* to a cysteine, and in mi-3 a tryptophane replacement was made by an as yet unidentified amino acid. In contrast, nuclear mutants showed *alteration* of the activity of MDH *in vitro* and in some cases *altered* ability of the MDH to complex with the mitochondrial structural protein.

Binding studies on the isolated proteins showed that MDH could form a 1 : 1 complex with SP and that *alteration* of the SP affected its ability to bind MDH but not the soichiometry of binding. *Mutation* of the structural protein also affected the binding of ATP and NADH, resulting in a much lower affinity for these *molecules*.

A comparison of the kinetics of malate oxidation by MDH in the presence of *mutant* and *wild-type* structural proteins *demonstrated* that *combination* of enzyme with SP has a marked effect on *activity*.

Table elsewhere in this chapter indicates the changes in Michaelis constants of wild-type and mutant MDH's resulting from addition of wild-type and mutant MSP. This last example is the most direct evidence for the role of SP in the catalytic process of mitochondria by virtue of a structural effect on activity.

Binding of lipids to SP has been studied in detail. The ,preparation of Richardson *et al.* shows markedly different lipid binding capacity than does the original preparation of *Criddle et al.* Richardson, Hultin and Fleischer have studied this binding and have concluded that the *interactions* between these substances are nonpolar in nature.

It is difficult to draw any conclusions concerning the importance of lipid binding to SP, as there is no readily measurable physiological property to serve as an indicator of *lipid binding*.

Other substances, in addition to ATP and NADH, shown to bind to SP include desaspidin and atractyloside. The binding of *nucleotides* and other anions has been studied by Palmieri and Klingenberg. Their conclusion was that binding of these molecules and their displacement by *atractyloside* is a *nonspecific* anion effect.

A completely different line of evidence for the role of SP in *mitochondrial* enzyme functioning come from studies on the mechanism of action of the *murine toxin* of *Pasteurella pestis* and *diphtheria toxin*. Those toxins inhibit the *respiration* of heart mitochondria.

While early observations suggested that the inhibition was due to *toxin inhibition* of cytochrome formation, 1 ore recent evidence suggests an alteration of mitochondrial structure by association of the toxins with SP.

Montanaro and Sperti demonstrated that the diphtheria toxin is capable of solubilizing mitochondrial structural protein, when the two are *incubated* together at pH 8. Maximum *solubilization* was obtained with excess toxin.

Immuno diffusion and *immuno electrophoresis* experiments were used to demonstrate actual complex formation between the two proteins. Attempts to locate the site of inhibition by the *plague toxin* more precisely were made by Kadis and Ajl.

They were able to show that this toxin inhibits primarily the enzymatic activity of Complex I of the electron transport chain [theNADH-CoQ reductase of Hatefi *et al.*] in *isolated beef heart* mitochondria.

No evidence could be found, however, for an effect of the toxin on any of the major individual electron transport components of this complex. Thus the activity of NADH *dehydrogenase flavoprotein*, *nonheme iron*, and *coenzyme* Q_{10} were not detectably altered by the toxin.

Kadis *et al.* were, however, able to demonstrate a *solubilization* of SP with the plague toxin analogous to that with the *diphtheria toxin*.

Again, complex formation was demonstrated by *immunodiffusion* experiments but was also studied by following the decrease in toxicity of the toxin as it was bound to the SP.. At SP: toxin ratios approaching 20 : 1, the toxin had lost all its *toxicity* for mice and *precipitin* bands for free toxin could no longer be detected.

These *experiments*, while aimed at defining the mechanism of *toxin inhibition*, also indicate the requirement for SP in, the ordered *electron transport chain*.

It appears that whew toxin reacts with the structural protein, the behaviour of the catalytic components is altered, and this alteration is only observed in the *particulate system*. This is entirely consistent with what may be expected if SP serves in the capacity of any organizing and *stabilizing* entity of the *membrane*.

Optical rotatory dispersion measurements of membranes. Recent studies of membrane structure using optical rotatory dispersion have shown that membrane systems as a class have spectral properties which distinguish them from soluble proteins or polypeptides.

In membrane systems such as *chloroplast* fragments *Bacillus subtills* membrane, and mitoehondriat vesicles a the entire Cotton effect show a red shift of 2 to 3 mμ. Steim and Fleischer have studied the effect of *aggregation* of MSP on this spectral change.

It was observed that while the solubilized SP is observed to have an optical rotary dispersion (ORD) spectrum characteristic of a protein or *polypeptide* containing α-helical structure, aggregation resulted in the spectral shift.

Steim and Fleischer therefore conclude that the typical ORD spectrum of mitochondrial membrane systems may be explained by SP interaction within the membrane.

Care must be taken in any extrapolation of this data not to suggest that this ORD shift is a specific property of interacting. membrane proteins, as it was demonstrated by Cassim and Yang that similar ORD spectral shifts are observed upon aggregation of a-helical poly-L-glutamic acid.

The relation of these measurements to membrane structure must yet the established.

Gel Electrophoresis

The application of disc gel electrophoretic techniques to the study of membrane protein has permitted a study of sample *heterogeneity* in detail not *previously* possible. This method, however, has a great many difficulties which currently make *interpretation* difficult.

The first problem comes in selecting a buffer system which wilt,. *solubilize* the membrane protein, limit aggregation, and allow migration of individual discrete components.

Several solventsystems have been proposed but at present none is completely satisfactory. Membrane proteins dissolved in these systems still' have only marginal solubility, so that aggregation, particularly during the boundary sharpening process, is marked.

This is evidenced by a heavy layer of insoluble material at the remaining top of the gel (e.g.,). Other lower molecular weight: *polymers* may still penetrate the gel under these conditions. and appear as *individual* bands.

While methods are available for *determining* differences between true heterogeneity and polymerization products on acrylamide gels by *altering gel* composition these have not been applied *generally* to studies of *membrane* proteins.

One of the major benefits of the use of gel electrophoresis on membrane proteins has been the demonstration by Green and co-workers of a number of *impurities* in the standard SP *preparations* of beef heart MSP and the ability to remove these components in some cases by urea *extraction*.

Other results cited in this same series of papers, however, are equally good examples of the necessity for careful *consideration* of the results obtained. It is obvious in these studies that a large and undetermined amount of protein failed to penetrate the gel yet one finds in the urea extracted sample only one *migrating* band.

To reduce the amount of material at the origin, the samples were subjected to performic acid *oxidation*. The sample subsequently yielded three *additional* bands upon electrophoresis which, taken all together, were stated to be four *species* of MSP.

The three *additional* species appear to be formed from

the original single band and not from the insoluble material, as it was reported that the *material* held at the origin was identical to that which *migrated* into the gel.

At present, the origin of the three additional bands is not clear whether they are separate protein species more clearly resolved after oxidation, whether they were produced by chemical side reactions during the *performic acid* treatment, -or whether they correspond to some of the various *conformation* states proposed by these authors.

It is apparent that these are not present in other solvent systems and that they are not always observed. Liver MSP has been stated to have only one and four components by the same workers at different times.

Gel electrophoresis has been used successfully to demonstrate that protein synthesis in isolated mitochondria results in the incorporation of C amino acids into the membrane proteins.

Some correspondence between the distribution of radioactive label and the major components of coupling Factor 4 proteins has been noted. ,With further development of this technique, it may become as important tool in studies allowing the description of products of mitochondrial syntheses.

Role of SP in mitochondrial synthesis

Recent widespread interest in SP has resulted from observations that *in vitro* incorporation of C^1 amino acids into isolated mitochondria results in a rather specific labeling of the mitochondrial membrane proteins.

A recent review of this subject may be found in the book by Roodyn and Wilkie. Here only the relation of these findings to structural protein will be discussed. It was shown in 1961 by Roodyn *et al.* that addition of labeled amino acids to a simple medium containing *mitochondria*, *adenine nucleotide*, Mg^{++}, and an energy source resulted in *incorporation* of label into proteins.

The major radioactive product was shown to be insoluble

protein associated with the membrane, while the soluble *enzymes* and *cytochromes* were labeled little, if at all.

Many recent studies have confirmed these original findings on isolated mitochondria. Neupert *et al.* have indicated further that amino acid incorporation *in vitro* occurs only in the *inner membrane*.

In vivo studies following the time course of *amino acid incorporation* into mitochondrial fractions, and also studies using specific inhibitors of cytoplasmic or mitochondrial protein synthesis, have confirmed and extended the earlier conclusions that the *mitochondrion* is the site of synthesis of proteins from the mitochondrial membrane.

The identification of the products of mitochondrial protein synthesis is not nearly so clear and reflects the difficulties apparent in *solubilizing* and *characterizing* the proteins of the membrane.

The *predominant site* of the incorporation, however, is into the structural protein fraction. The work of Haldar *et al.* has shown that SP prepared by the method of Richardson *et al.* is labeled (by *In vitro* synthesis).

Their data show radioactive label in a number of components separable by gel electrophoresis from a SP preparation, indicating several, products of synthesis. Kadenbach in similar experiments found that 65 per cent of the *radioactivity* was in the SP.

Wheeldon and Lehninger, following the time course of synthesis in isolated mitochondria, showed that while the initial labeling is rather uniform throughout their membrane fractions as synthesis proceeded SP became relatively more radioactive.

Kadenbach has pointed out the need for caution in *interpreting* such studies on radioactive incorporation when the showed that some of the radioactive product could be released from the membrane by treatment with *phospholipase*.

A tight nonspecific adsorption of the labeled amino acids onto structural protein has also been observed and thus further care is required in interpretation of these experiments. Strong support for the structural protein being at least one major product of mitochondrial protein synthesis comes from the work of Woodward and Munkres on the *pokey mutants* of *Neurospora crassa.*

Certain such respiratory-deficient mutants in which an amino acid replacement in the peptide chain of SP has been noted show a maternal or cytoplasmic inheritance pattern. The resulting change in the structural protein alters its ability to combine with the enzyme malic dehydrogenase and with nucleotides and may disrupt the system for mitochondrial assembly.

Other mutants requiring malate were studied to show that observed differences in the properties of the malic dehydrogenase enzyme were dependent in part on the malic dehydrogenase-SP complex which could be formed either *in vivo* or from the isolated components.

This latter observation was also cited as strong support for a functional role for the SP in membrane function *in vivo* and suggests that at least some of its specific properties are not lost in the isolation process. The evidence thus far accumulated strongly suggests that protein synthesis does occur in the *mitochondria* and that SP is one of the products of this synthesis.

It is of interest to note that evidence has also been presented to suggest that the half life of structural protein in rat liver mitochondrial *in situ* is considerably longer than that of catalytic protein. While this further suggests that SP may, therefore, be a direct gene product of a mitochondrial gene, there has as yet been no direct demonstration of this.

Such direct evidence can come only after more through analysis of the insoluble structural protein fraction. The observations that mitochondria from cytoplasmic petite mutants of yeast may have a greatly altered DNA and lack mitochondrial r-RNA and yet still make an apparently normal SP are difficult to reconcile with the conclusion that

SP is solely a product of the mitochondrial gene, however, and a much ,more complicated relationship may exist.

While studies of the biosynthetic apparatus of chloroplasts have progressed further than corresponding studies in mitochondria the identification of protein products of the chloroplast DNA-directed synthesis are presently even more uncertain.

There is evidence that some of the structural genes concerned with the synthesis of photosynthetic enzymes are located in the nucleus, but there is no such evidence that the structural gene for any chloroplast protein is located in the chloroplast DNA.

Isolated chloroplasts are capable of incorporating C^1 amino acids into acid insoluble products. Again, as in mitochondria, much of this incorporation is into the insoluble or membrane proteins. It has been reported, however, that incorporation into some of the soluble enzymes of the chloroplast may also occur.

Whether synthesis of chloroplast structural proteins is directed by the chloroplast DNA is again a question that must await further study. The mass of data accumulated to date allows us to conclude that a protein fraction termed SP can be isolated in large yield from mitocho-ndrial of chloroplast membranes by numerous procedures.

While it is quite probable that none of these procedures gives rise to a completely homogeneous preparation, and that all have a different group of contaminating species present in varying amounts, the same major protein components are probably isolated in all cases.

It is difficult to assess the purity of these preparations when there is no means of determining a "*specific activity*" to follow the purification process, and when physical measurements are hampered by problems of solubility.

The final demonstration of whether purified SP is one species or a family of closely related peptide components must yet be made. Nonetheless, the *demonstrations* of binding by structural protein and indications of its effect on enzymic activity lead to the conclusion that this material plays an important role in the structure of membrane systems.

In addition, suggestive results of biosynthesis of SP by the protein synthesizing systems of mitochondria and chloroplasts points to an important role of this material in organization and assembly as well. It is clear that SP will be the subject of much future study and that these studies will be central to further studies on structure, assembly and function of organelles.

BIOCHEMISTRY OF TOXINS

The *living plant* must be regarded as a complicated biochemical factory carrying on a series of intricate and well organized processes essential for life. Any *disturbance* of these processes or the forces *integrating* them leads to a condition of "*ill health*" or disease.

Recent studies on antibiotics have drawn attention to the high *biological activity* of many products of *microbial fermentation*. It is not surprising, therefore, to find that increasing *attention* is being focused on the role of *toxic* substances in plant disease.

The difficulties of defining the boundaries of this discussion as distinct from a general discussion on the biochemistry of plant *disease* are obvious. The term "*toxin*" has been adopted in the plant pathological literature to describe a toxic substance rather than in the more restricted sense originally *implied* in the *terminology* of *mammalian pathology*.

It is defined for purposes of this chapter as a product of a *microorganism* or a *microorganism-host* interaction which acts directly on living host protoplasts to *influence* either the course of disease development or *symptom expression*.

The *plant viruses* have been deliberately excluded from consideration here. *Enzymes*, unless they are themselves toxic cannot be considered as toxins. *Death* of tissues in the soft rots for example may result from *cellular disor-*

ganization following the utilization of the materials of the middle lamella as an *enzyme substrate.*

Gaumann (1954) states "*Microorganisms* are *pathogenic* only if they are *toxigenic* : in other words, the *agents* responsible for diseases can damage their hosts only if they form *toxins-microbial poisons*—that penetrate into the host *tissues.*" This concept would seem, on the basis of current evidence, to be too *embracive.*

In *Fusarium* wilt of tomato, for example, the organism enters the vascular system, often -through root *wounds* and *proliferates* in the xylem vessels to which it is confined. Evidence, recently summarized by *Dimond* (1955), suggests that *pectic enzymes* are produced which, acting on the cell wall, hydrolyze or *partially hydrolyze* pectic *materials* with the resulting production of pectic gels and perhaps ultimately gums which plug the *xylem vessels*, thus interfering with water conduction and resulting in wilting and ultimate death.

This situation does not involve toxins or -any direct effect on living cells. The so-called *wilt toxins* (Dimond, 1955) ; *undoubtedly* responsible for some of the commonly recognized *symptoms* of the disease, may play an entirely secondary role.

They will be considered in more detail in a later section. Dimond and Waggoner (1953), concerned with distinguishing between *phytotoxic* products produced in *culture media* and those associated with disease in plants, coined the term "*vivotoxin*".

The defined a "*vivotoxin*" as a substance produced in the infected host by the pathogen and/or its host, which is not itself the initial causal agent of disease. Influenced by Koch's "rules of proof" they propose three criteria for the establishment of a "*vivotoxin*," namely: (*a*) isolation from diseased but not from healthy plants, (*b*) chemical characterization, and (*c*) production of disease symptoms or a portion thereof on reintroduction into a healthy host.

The only clearcut examples of toxic materials that

appear to meet all these requirements are ethylene, Dimond and Waggoner's own example, and fusaric acid.

This concept, now rather widely accepted in plant *pathological literature*, has served a useful purpose in helping to clarify our thinking with regard to toxins and plant disease.

It would seem, however, to be too *restrictive* since it is difficult to apply to a nonspecific toxin such as that produced by *Helminthosporium sativum* or *Rhizoctonia solant* where initial production may be external to the host and the effect one of *preconditioning* the host to the advance of the *pathogen*.

The term *vivotoxin* might usefully be retained to describe a certain type of *phytotoxin*. The chain of biochemical events occurring when a *pathogen* invades its host may work in favour of the host rather than the pathogen. Thus, *Millerd* and *Scott* (1956) found that an agent *uncoupling* respiration from its normally associated phosphorylations occurred in *mildewinfected* plants. This *resulted* in cell collapse and the *liberation* of *phenolic* substances.

The latter appear to inhibit further mildew development and a "*resistant*" type of reaction is the result. Muller (1956) suggested that the term "Phytoalexin" be used to describe antibiotic principles present in hypersensitive host tissues.

They cannot, however, be readily set apart from substances included under the general term toxin. The significance of antibiotic materials occurring normally in the host and conferring disease resistance is just beginning to be appreciated.

Catechol responsible for resistance to onion smudge and 2,3-benzoxazolinone for snow mold in rye are good examples. Such materials are *beyond* the scope of this chapter.

TOXINS AND ROOT INVASION

In 1918, Skinner published his *classic monograph* showing that aromatic aldehydes are produced in soil and might accumulate sufficiently under certain *circumstances* to be detrimental to crop growth. Among the more active of these *aldehydes* are *salcylaldehyde* (I) and *vanillin* (II).

They are found especially in soils of low *productivity* and disappear rapidly from fertile soils having "strong biological activities and good *oxidative* powers." Poor *fertility* often favours root disease Rands and Dopp (19;8) showed that apparently non *injurious* amounts of *salicylaldehyde predispose* sugar cane to *Pythium* root rot.

Similar observations have been made in connection with *Pythium* root rot of wheat. Aldehydes of this type are among the first products of the microbial *degradation* of lignin although occurrence in nature may not be confined to this source as evidenced by the work of Gray and Bonner (1948), and Bonner (1950) on the *phytotoxic* principle in *Encelia* leaves.

This principle, shown to be 3-acetyl-6-metboxybenzald-ehyde (III), inhibits growth of sensitive plants such as . tomato at concentrations as low as 20 p.p.m. Fallen *Encella* leaves retain their *toxicity* toward tomato for at least a year and the toxic factor can be leached into the soil by water.

Finally, Schreiner and Shorey isolated a-*methylisonicot-inic* acid (IV) from infertile soil in the Tacoma district of

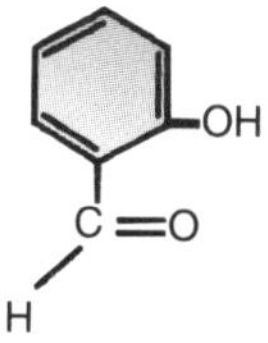

(I)
salicyladehyde

(II)
vanillin

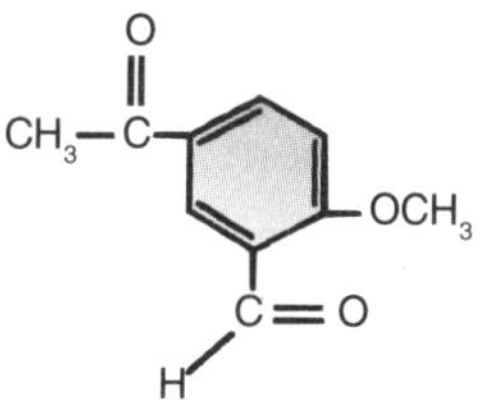

(III)
3-acetly-6methoxybenaldehyde

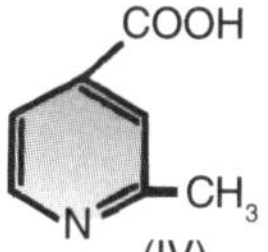

(IV)
e-methyl isonicatinic acid

Washington and found it to possess strong growth *inhibitory* properties.

Ludwig *et al.* (1956) showed that artificial infestation of soil by spores of *Helminthosporium sat hum* PK and B **is** ineffective in inducing disease development in *barley seedlings*.

Whole culture organic inocula were *highly* potent but their activity could be reduced or *eliminated* by *leaching* with water. Heat *sterilization* sufficient to kill the *organism* failed to *eliminate activity*.

They found further that the addition of sterilized inoculum to nonsterilized planting soil predisposes, the barley seedlings to invasion by a variety of organisms including *Pythium* and *Fusarium* species.

Seedlings treated with active culture filtrates or crude preparations of the toxin show stunting, chlorosis, loss of normal "*tropic responses*, and, death; symptoms characteristic of *Helminthosporium seedling* blight but no necrosis unless invaded by secondary microorganisms.

Ludwig (1957) found the toxin to be nonspecific in relation to host, affecting wheat, oats, and barley equally.

While strains of the fungus varied in their ability to produce toxin, and high toxin production was associated with high pathogenicity, some other factor of organism, perhaps a second toxin, appeared to be involved in disease develop-ment.

The conclusion is reached that the toxin (or toxins) produced by *Helminthosporium sativum* predisposes barley seedlings to invasion by inducing premature senescence.

In nature, the organism growing on infested seeds, crop debris, or *senescing coleoptile sheaths* would have ample opportunity to produce the toxin which could then affect actively growing crown tissue and *predispose* it to invasion.

This seems to be parallel to the response described for aromatic aldehydes. Preliminary work on the chemical nature of the *Helminthosporium* toxin suggests that it is an unsaturated aliphatic aldehyde with a molecular weight of about 220.

Helminthosporium oryzeae (*Ophlobolus miyabeanus*) causes a disease in rice similar to that produced in barley by *H. sativum*. Orsenigo (1957) demonstrated the presence of a toxic substance in culture filtrates which reduced germinability and produced *abnormalities* in rice seedlings. He extracted the principle with *chloroform* and partially purified it by further *solvent* extraction.

This product, cochliobolin, was found to be extremely toxic to rice seedlings, affecting root and shoot growth at low concentrations. Kerr (1956) reported on infection studies with *Rhizoctonia solani* in which he employed a dialyzer tube to separate plant from *inoculum*.

This barrier effectively *prevented* the passage of the organism but *permitted* the outward diffusion of chemicals from the root and the inward diffusion of products of *microbial* origin. *Rhizoctonia* was *obviously* affected by root excretions since its growth followed lines of root contact on the cellophane.

Further, discoloration of roots occurred beneath the fungal mats, thus *demonstrating* a *phytotoxic principle* produced by the fungus. These results suggest that *diffusing* plant substances encourage the growth of the *pathogen* on the root where it evolves toxins which condition the host to invasion. There is some *evidence* for toxin production by *species* of *Pythium*.

Vanterpool (1933) found evidence of a toxin in his studies on *Pythium* root rot of wheat. More recently, *Brandenberg* (1950) studied the physiology of a species of *Pythium* found attacking the fine roots of beet. A toxic substance was found to be produced and it is *postulated* that it is swept from the root source to the foliage where *symptoms* are produced.

The possibility of its being a pectic enzyme is not excluded. Difficulty is often experienced in establishing a peach transplant in a site where an old tree has been removed. A, number of workers have shown that a *toxic condition* of the soil is associated with the "*peach replant problem.*"

Peach roots contain the *cyanogenic glucoside amygdalin*. Patrick (1953) demonstrated that both peach roots and pure amygdalin. when subjected either to direct enzymatic or microbial breakdown produce substances toxic to peach *seedlings*. Among these degradation products are benzaldehyde and *hydrogen, cyanide*. *Broadfoot* and Cormack (1941) and Cormack (1948) studied a disease of alfalfa caused by an as yet unidentified', low temperature *Basidiomycete* which they named *descriptively* "*winter crown rot.*"

Lebeau and Dickson (1955) demonstrated that the organism possessed the necessary enzymes for HCN production when an appropriate *substrate* was provided. Organic inocula, particularly those prepared from grou-nd *alfalfa crowns*, promoted both kill and HCN accumul-ation in affected tissues. Since HCN levels as high as 2400 p.p.m. were *demonstrated* in some tissues, they logically suggest that it is, the agent responsible for death of cells.

Winter snow and ice cover would block the outward *diffusion* of the gas that might be expected under other *circumstances*. The *disease* optimum of 2-4°C. is lower than the optimum of 12°C. for HCN production. The lower temperature might however be expected to favour *accumulation*. Here again then we would appear to have a situation in which the production of a toxin paves the way for tissue invasion by a *microorganism*.

It is tempting to suggest in relation to the peach replant problem that *microbially produced* HCN affects the young tree and paves the way for root invasion perhaps by other normally nonpathogenic organisms, i.e., a root disease *complex* composed of two or more *organisms* none of which alone can establish themselves in the host.

TOXIN PRODUCTON BY ALTERNATA

Toxin production has been associated with the development of early blight in *Solanaceous* hosts Thomas (1948) observed chlorosis and necrosis in the top of *tomato plants* apparently only carrying the causal fungus, *Alternaria solani,* in a basal stem lesion.

He also noted the rapid necrosis of *leaf tissue* around a point of infection. He concluded that these observations were most easily explained on the basis of a toxin produced by the *fungus*. *Pound* and *Stahmann* (1951) provided further positive evidence of the *involvement* of a toxin in the disease by studying the effect of various types of *inoculation*.

Inoculation of the petiole on one side resulted in cblorosis or necrosis of the leaflets on that side. The fungus could readily be *reisolated* from the lesion but not from *chlorotic* or *necrotic* tissue away from it. A *similar* effect on the top of the plant resulted from one-sided lesions at the stem base.

Here the leaves supplied by that portion of the *vascular* system under the lesion appeared to be the ones affected. Lesions on nonvascular leaf tissue had only a local effect. Brian *et. al.* (1949) isolated a biologically active substance from culture filtrates of *Alternaria solani.*

They proposed the name "*alternaric acid*" for it. In later work, Grove (1952), showed it to he an unsaturated dibasic acid with an empirical formula of $C_{21}H_{30}O_{8}$. The details of its structure, however, yet remain to be elucidated. An apparently identical product was isolated by Pound and Stahmann (1951).

Darpoux *et at* (1952) described a biologically active material that they isolated from *A. solant* and gave it the name alternarin. It was inactive when sprayed on tomato plants but inhibited the growth of a number of fungi.

Alternaric acid possesses strong antifungal properties. 'Spore germination in some species is prevented by 1 µg./ ml. or less, while in others it is unaffected by 100 µg./ml. but growth of germ tubes is retarded soon after *germination*.

Very low concentrations (0.01 µg./ml.) are required for the latter effect and hence, this phenomenon was employed as a principle of *bioassay* in isolation studies with *Botrytis allii* as the test *organism*. Using this technique, production of alternaric acid -or a *biologically* similar product was *demonstrated* in tomato fruits bearing *Alierraria* lesions, thus furnishing evidence of in vivo *production*.

Crude culture *filtrates* and *alternaric* acid itself are highly phytotoxic and when introduced into tomato shoots either through cut *stem ends*, *petiole tips*, or *intact root* systems, produce *symptoms* of *chlorosis* and *necrosis* characteristic of early blight.

It can, then, be carried upward in the vascular system. Alternaric acid is a relatively *nonspecific toxin*, although some plant species. can *withstand* a somewhat higher level than others, and it can produce lesions resembling those of *Alternaria* in plants outside the host range of *A. solani*.

The extreme potency of *alternaric* acid, the *striking* similarity of its *toxicity symptoms* to natural infections, its translocatability and its known production on infected *tomato fruits* are all strong points of evidence in favour of its *involvement* in the early blight disease.

Brian *et al.* (1952), however, found only 2 of the 12 strains of *A. solani* examined to be able to produce it in, culture and these were the least *pathogenic* of those studied.

This is not altogether surprising since *Alternaria solani*, in common with *Helminthosporium sativum* discussed in the previous section, tends to attack old or senescent tissues. Any factor tending to induce this condition whether it be age, adverse *growing* conditions, or the production of a *nonspecific* toxin would predispose the plant to attack.

It would be interesting to know if unilateral petiole inoculations of all 12 -of Brian's isolates would produce least, necrosis as demonstrated by Pound and Stahmann (1951) with their isolate. Finally, there is indirect evidence (1951) that other toxins may also be involved. If this is the case it would further complicate the *situation*.

Black spot of Japanese pear caused by *Alternaria kikuchiana* is confined to a few varieties, all varieties of European pear and most of the Japanese varieties being either *immune* or *highly* resistant. Hiroe and Syoya (1954) found that *sterile* culture *filtrates* of the organism when applied to pear *foliage* induced *symptoms* identical with those of the disease itself. *Pathogenesis* of the organism and toxin production were *correlated.*

These workers affected partial purification of the toxin and obtained some evidence of its production on infected' fruit. The name "*phyto-alternarin*" was given to the toxin.

It was shown to be different from alternaric acid. It is not clear whether or not the action of this toxin has the same host specificity as the organism.

DIAPORTHEN AND CHESTNUT BLIGHT

Chestnut blight caused *by Endothia parasitica* appeared in New York in 1904 and finally destroyed virtually all the chestnuts on the North American Continent. In 1953, Bazzigher showed that culture filtrates of the organism contained a toxin which he named "*diaporthin.*"

This substance was nonspecific in that it was shown to affect a variety of plants including *chestnut* and *tomato.* Further studies showed. that at least two toxins are produced *in vitro* by *Endothia parasitica.*

These are diaporthin with unknown chemical structure but empirical formula of $C_{13}H_{14}O_6$ and a bianthroquinone, "*skyrin,*" with empirical formula $C_{30}H_{13}O_{10.}$ The former is known to be produced only by *Endothia* while the latter synthesized by both *Endothia* and *Peniciilium islandicum.*

Both substances are relatively *nonspecific* in their action. As with. many other *toxins*, the role of these materials in disease development has yet to be *demonstrated.*

RICE BLAST

Blast, caused by *Piricularia oryzae,* is the most destructive disease of rice in Japan and other humid areas. The symptoms consist of spotting and severe *necrosis* on the leaves, culms, *panicle branches*, and *floral structures.*

Tamari and Kaji (1955) isolated two toxins from the culture filtrates of the organism.. The first of these, "*toxin A*", with an emmpirical formula of $C_6H_5NO_2$ proved to be

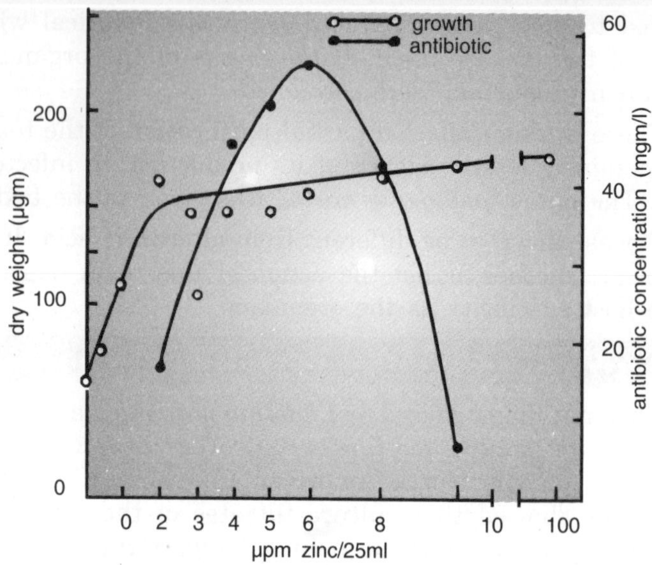

Figure 5.1: The influence of zinc on growth and fusaric acid production in Fusarfum oxysporum f. vasinfectum.

α-picolinic acid. The second "*toxin B*," with an empirical formula of $C_{21}H_{18}N_2O_3$ yet remains to be identified. The authors applied the name piricularin to toxin B'.

Piricularin was found to be a much more potent growth inhibitor than a*-*picolinic acid*, being active at a dilution of 1/400,000. At 1-1,000,000 it was stimulatory. *Chlorogenia acid*, stated to be the principal *polyphenol* of the plant, completely eliminated the growth *inhibitory* action of *piricularin*. The resistance and *susceptibility* of rice *seedlings* seemed to be related to their sensitivity to the combined toxins.

CONCERNING TOXINS AND THE VASCULAR DISEASES

The so-called vascular diseases are caused by a group of *pathogens* capable of *penetrating* through the external tissue of the host and establishing themselves in the water *conducting* tissue or *xylem*.

Here they are usually confined to nonliving elements

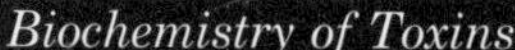

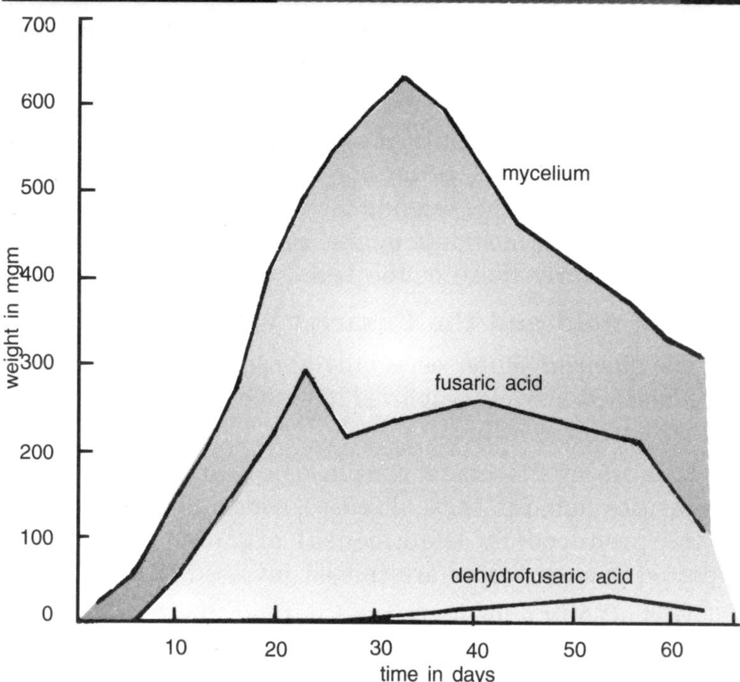

Figure 5.2: Relationship between growth, fusaric acid production, and dehydrofusaric acid production in Fusarium oxysporum f. iycopersici.

until the disease is in an advanced state of development, at which time they proliferate in the *surrounding* tissue. The fungi involved area specialized group in that they can survive and multiply in this sheltered environment.

They are generally nutritionally nonspecific and with the possible exception of the penetration phase of their life cycle lead a semisapr-ophytic existence and can be considered as showing a low order of parasitism, a characteristic in common with most of the *fungi* mentioned in the section on *root diseases*.

By virtue of their location toxic substances produced can be either readily absorbed by surrounding cells or swept through the plant with the transpiration stream depending on their chemical nature and concentration.

The most *conspicuous symptom* common to these

diseases is a *wilting* and, hence, they are generally referred to as the wilts. Two *theories* have been advanced to account for the wilting.

The first, the bundle *plugging* or occlusion theory assumes a *vascular plugging* interfering with water translocation and the second, the toxin theory, postulates plasma poisons which destroy the *osmotic* function of living cells particularly those of the leaf.

Fusaric Acid and the Fusarial Wilts

The *fusarial wilts*, especially those of annual species have been extensively employed in studies on the physiology of *hadromycotic* wilting.

Because of the many morphological and *physiological* similarities found in these diseases, some *amity* among the toxins produced by their causal organisms would be expected if such toxins are indeed involved.

This affinity appears to exist in their ability to produce fusaric acid. *Fusaric acid* was *originally* isolated from *Fusartum heterosporium* Nees. by Yabuta *et al.* (1934) and shown to be 5-butylpicolinic acid (V). Associated with it in some instances, for example in cultures of *F. oxysporum flycopersiei*, is *dehydrofusaric* acid (5-butylenepicolinic acid).

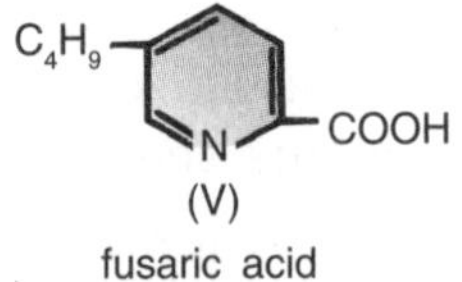

(V)

fusaric acid

Its in *vitro* production by a number of fungi, all belonging to the family Hypocreaceae has been demonstrated. These include Gibberella fujikuroi ; Fusarium oxysporum (*f. lycopersici*, *vasinfectum Nevis*, *f. batatos*, (*f. nicotianae*) ; *F. solani*, *F. lateritium*, *F. monilformae*, *F. monilformae f. majus* and *Nectria cinnabarina*.

Undoubtedly, this range will be extended as more species and forms are examined. Studies on the *in vitro* production of fusaric acid are often complicated by the presence of other toxic substances. The difficulty created by lycomarasmin production in the case of *Fusarium oxysporum f. lycopersici* was resolved by Kern (1952) who found that the fusaric acid inhibited spore germination in *Ustilago zeae* while the lycomarasmin was. innocuous.

The nutritional conditions required for the production of fusaric acid appear to be relatively nonspecific, a C : N ratio of approximately 5 : 1 being more important than any specific feature of carbohydrate or nitrogen metabolism. Zinc has been found to be essential for both growth and fusaric acid production in *Pusarium oxysporum f. vasinfectum*.

This is illustrated in Figure elsewhere in this chapter reproduced from *Kalyanasundarem* and Saraswathi-Devi (1955). It is particularly interesting to note that the *critical range* for fusaric acid production is much *narrower* than that required for growth. *Fusaric acid* production is not associated with *autolysis*. This is well illustrated in Figure elsewhere in this chapter adapted from Gaumann (1951).

Debydrofusaric acid, however, may well be an autolytic product Kern (1952) compared *lycomarasmin* and *fusaric acid* production by a *virulent* and an *avirulent straian* of the tomato *wilt fusarium* and found the latter to produce slightly greater quantities of both substances, thus apparently confirming aria extending the earlier observations of Gaumann *et al.* (1950) with respect to *lycomarasmin*.

This might be interpreted as an *argument* against these substances playing an important role in disease development. The possible fallacy of such an argument was, however, demonstrated by Sanwal (1956) who found that this relationship could be reversed by a simple reduction in the. nutrient concentration of the medium.

Lakshminarayanan and *Subramanian* (1955), and Kalyanasundaram and Venkata Ram (1956) using chromotographic techniques demonstrated the *in vivo* production of fusaric acid in cotton plants infected with *F. oxysporum f. vasinfectum.* Yields of at least 17 mg. per kilogram of fresh weight were obtained.

Kern and Kluepfel (1956), using isotope methods, were able to demonstrate a fusaric acid-like compound in tomato plants 10 days after inoculation. Fusaric acid production in wiltinfected watermelon plants has also been demonstrated.

The probable production of fusaric acid within .the plant suggested by *In vitro* studies has thus been confirmed *in vlvo*. The symptoms of fusaric acid injury to tomato are not typical of the symptoms observed in infected plants.

Damage appears first in the stems where cortical tissue over the vascular bundles is destroyed resulting in a "*furrowing*." This gradually extends out into the petioles as injury progresses. *Leaf injury*, *occurring* later, usually takes the form of necrotic spots in the interveinal area. *Epinasty* follows *stem injury*.

As would be anticipated, degree of injury and rate of development are functions of toxicant concentration. The treatment of tomato cuttings with fusaric acid results F in an unfavourable *disturbance* of the *transpiration-absorption* balance and attempts have been made to relate this to changes in the water *permeability* of plant protoplasts.

In the case of epidermal cells of *Rhoeo discolor,* a doubling of the rate of water movement was found to occur at a concentration of 1×10^{-7} M. This effect decreased to a concentration of 1×10^{-7} M after which a reduction in rate occurred.

Comparisops, of the cation content of diseased and healthy cotton shoots showed a substantial reduction of potassium accompanied by some increase in magnesium, calcium and iron in the -infected plants. This is interpreted by the authors to mean a -dearrangement of selective absorption and to be evidence against vascular occlusion as a primary cause of wilting.

Fusaric acid is a weak acid with percentage dissociations of approximately 2, 50, and 100 at pH's 4.3. 6.0, an 8.7, respectively. Cell penetration occurs most readily in the undissociated form and hence would be expected to increase as pH decreases. The practical application of this principle was demonstrated in an experiment in which tomato cuttings were placed in solutions at various pH's. Stem injury was found to decrease as the pH increased from 4.3 to 6.8 while leaf injury increased.

Presumably, at low pH, the fusaric acid molecules diffused into cortical cells of the stem, whereas at high pH it was swept up to the leaves in the transpiration stream in ionic form.

Gaumann (1957) points out that data on pH conditions prevailing within a tomato plant are not available but over the range given by Small (1955) for potato (xylem 4.0-4.4 to tubers, 6.2) the degree of dissociation would range from over 50% to virtually zero.

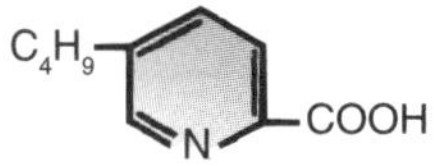

C_4H_9 — COOH
(V)
fusaric acid

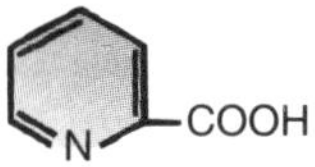

COOH
(VI)
picolinic acid

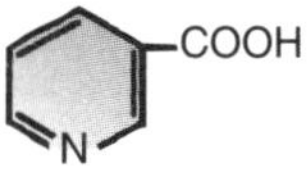

COOH
(VII)
nicotinic acid

C_4H_9 — $COOCH_2CH_3$
(VIII)
ethylester of fusaric acid

Bachmann (1956), studying the effect on water permeability in cells *of Rhoeo discolour* and *Spirogyra* found p11 to be only important at concentrations greater than 1 × 40-5 M. Below this level, permeation was pH independent.

This finding may be a reflection of the cations readily available for chelation with the fusaric acid molecule. At low concentrations, cell penetration might be facilitated by metal complexing and the effect of pH on dissociation consequently masked.

Once the supply of cations became exhausted, the degree of dissociation would then become important. Deuel (1954) has recently reviewed the literature pertaining: to the metal relationship of the wilt toxins.

Fusaric acid (V) and picolinic acid (VI) are equally effect-

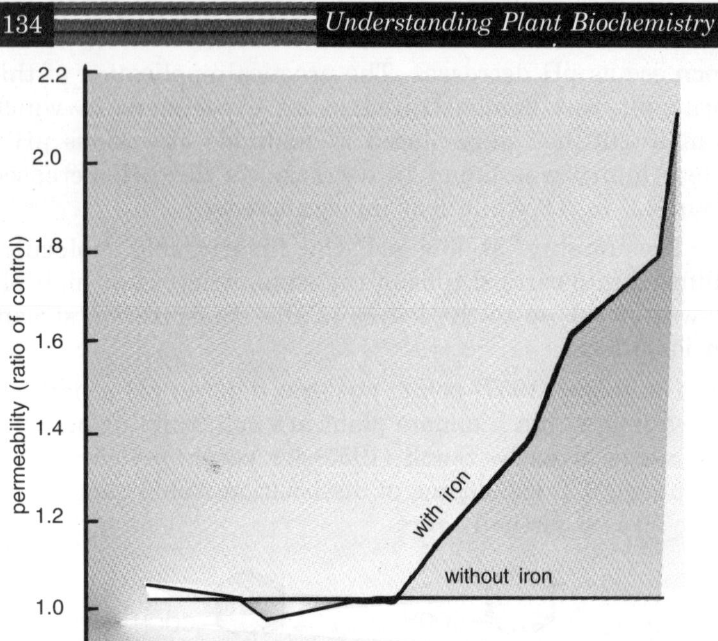

Figure 5.3: The effect of lycomarasmin and its iron chelate on the water permeability of Rhoeo cells. The chelate was prepared by adding an equivalence of iron to each of the test solutions.

ive as growth inhibitors while nicotinic acid (VII) and the ethyl ester of fusaric acid (VIII) show little activity.

The first two can form metal chelates while the latter two cannot. Bachmann (1956) found the *ethyl* ester to be as effective as fusaric acid itself in altering the water permeability of *Rhoeo* protoplasts. She concluded from this that metal chelation was not an important factor in activity.

This *discrepancy* may be *explainable* on the basis of hydrolysis in certain *biological* systems. Considerable emphasis has been placed by the Madras school on the metal *chelating* properties of fusaric acid in the physiology of wilt development.

Lakshminarayanan (1955Y found the activity of fusaric acid to be *potentiated* by iron. In analyses of resistant and *susceptible plants cystine* was *demonstrated* in the former but not in the latter. Increasing *tempereature* from 325° to 37-M resulted in a *progressive* increase in detsotable fusaric acid and decrease in wilt in *infected plants.*

Cystine was present at 37.5°C. but not at 32°C. Preferential chelation of the iron by cystine, rendering available to the toxin, is suggested as an explanation of resistance. It has been demonstrated further that pretreatment with 8-hydroxyquinoline protected cut shoots from the *toxic* effect of *culture* filtrates and functioned also as a *chemotheropeutant* on infected plants.

Again preferential metal chelation is advanced as the *explanation.* While *metal ions* may influence the in vivo production and *potentiation* of the toxin, a *poor chelator* such as *fusaric acid* would not be expected to disturb trace *elements* present in a bound form and thus create deficiency *symptoms.* Finally the reaction of a susceptible cotton variety grown in *infested soil* was found to be altered to that of a resistant one by zinc *fertilization.*

Other Toxin Produced by the Wilt Fusaria

Lycomarasmin, isolated from cultures of *Fusarium* oxysporum *f. lycopersici* was the first of the so-called wilt toxins to be characterized. It is a dipeptide with a *molecular weight* of 277 and an empirical formula of $C_9H_{15}O_7N_3$. Woolley (1948) reviewed the chemical evidence and concluded that it is. N-(α-α-hydroxypropionie acid))-*glycylasparagine.*

Lycomarasmin has been isolated only from culture filtrates of the tomato wilt *Fusarium* and apparently it either has not been recognized or does not occur in similar culture *filtrates* of other closely related *wilt fusaria.*

Dimond and Waggoner (1953), in their studies on the *in vitro* production of *lycomarasmin* concluded that it was a product of lysis rather than of actively growing *mycelium.* Gaumann (1957), however, takes exception to this conclusion and states that lycomarasmin can be demonstrated in the *mycelium* of *F. lycopersici* as early as the seventh day but reaches a maximum by the forty-fourth day.

While in vivo production has not been *demonstrated*, the *nutritional requirements* for its production are relatively nonspecific and its actual production within the conducting tissue of the living plants must certainly be considered a possibility.

Although lycomarasmin when applied to tomato cuttings does not produce symptoms typical of *Fusarium* wilt, this does not preclude the possibility that it plays a vital role in the development of the disease since a continuous low level of production within the host may have an effect quite different from a large single application applied to the base of a cutting.

Lycomarasmin forms a chelate complex with iron that is far more toxic than lycomarasmin itself although it produces an identical symptom picture. The *copper complex*, by contrast, is *nontoxic* (Kern, 1956). Gaumann and Naef-Roth (1956) recently reported on the interaction between lycomarasmin, a weak chelator, and a series of cations chosen according to Mellor and Malley's (1947, 1948) stability series for coordinate bonding. "*Komplexon III*," a strong chelator was also included for purposes of *comparison*. *Magnesium* had no effect on either *chelating agent*.

Manganese reduced the toxicity of the strong *chelator* but had little effect on lycomarasmin, a *weak chelator*. *Cobalt*, *nickel*, and *copper detoxified* both agents although increasing above a 1:1 M ratio resulted in metal ion toxicity. Iron is apparently carried to the leaves as the *lycomarasmin* complex.

This then breaks down under the influence of light to liberate an excess of iron which is phytotoxic. When lycomarasmin is applied to the basal end of a tomato *cutting*, there may be a twofold effect : iron *deficiency* in lower regions resulting from the binding of iron and its *translocation* upward to the leaves and iron toxicity resulting from the release of an excess of iron in the *leaf itself*.

Further evidence for this pattern of *behaviour* was obtained by Gaumann and Bachmann (1957) who studied the effect of *lycomarasmin* on the protoplasts in cells of *epidermal* strippings of *Rhoeo discolor*. *Lycomarasmin* applied alone was found to have no effect on water *permeability* but when applied in a 1:1 M ratio with iron, produced a progressive increase in the rate starting with no effect at 10^{-4} M to a doubling at 10^{-2} M.

This effect is illustrated in Figure elsewhere in this chapter. It explains the fact that doses of lycomarasmin applied on successive days showed progressively less effect since available iron is swept away on the first day. Gaumann *et al.* (1952) and Kern (1956) studied the effect of *lycomarasmin* on the water balance in tomato cuttings: "If tomato cuttings are allowed to take in the *lycomarasmin-iron* complex saturated with iron 1:1 they show the same characteristic curve of disturbed transpiration as they do with pure *lycomorasmin* although the saturated *lycomarasmin-iron* complex cannot chelate iron ions of the host on the way.

The opposite occurs if *lycomarasmin* is shielded from iron so that on the one band it carried no iron and on the ether hand it cannot chelate on its way through the shoot *iron ions* of the host. In this case the *transpiration* of he tomato shoot does not show the characteristic curve of *lycomarasmin* injuries.

Hence, *lycomarasmin* without iron is without effect in the field of excessive *transpiration*." Hiroe and Nishimura (1956) demonstrated the presence of a *toxic principle* in culture filtrates of the watermelon wilt *Fusariuvn (F oxysporum f. niveum)* and succeeded in isolating it in *crystalline* form.

They named the substance phytonivein. It was found to have an *empirical* formula of $C_{29}H_{46}O_2$ and to show many of the reactions of a steroid substance. Its occurrence in diseased *watermelon* plants was demonstrated. *chromatographically*.

There seemed to be a good correlation between *in vitro* production and the *pathogenicity* of strains of *Fusariurn*. Cut shoots and seedlings of watermelon werepermanently wilted by toxin concentrations of 10^{-6} *M. Phytonivein* showed some chelating properties and appeared to affect the *respiratory cycle*. Dimond and Waggoner (1953) demonstrated the *In vitro* and *in vivo* production of ethylene by *Fusarium oxysporum f. lycopersict* and showed it to be the cause of the epinastic symptoms of tomato wilt.

Ethyl alcohol has been suggested as a *possible* cause of fusarial wilt induced *epinasty* in the tomato. Dimond and Waggoner (1953) investigated this possibility and discounted it since amounts of ethanol greatly in excess of those *demonstrable* in either infected plants or *artificial* culture failed to produce the *response*.

Scheffer and Walker (1954) inoculated plants of the resistant *Jefferson* variety and grew them in nutrient solutions containing 1.0, 0.5, and 0.2% ethyl alcohol. The treated plants were characteristically wilted in 12 to 15 days while the *comparable uninoculated* controls were apparently *unaffected*. No epinasty was reported in the latter.

Resistance was unaffected in parallel experiments with methyl, isopropyl, and n-butyl alcohol. Alcohol concentrations as high as 2.1% have been reported for artificial cultures of *F. oxysporum f. lycopersici.*

The Role of Toxins in Fassriam Induced Wilt

Before discussing the possible role of toxins in the *fusarial* wilt *diseases*, brief reference must fife made two *enzymatic processes*. Ludwig (1952) advanced evidence to show that actual wilting is the result of occlusion of the *conducting* tissue.

This conclusion was later strengthened by the findings of Scheffer and Walker (1953) who also showed that the active principle in *culture filtrates* is beat labile and *nondialyzable* indicating a substance or substances *enzymatic* in character.

In *subsequent* work pectic enzymes, *primarily pectin methyl esterase*, have been identified with this activity. The exact mode of action is not clear but *presumably* occluding plugs of pectic *material* form in the *xylem vessels* at the expense of the *pectins* in the cell wall.

Evidence for this is to be found in the wilt-producing effects of enzyme *preparations* and *histological* evidence of pectic plugs and wall dissolution. *Vascular browning*, another symptom *characteristic* of wilt, has also been ascribed to *enzymatic* action.

It appears to be due to the *oxidation* of phenolic substances to melanins by the polyphenoloxidases. The phenols involved may arise from the *splitting* of *conjugated phenols*, perhaps. β-*glucosides*, by *fungal enzymes*. Gaumann *et. ai.* (1953) isolated a browning factor from culture *filtrates*.

They called it vasinfuscarin, and suggested that it was enzymatic in character. Many preparations of the pectin *esterases* have also produced vascular browning. This is probably due to impurity rather then to the enzyme itself. According to the concepts laid down in the introductory paragraph of this chapter, none of the enzymes involved here can be classed as toxins.

The phenols could, however, be considered in this category since they exist in the stem of diseased but not healthy plants, and are directly responsible for the browning symptoms and may exert other *physiological* effects, perhaps even wilting. In *fusarial* wilt of tomato, a multiplicity of *morphological*, *symptoms* precede and ultimately end in wilting and death.

An attempt to reconcile all observations relating to the physiology of the *pathogenism* of the disease leads almost inevitably to the conclusion already published by Dimond (1955), namely, that what we observe is "the combined effect of many causes."

Some symptoms such as epinasty, where ethylene is involved, can be traced to a single causal factor but this is the exception rather than the rule. Toxins are deeply involved as the previous discussion indicates and the work of Gottlieb (1944) on tracheal sap clearly demonstrates. Yellowing might be due to an effect of ethylene or to a *robbing* of iron from the *chloryphyll* molecule by *lycomarasmin* or an indirect effect *accompanying* a general senescence and decline of the plant. The *evidence* implicating toxins as a primary cause of wilting is not strong.

It consists first of the demonstration that a collapse in water economy occurs when cut tomato shoots are allowed to take up substances such as lycomarasmin, and second the demonstration that *lycomarasmin* and *fusaric acid* alter the water permeability of plant *protoplasts*.

In the first instance, as already pointed out, the morphological symptoms produced by high dosages do not *coincide* with those associated with the *disease*. A *collapse* in water economy and wilting may be expected to result from the *application* of *sufficiently* large amounts of any *translocatable nonspecific toxicant*.

Low dosages of *lycomarasmin* produce an increase in *transpiration* rate but no general breakdown. This certainly indicates a disturbance of physiological processes but is not *convincing* as the primary cause of wilting when the large changes in transpiration rate, occurring from day to day as a result of *environmental* changes, are considered.

The same may be said for observed changes in the water *permeability* of the *protoplasts* where a doubling in rate has been recorded. The permeability of onion pulp cells, for example, has been reported as 0.3 ml. sq. cm. of cell surface per minute per *atmosphere* of difference in *osmotic pressure*.

The potential for water flow through a normal protoplast is, therefore, much greater than the actual flow. *Irreversible* increases in water and solute permeability are to he expected as death approaches and the osmotic system breaks down. It is easy to *confuse* cause and effect here and difficult to separate them *experimentally*.

The recovery of *detached* wilted leaves and leaflets when placed in water is evidence strongly in favour of an effect rather than a cause. *Biochemical comparisons* of resistant and *susceptible* cotton plants have shown a number of physiological differences in addition to the differences in *cystine* content that have been correlated with wilt development.

Resistant plants have also been shown to have a *higher carbohydrate* and ascorbic acid content than *susceptible* ones. Further, the pectin content of the roots of susceptible varieties has been found to be higher than that in resistant ones, *synthesis* and storage tending to be in the *roots* in the former and leaves in the latter.

There appears, in other words, to be a correlation between root *pectic* reserves and resistance. The *ability* of the organism to *establish* itself in the xylem vessels of a given plant appears to be governed by factors within the host and is thus independent of the *toxin*-producing capabilities of the *pathogen*.

During the early stages of the disease, in a susceptible variety, the *fungus* remains confined to the xylem and again is *presumably* excluded from the *cortical*. tissue by the resistance factors of the host. Under cool conditions a plant may show little outward evidence of infection for a '*protracted* period of time.

At the onset of wilting, the organism grows out of the xylem vessels and proliferates rapidly in the surrounding living tissue. It is suggested that the nonspecific toxins produced by the organism pave the way for this final stage of the disease.

Actual wilting may result from the combined effect of impaired osmotic function and the increased resistance to water movement resulting from vascular occlusion.

The general association of fusaric acid with the fusarial wilts indicates that it may be the primary toxin concerned; further, the association of α-methyl isonicotinic acid with infertile soil (Skinner, 1918) and α-picolinic acid with rice blast suggests that a family of similar toxins may be involve, in a broad group of diseases caused by weak parasites.

THE VERTICLLIUM WILTS

Verticiilium albsstrum is an unusual pathogen in that it -attacks a wide variety of plants including trees, shrubs, ornamentals, vegetables, and weeds with very little evidence of host specialization. Donandt (1932) for example isolated it from more than 70 plant genera and found each isolate to be transferable to each other host.

Some differences in pathogenicity were noted but this would also be expected among a comparable number of isolates from a single host species. Bewley (1922), in his early studies on the sleepy disease of tomato, demonstrated that culture filtrates of the causal fungus could produce many of the symptoms of the disease itself when introduced into cut shoots.

He concluded that the activity factor was enzymatic in character and that the wilting symptoms arise as a result of vascular *plugging* by pectin-like *material*. Others, have suggested nitrites as the wilt inducing toxin of *Verticillium albo-atrum.*

More recently, Green (1954) reinvestigated the nitrite theory and found no evidence to substantiate it. The presence of wilt-inducing toxic substances in culture filtrates was reaffirmed. The fraction responsible for the responses, other than vascular *browning*, was found to be a *proteinaceous* material which did not appear in *detectable* amounts until after the onset of *autolysis*.

A polysaccharide fraction also was isolated. This produced vascular *discoloration* and gummosis but only in the absence of the *proteinaceous* material. Green concluded that this discoloration is atypical and results simply from the *inhibition* of the *amber* colour of the *polysaccharide*.

In view of the association between activity and autolysis it is difficult to see any relationship here between *in vitro* and possible *in* vivo activity. Scheffer *et al.* (1956) found transpiration to be depressed before and during wilting and concluded that this is due to *vascular blocking*.

Culture *filtrates* were found to contain a heat *labile* vascular browning factor. The pectic enzymes produced differ quantitatively from those previously reported for *Fusarium oxysporum f. lycopersfci* but the study of a broader range of material is necessary before any definite conclusion can be drawn in this regard. Talboys (1957) :found some evidence that toxins are involved in *Verticll-lium* wilt of hops. These are, however, nonspecific since symptoms of desiccation and necrosis induced by culture filtrates bear no relationship to either the pathogenicity of the fungal strain or the wilt tolerance of the hop variety.

The author suggests that there is a "*determinative phase*",, in which the organism establishes itself in the vascular tissue and a later "*expressive phase*" in which visible symptoms appear and in which toxins are operative. Young cotton shoots were found by Kamal and Wood (1956) to wilt rapidly when placed in culture filtrates of *Vertlcillium dahliae.*

Toxicity of these filtrates to parenchyma -cells appeared to be related to protopectinase activity while wilting seemed to result from the uptake of *thermostable* compounds of high molecular' weight. Vascular browning was obtained only when solutions containing protopectinase were used. Here, however, only crude preparations were *employed* and hence the *possibility* of a *contaminant* cannot be *excluded.*

SOUTHERN BACTERIAL WILT

Pseudomonas solanacearum attacks a wide range of solanaceous and other hosts. Hachinson (P913) introduced the toxin theory of wilting as a result of his work on the Rangpuror Southern bacterial wilt of tobacco. His conclusions were drawn froth the observation that an aqueous solution of an alcohol precipitate from Died broth cultures induces wilting when introduced the *tobacco plant.* This view has recently been by Kunz (1952) who separated two toxic fractions Own from 2- to 5-mouth-old culture filtrates.

One of these was thought to be a *bacterial* slime, complex polype-ptide in nature, that occluded water *conducting* tissue and the second a plasma poison *causing* an osmotic *disturbance* in the leaves.

Other workers found no evidence of toxins and concluded that wilting is caused by a mechanical plugging of vessels by masses of bacteria. In an attempt to clarify this situation, Husain and Kelman (1958) made a detailed comparison of the behaviour of strains of *Pseudomonas solanacearum* differing widely in their pathogenicity.

Culture filtrates from young. (24-48 hour) colonies of the virulent strain caused wilting in tomato cuttings while comparable filtrates from a weakly virulent and nonvirulent strain were without effect.

Further, a heat stable *viscous substance* causing reversible wilting in tomato cuttings was isolated from filtrates of the virulent strain but not from the *nonvirulent* or *avirulent* type.

This substance appeared to be a high molecular weight polysaccharide with glucose as its main component. *Tracheal sap* from plants inoculated with. a virulent strain also induced wilting. This *sap* was shown to contain a *polysaccharide* similar to the one produced in culture.

When grown on solid media, the cells of the *pathogenic* form were found to possess a slime sheath while the avirulent oness did not. This sheath appeared to be composed of the extracellular *polysaccharide previously demonstrated.*

The evidence, to indicate that wilting results from a restriction of water flow caused by increased viscosity of the tracheal sap, is, thus, very convincing. Polysaccharide production has also been demonstrated fora number of other plant pathogens and associated with wilting. These include *Ceratostomella ulmi*, *Fusarium solant f. eumarttt*, *Verticillium albo-atrum* and various *bacteria*.

TOXINS AND THE WILTS OF WOODY PLANTS

There are a number of wilts of woody plants that bear at least a *superficial resemblance* to the fusarial wilts in that their causal organisms are primarily vascular parasites and they are characterized by a *yellowing* and *rapid* wilting of *foliage*.

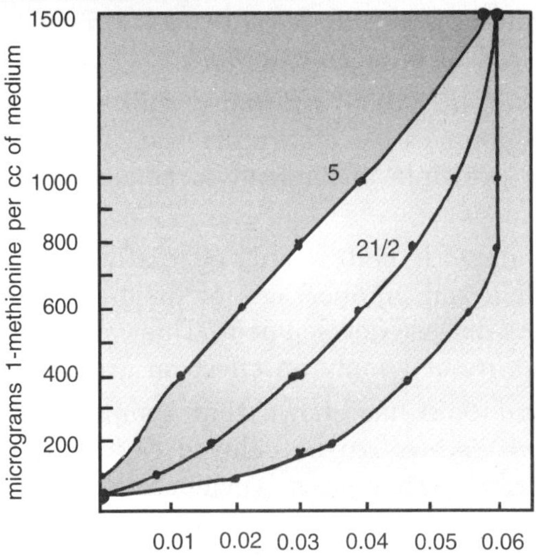

Figure 5.4: Data obtained in an experiment in which three concentrations of chemically pure toxin were tested against a range of concentrations of L-methionine. Chlorella vulgaris was used as the test organism. Note that at half growth (X), an excellent competitive relationship-exists between methionineand toxin concentrations. Five times as much L-methionine is required in a culture medium containing a 5-fold concentration of toxin as is needed to obtain the same amount of growth in a medium containing 1/5 that concentration. The results shown above were obtained after a 3-day incubation period at 25°C.

Some progress has been made toward an understanding of the physiology of disease development despite the fact that the nature of the host makes *experimentation* much more difficult than with annual hosts. Although frequent reference is made to toxins in the literature on Dutch elm disease, there is very little direct *information* concerning them.

Zentmeyer (1942) freed culture filtrates of. *Ceratostomella ulmi* of mycelium by passage through a Berkfield filter and injected them into young elm trees. After 3 days typical symptoms of Dutch elm *disease* appeared.

The principle involved was apparently nonenzymatic in nature since it with-stood *boiling* for 5 minutes. Dimond (1947) obtained essentially similar results and showed that culture filtrates contain at least two toxic factors, one of which appeared to be a *polysaccharide*.

Feldman *et. al.* (1950) concluded that polysaccharides are not the main cause of the disease. They found the second toxic principle of Dimond to be unstable at high pH's.

It accumulated in culture only at relatively low pH(4 to 5). In the field soil, applications of toxic chemicals were found to delay disease development. This could be an effect on *toxin stability* or simply an effect on growth.

Beckman (1958) has shown that symptom expression in *Datch elm* discase can be delayed by treatments that retard tree growth. There is then evidence of the application in culture filtrates of toxic substances which are circumstantially linked to disease development. *Oak wilt* has been described as one of the most destructive tree diseases.

While all oak species spear to be affected by the disease, it is most severe in trees of the red oak group. Symptoms progress from the crown of the tree downward. The leaves typically wilt, turn brown, and fall.

The causal fungus, *Endoconidiophora fagacearum* (*Chalara quercina*), is a typical vascular pathogen and appears to spread through a tree by movement in the *transpiration* stream.

Young (1949) found that oak cuttings, placed in cell-free culture filtrates of the *organism*, wilted rapidly and developed symptoms characteristic of those observed in small *greenhouse inoculated plants*.

White (1955), in a more detailed study, found two *nonvolatile* thermostable toxins to be involved; one was responsible for the wilting and drying of the leaves while the other produced necrosis. *Nectria cinnabarina* causes a disease of numerous trees and *shrubs* including apple and currant, frequently referred to as coral spot.

This organism is a wound pathogen and invades the cortex and xylem causing a brown discoloration of tissues.

The vessels become invaded by hyphae and their *plugging* by a brown *gummy material* is obvious. *Invasion* is limited and the mycelium of the *fungus* does not appear to extend much beyond the *discoloured* area.

The *necrosis* and *wilting* frequently noted in leaves above a diseased area have been variously attributed to a cutting off of water supply and to the formation of *translocatable* toxins. Gaumann (1957) states that this organism also can produce *fusaric acid.*

Kobel (1951) concludes that wilting, the major symptom, is due to an interference with translocation but that leaf spotting is due to the action of a toxin. It must be concluded in relation to this group of diseases that toxins are definitely "*suspect*" but that a knowledge of their nature and, role must await the outcome of future *investigations.*

ETHYLENE AS A FUNGAL TOXIN

A study of substances which affect the *physiological* processes of the plant and in so doing may *predispose* them to disease leads almost inevitably to ethylene.

This substance has been studied extensively by plant physiologists in relation to fruit ripening and is now generally accepted as the cause of the climacteric rise in the *respiration* of *ripening* fruits.

It also induces fruit softening associated with pectic changes, notably an increase in soluble *pectin* and a corresponding decrease in insoluble protopectin. *Ethylene* has also been studied extensively in relation to *auxins* balance and foliar abcission.

The literature relating to this. question has been reviewed by Hall (1952). Ethylene promotes abscission but its effect can be counteracted by auxin treatment.

Although both auxin and ethylene are less abundant in older tissues than they are in actively growing tissues it is the balance rather than the absolute amount that seems to be important in *regulating* the level of *physiological* activity in cells.

Williamson (1950) confirmed the fact that a low level of *ethylene* production is normal in plant tissues and showed that it frequently appears in greatly increased amounts in *response* to *injury* or disease.

He suggested that it might be responsible for rapid yellowing and early leaf abscission. It is a metabolic product, of the green mold fungus *Penicillium digitatum* and lemons infected with this organism show a respiratary rate as much as 100% greater than the controls.

Dimond and Waggoner (1953) investigated the cause of epinasty, an early symptom of tomato fusarial wilt. They found ethylene to be produced by the organism in culture and by diseased plants. The amounts demonstrated were adequate to cause epinasty and yellowing.

Crude enzyme preparations from *Penicillium digitatum* and apple juice were found by Hall (1951) to produce ethylene from a variety of substrates, the best being ethyl alcohol, arabinose, and pectin.

The observation with respect to ethyl alcohol is a surprising one and may, as the author suggests, indicate that it is the terminal substrate. *Fusarium oxysporum f. lycopersici* is known to produce ethanol both *in vitro* and *in vivo.*

This could be of significance in relation to the appearance and role of ethylene in infected tomato plants. Pectin hydrolysis and ethylene production are not correlated since *Rhizopus nigricans* and *Penicillium italicum* failed to produce it although both are active pectin hydrolyzers.

Evidence summarized by Allen (1953) suggests that ethylene indirectly uncouples respiration from the energy-requiring activities of the cell.

All these results show that ethylene is biologically active in small amounts and that it seems to regulate the state of maturation of plant cells which in turn affects susceptibility to microbial attack. Studies on the role of ethylene in the physiology of a great variety of diseases would undoubtedly be very rewarding.

WILDFIRE AND ANGULAR LEAF SPOT OF TOBACCO

Wildfire and angular leaf spot are two important bacterial diseases of tobacco. The former is characterized by localized chlorotic halos 1 to 2 cm. in diameter surrounding a central, usually small, necrotic spot while the latter appears as a small angular necrotic spot without the halo.

The chlorotic area in the case of wildfire is free of bacteria. The causal organisms are *Pseudomonas tabaci* and *Pseudomonas angulaium, respectively.* Johnson and Murwin (1925) demonstrated that sterile culture filtrates of *P. tabaci* would produce wildfire symptoms.. This observation was confirmed by Clayton (1934) who showed the toxic principle to be heat stable.

Leaf prick inoculations with either the toxin alone or the toxin plus bacteria resulted in the development of typical wildfire symptoms on many plant species. Comparable inoculation with the bacteria alone, however, only gave consistent positive results on *Nicotiana* species.

Thus, the toxin was shown to be nonspecific but its production dependent on the ability of the organism to multiply on the host concerned. Braun (1937) made a detailed comparison of the two organisms, *P. tabaci* and *P. angulatum,* and found them to bemorphologically, physiologically, and serologically indistinguishable.

Strains could, however, be readily separated on the basis of host symptomology. Nontoxin producing strains of *P. tabaci* were relatively easy to produce. These produced symptoms similar to those of *P. anguiatum* on tobacco leaves.

Since no evidence of the reversion of a *nontoxin*-producing strain to a toxin-producing one was obtained it is suggested that *P. angulatum* may be a strain of *P. tabaci.* Clayton (1936) described epidemic forms of the two diseases that are indistinguishable.

Here the organism appears to spread so rapidly through water-soaked leaves that general necrosis precedes the development and diffusion of the toxin. A tobacco leaf assay procedure has been developed for the wildfire toxin which was employed to monitor steps in isolation procedures and an apparently pure product was obtained.

This product was highly active, 0.1 µg./ml. producing a halo on a tobacco leaf. It was also highly unstable, particula-rly at high pH's, and very hygroscopic. Analytical findings indicated the toxin to be an a-amino acid. This work was continued and the toxin found most probably to be the lactone of α-lactylamino-β-hydroxy-Σ-aminopimelic acid. Complete acid hydrolysis gives rise to the amino acid, α, Σ-diamino-β-hydroxypimelic acid, and lactic acid.

The name tabtoxinine was applied to the former. It is inactive in either the formation or inhibition of wildfire halos. Treatment with dilute alkali results in an opening of the lactone ring. Parallel to the work on characterization, studies on biological activity of crude toxin preparations were in progress. Braun (1950) found growth of the green alga *Chlorella vulgaris* to be inhibited by the wildfire toxin.

Since this alga can be readily cultured, it lends itself to studies of this kind. The deleterious effect of toxin concentrations sufficient to inhibit growth completely was found to be completely overcome by the addition of liver extract to the medium.

A large number of compounds, including those found in liver extract, were tested and of them only DL-methionine proved to be effective. The results indicated further that the effect was on methionine utilization rather than on its synthesis and that a constant ratio existed between the amount of toxin and the amount of methionine required as an inhibitor.

Methionine is, in other words, synthesized by *Chlorella* in the presence of toxin but its normal utilization is impaired, i.e., competitive inhibition. Methionine sulfoximine, a known methionine antagonist, behaved in the same way as the wildfire toxin, with regard to both *Chlorella* and halo production on tobacco leaves.

This work was confirmed and extended with chemically pure toxin. The competitive reversal of the toxic action by methionine is well illustrated in Figure elsewhere in this chapter.

This reversal could not, however, be demonstrated on tobacco leaves. A number of structural analogues of methionine were examined for ability to produce halos on tobacco leaves and again methionine sulfoximine and the related ethionine sulfoximine were the only ones that proved to be effective.

Mutants of *Chlorella* selected for resistance to the methionine sulfoximine were equally resistant to the wildfire toxin. The evidence then suggests strongly that the wildfire toxin functions as an antimetabolite of the essential amino acid methionine.

BACTERIAL CANKER OF STONE FRUITS

The physiological relationship exemplified so well by the wildfire and angular leaf spot diseases may not be unique *Pseudomonas morsprun-orum* Wormald is described as the organism causing bacterial canker and gummosis in stone fruits.

This organism belongs to a group of organisms of the *Pseudomonas syringae* type apparently only separable on the basis of host range and pathogenicity. Erikson (1945) and Erikson and Montgomery (1945) found that the organism invades the cells of the bark intercellularly causing plasmolysis of cells and later disintegration in advance of invasion.

This paves the way for further advance of the organism. Cell-free filtrates, from old cultures of the organism grown on either a synthetic medium or bark decoctions, when injected into the bark of susceptible - plum trees produce injury symptoms identical to those from an infection.

Parallel filtrates from young oultuses have little effect

indicating that the active principle is a product of autolysis. A partially purified product was also found to be active.

It is suggested that the killing action of *Pseudomonas morsprunorum* may he due in part to an eadotoxin of a proteinaceous nature. Varieties of cherry and plum resistant to the disease are little affected by the toxin preparations while susceptible varieties are severely damaged. Some strains of the closely related *Pseudamonas syringae* produce active filtrates while others do not. An understanding of the toxins produced by this complex group of microorganisms may well provide theanswer to many of the problems posed by them.

TOXINS AND THE VICTORIA BLIGHT OF OATS

In the preceding section, an example was .given *(Pseudomonas morsprunorum)* in which resistance and susceptibility appears to be regulated by sensitivity to a toxin.

The most clear-cut illustration of toxin regulated host specificity is, however, to be found in the case of the "*Victoria*" blight of oats. The South American oat variety Victoria, an *Avena byzantina* type shows a hypersensitive reaction to crown rust and beginning in the 1930's was used extensively in Canada and the United States as a source of resistance in the oat breeding program.

Between 1944 and 1946 a new oat disease,. confined to the Victoria progeny, appeared and increased to devastating proportions. It was characterized by a striping and yellowing of leaves, basal necrosis, and weakening of the lower culms resulting in severe lodging. The symptoms of the disease, its distribution, and the casual organism, a species of *Helm inthosporium* resembling *H. sativum* were described by Mechan.

And Murphy in 1946. They named the causal organism *Helminthosporium victoriae.* Later they produced evidence to show that a toxin is involved. The fungus is confined to the basal infection and cannot be isolated from blighted

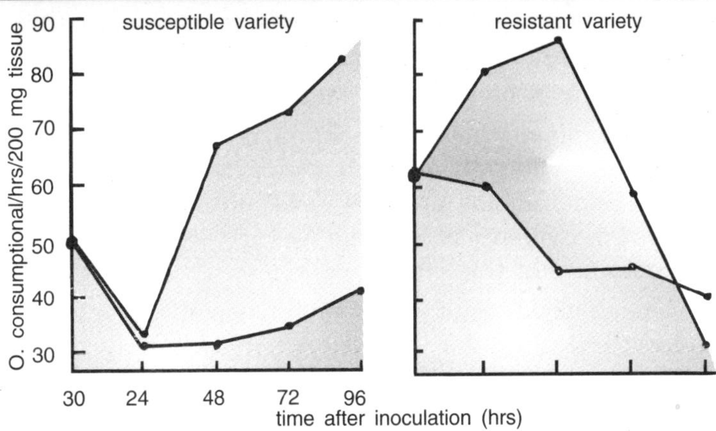

Figure 5.5: Comparison of respiration of non-infected and infected barley leaves from a resistant and susceptible variety.

leaves till complete necrosis has occurred. Culture filtrates at high dilution produced leaf yellowing and streaking in the Victoria varieties characteristic of the disease but were without effect on resistant oat varieties. Finally, leaves of the Victoria varieties could be killed by spraying with culture filtrate while the resistant varieties were relatively unaffected.

The principle In the culture filtrate was found to be heat stable since it withstood autoclaving for 20 minutes at 15 lb. pressure. These findings were later confirmed and extended by Litzenberger 1949) who demonstrated the presence of the specific toxic principle in infected plants as well as in culture filtrates.

The fungus grew in the stems of both resistant and susceptible varieties when inoculated by needle puncture but only in the latter did symptoms develop.

Luke and Wheeler (1955) developed a chemically defined medium favorable to toxin production. Culture filtrates reduced root growth in susceptible types by 50% at dilutions of 1:1,000,000 but had virtually no effect on resistant varieties at 1:10.

Further, a good correlation was found between pathogenicity, growth, and toxin production among strains of *H.*

victoriae. The peak of toxin production coincided with the maximum growth. The toxin was found to be unstable at high pH but to be relatively stable at a pH of 4.

This explains the success obtained with a medium containing ammonia as a nitrogen source, where the pH drops rapidly and remains at a low level until the ammonia is exhausted. Evidence of a second less active nonspecific toxin was obtained in this work.

Unpublished results obtained by the author confirm this and suggest that the second toxin is similar to the one described for *Helminthos-porium sativum.* Wheeler and Luke (1955), through the use of the toxin, were successful in obtaining resistant plants from a susceptible variety by a mass selection process.

Some of these seedlings were also resistant to crown rust. Pringle and Braun (1957) isolated the toxic substance in what they consider to be pure form. They found that the toxin becomes less stable as purification proceeds and were unable, because of this instability, to obtain an elemental, analysis, or to characterize structure.

The product, however, was extremely potent, being active at 0.01 fag. per milliliter and produced the same host response as the crude culture filtrate and the disease itself. It appears to be polypeptide in nature.

Fresh biologically active preparations of the toxin are ninhydrin negative but this reaction appears as activity is lost. Two ninhydrin spots appeared on paper chromatograms following mild alkaline hydrolysis. One of these was found to be produced by a compound having the empirical formula $C_{17}H_{29}NO$ and was given the name "*victoxinine.*"

The other appeared to be a peptide. Victoxinine completely inhibited root growth of both resistant and susceptible varieties at a concentration of 2.5×10^{-7} M. Since it is nonspecific in its action, the authors suggest that the toxicity of the parent toxin may be due to the victoxinine while the specificity is a function of the peptide portion of the molecule.

The exact chemical nature and the mode of action of the Victoria blight toxin yet remain to be elucidated. It is one of the most intriguing of the phytotoxins demonstrated thus far, not only because of its extreme potency but also because of its host specificity.

A final clarification of the problem may provide a clear-cut biochemical explanation of one type of disease resistance.

PLANT GROWTH REGULATORS

Plant growth is controlled by hormones and it is not unreasonable to assume that the effective level prevailing varies with species and variety and is genetically controlled. Vent and Thimann (1949) for example demonstrated that growth in certain *Epilobium* hybrids is limited by an auxin deficiency and they were able to correct this by the application of auxin.

Similarly, it has recently been demonstrated that dwarfism in certain varieties of corn and peas can be overcome by treatment with the gibberellins. The question can plant growth regulators sometimes be toxins?" is not an easy one to answer.

It will be considered here in relation to the two main classes of plant growth hormones, namely, indole 3-acetic acid and the gibberellins. Much of the voluminous literature pertaining to this subject has been recently summarized in reviews by Brian (1957) and Stowe and Yamaki (1957).

The latter review is particularly valuable since it summarizes Japanesework on the gibberellins, much of which is otherwise unavailable to Western readers.

Indole Acetic Acid

Indole 3-acetic acid (IAA) is a fairly common metabolic product of fungi and bacteria if tryptophan is supplied in themedium. Some fungi at least are also capable of producing on IAA-destroying enzyme. There are many plant diseases, particularly among those caused by obligate and semiobligate parasites in which symptoms suggest an overdose of auxin. This observation has led to detailed studies, many of which have shown a high IAA content to exist. Crown gall is the best example. However, here, as pointed out by Brian (1957), there is no proof that the extra IAA in the tissues is of microbial origin.

Further, there are two phases to tumor formation (a) inception and (b) unregulated cell proliferation. The inception, or transformation of normal cells into tumor cells, apparently occur's under the stimulus of a tumor-inducing principle secreted by the bacterial cells.

Similar demonstrations. of a high IAA content have been made in connection with theso-called "witches'-broom" diseases, such as those caused by various rusts.

Here again there is no evidence of in vivo IAA. production by the microorganisms involved. Shaw and Samborski (1956) demonstrated that an area of high metabolic activity occurs in the vicinity of stem rust postules and mildew infections on wheat.

These areas were high in IAA content even though no cell proliferation was induced. The evidence then would suggest that IAA is a result of enhanced metabolic activity rather than the cause of it. It is not, in other words, to be regarded as a toxin.

The Gibberellins

The temptation to regard the gibberellins as potential toxins is great as a result of the manner of their discovery. The, bakanae or "*foolish seedling*" disease of rice is caused by a soilborne fungus, Gibberella fujikuroi (Fusarium moniliforme).

Early attack by the organism results in a seedling blight. Tillering is suppressed in plant which survive the early attack of the organism and the remaining shoots as a result of excessive internode elongation grow taller, than do those of the surrounding healthy plants.

In humid areas, scab symptoms similar to those found in corn and wheat occur at heading time. The Japanese workers demonstrated that the symptoms of the bakanae disease could be reproduced by treatment with cell free culture filtrates of *Gibberella fujikuroi.*

Early work was made difficult by the presence of a growth-inhibiting: factor in culture media. This complication was resolved with the identification of fusaric acid which has already been discussed.

They eventually isolated a crystalline product that they called gibberellin A, (found to be a mixture of gibberellin A_1, $C_{19}H_{24}O_6$, and gibberellin A2, $C_{19}H_{26}O_6$; sec Grove *et. al.,* 1958). Later, a second product, gibberellic acid, with the formula $C_{19}H_{22}O_6$ was isolated independently by British and American workers. Gibberellic acid and gibberellin A, although chemically distinct, appear to be physiologically identical.

Gibberellic acid reproduces the symptoms in the host characteristic of the bakanae disease and Brian (1957) concluded: "It is therefore virtually certain that the overgrowth in bakanae disease is caused by production of gibberellin A or gibberellic acid in the host plant tissue by the invading fungus."

In the seedling blight stage of the disease, root growth is often inhibited while the coleoptile expands normally. These are symptoms of fusaric acid injury. The gibberellins cbaracteristically stimulate shoot elongation and are either without effect or stimulatory to roots.

It would seem, therefore, that both substances are operative in the disease, the nonspecific toxin, fusaric acid, tending to inhibit growth and perhaps predispose the plant to attack, and the gibberellins producing overgrowths in surviving less severely affected plants.

The overgrowths characteristic of the bakanae disease are not caused by strains of *Fusarium moniliforme* other than those isolated from rice and parallel symptoms are not observed in such corresponding diseases as those of corn and wheat.

Following the demonstration of gibberellin production

by *fujikuroi,* a number of workers have demonstrated the presence of gibberellin-like substances in higher plants. Recently, MacMillan and Suter (1958) have succeeded in isolating and -characterizing gibberellin A from immature bean seeds, thus leaving no doubt that it is a new type of naturally occurring -plant growth regulator and may be the forerunner of a series of hither to unsuspected plant hormones.

The gibberellins can, from this standpoint, scarcely be classed as toxins even though they are known to be responsible for one type of pathological overgrowth.

TOXINS AND THE OBLIGATE PARASITES

The toxin relationships involved in obligate parasitism must obviously be much more subtle than those prevailing in most of the examples considered in previous sections of this chapter.

An ideal condition from the standpoint of the pathogen would be one creating the least pathological disturbance in the host. In the early stages of disease, substances produced by the organism might function as modifiers rendering the host more suitable for the further growth and development of the pathogen.

The least favourable condition for the pathogen is the one involving a hypersensitive reaction where 'host cells die quickly, thus cutting off the development of the parasite. There is considerable circumstantial evidence for the association of host stimulating substances with rust and mildew infections on susceptible hosts.

Yarwood and Jacobsen (1955) demonstrated that radiophosphorous accumulates around rust pustules on the leaves of Pinto bean. In one instance, one-half of a primary bean leaf was inoculated 'with rust. The shoot was then placed with the opposing, noninoculated, leaf in $H_3P_{32}O_4$ solution and the inoculated leaf to water.

Under these conditions, 7870 times as much P^{44} accumulated in the rusted as in the nonrusted portion of the same leaf. In this experiment, as in many others, where the leaves were either immersed in water or in a saturated atmosphere, transpiration could not be a factor in accumulation.

Further, accumulation was apparent shortly after infection and increased as the fungal development progressed. There was no sudden change in pattern as the developing pustule ruptured the cuticle. It might be argued that the accumulation represented uptake by the developing fungus rather than by host cells.

A parallel increase was observed,, however, with a number of mildew infections where the mycelium developing superficially could be removed, and with virus infections. Further evidence that the effect was one on host cells was provided by the fact that the accumulation of phosphorus also occurred after the rust had been destroyed by a. selective heat treatment.

In experiments with rust and mildew on wheat, Shaw and‘: Samborski (1956) found accumulation of C^{14}, Pa^{32}, and Ca^{45}. A number of sources of C^{14}, including sugars and organicacids such as indole acetic acid, were tested with essentially the same result.

Among these, protocatechuic acid accumulated sufficiently to cause visible damage around infections: while neighbouring healthy areas were apparently unaffected. The curves for accumulation paralleled those for enhanced respiration.

Either anaerobiosis or treatment with respiration inhibitors such as azide or dinitrophenol were effective in inhibiting accumulation. The results, in other words, suggest that the accumulation is similar to that observed in meristems, and other metabolically active regions.

The accumulation of indole acetic acid in the environs of an infection was not, accompanied by increased cell division. This may, however, be a matter of species since Yarwood and Cohen (1951) did report some hypertrophy in connection with bean rust, a finding suggestive of the "tumor inducing principle" of crown, gall.

Shaw and Samborski (1956), after a thorough discussion of their own and related findings, conclude: "The results obtained. with *Puccinia* and *Erysiphe* are in full accord with the hypothesis that a diffusible substance (or substances), produced at the incipient infection, either by the fungus, or by the host cell or cells under attack or both, stimulates the metabolic activity of the host tissue in the environs of the infections." Such a substance would be a toxin.

Its effect in the case of a susceptible reaction is to mobilize host reserves for the use of the pathogen. If, however, other translocatable phytotoxic subs tances are present, its effect might be to concentrate these at the infection site, thus causing death of cells and resulting in a hypersensitive reaction, i.e., an effect parallel to that reported for protocatechuic acid.

While there is apparently no direct evidence for the latter role, the nature and time of production of such phytotoxins could account for the various intergrading rust reaction types. "*Victoria*" oats, as has already been pointed out, are susceptible to attack by *Helminthosporium victoriae* but resistant to *Puccinia coronata*.

The host selectivity of *Helminthosporium victoriae* is clearly governed by the reaction of the host to a specific toxin. Litzenberger (194§) showed that extracts from oat leaves infected with *P. coronata* passe a similar host specificity, indicating that the two unrelated pathogens may produce similar toxins.

Damage to tissues in the cage of the facultative parasite would lead to susceptibility while With the obligate parasite it would lead to resist-ance. Allen (1953) reviewing the literature on "toxins and tissue respiration" notes that an enhanced respiration occurs in connection with a variety of plant diseases and that it is a response of the host cells to diffusible substances produced by the pathogen.

He cites a limited amount of evidence to show that this

results from an uncoupling of respiration from the energy requiring processes of the cell through an effect on oxidative phosphorylations.

This would not explain the rather prolonged period of enhanced metabolic activity associated with the growth of rusts and mildews on susceptible hosts.

A complete or partial uncoupling could, however, easily be the explanation of a hypersensitive or partially resistant reaction. White and Baker (1954), in a histological study of barley mildew caused *by Erysiphe graminis* var. *hordel*, found resistance to be related to the rapidity and degree of collapse of the mesophyll cells.

Infected leaves of a resistant variety showed a rapid rise in respiration followed by cell collapse at the infection site and return of the respiration rate to normal. The onset of increased respiration was delayed in a susceptible variety and the increase continued gradually as more cells became invaded.

These results are illustrated in Figure elsewhere in this chapter. The authors suggest that an uncoupling agent might be produced by the pathogen or boat pathogen combination Crude extracts from infected leaves stimulated respiration in non-infected leaves.

A phenolic compound, apparently liberated on cell collapse, was also isolated. It showed marked antifungal properties and was thought to prevent further development of the fungus. The "respiratory factor" caused cell collapse in leaves of a resistant but not a susceptible variety.

Brushing the leaves of the susceptible variety with a preparation of the respiratory factor just prior to inoculation caused subsequent cell collapse and inhibition .of growth of the pathogen.

The hypersensitive reaction in barley can then, in at least one instance, be attributed to the action of a toxin and resistance and susceptibility seem to be related to the relative toxin tolerance of the barley varieties involved.

The explanation of the Australian group, namely a

partial or complete uncoupling of oxidative phosphorylation from respiration could be the correct one. It seems more probable though that a stimulatory substance results in enhanced metabolic activity with resultant preferential accumulation of a phytotoxic substance. The latter might function as a respratory poisons.

PHOTOSYNTHETIC PIGMENTS

The concentration of photosynthetic pigments is commonly used as a measure of the amount of plant material in a sample, and photosynthesis rates are frequently normalized to chlorophyll a concentration.

In addition, assessments of pigment composition provides qualitative information on the physiological condition of natural samples by providing information on the presence of breakdown products and provides information on the taxonomic composition of algal populations *via* an analysis of accessory pigments.

Estimations of pigment content and complement are also the basis of quantitative assessments of the relationship among light harvesting, photosynthesis, and growth.

Chlorophyll a is the only photosynthetic pigment found in all oxygenevolving photoautotrophs and so provides a convenient and unambiguous measure of algal abundance.

However, the ratio of chlorophyll a to algal biomass ranges from 0.1% to 5% of dry weight, and varies in response to changes in irradiance, nutrient availability, and temperature.

In addition to chlorophyll a, algae contain accessory pigments that often account for most of the *in vivo* absorption. These pigments include chlorophylls *b* and c, carotenoids, and phycobiliproteins.

EXTRACTION OF CHLOROPHYLLS AND CAROTENOIDS

Chlorophylls a and *b* consist of a magnesium porphyrin complex with a long hydrophobic side chain, whereas chlorophyll c is actually a chlorophyllide that lacks the phytol tail. Carotenoids are long polyisoprenoids having conjugated double bonds with unsaturated unsubstituted cyclohexane rings at each end of the molecule.

There are two classes of carotenoids: carotenes, which are hydrocarbons, and xanthophylls, which contain oxygen atoms in their terminal rings. Chlorophylls can be characterized spectrophotometrically as having relatively sharp absorption maxima in both the blue and red spectral regions.

The carotenoids, in contrast, usually have a broad yellow absorption band, perhaps with several local maxima within this broad band. Chlorophylls and carotenoids can be extracted in organic solvents: acetone has been the solvent of choice for oceanographers, although investigators who study macroalgae and freshwater phytoplankton prefer the more polar solvent methanol, which provides a higher extraction efficiency.

Macroalgal samples are blotted dry, cut into small pieces, and extracted by grinding tissues in a mixture of solvent and an abrasive such as sand, whereas microalgae are commonly concentrated by filtration, followed by homogenization in a solvent using a tissue grinder.

Solubilized pigments are separated from residual material by centrifugation or filtration. The homogenization step is sometimes omitted in analyses of microalgae in order to decrease the processing time.

Specifically, a sample can be concentrated onto a filter, placed in a vial containing solvent, and allowed to extract overnight in the cold at 4°C or in a deep freeze at -20°C. Phinney and Yentsch (1985) recommend direct injections of samples into 100% acetone (to obtain a final concentration of 85%) for pigment extraction of microalgae.

Incomplete pigment extraction may be encountered with less laborintensive procedures, particularly when chlorophytes and cyanobacteria are present in samples extracted with 90% acetone. Complete extraction from microalgal samples can be obtained with either hot 100% methanol or a 1:1 mixture of dimethyl sulfoxide (DMSO) and acetone.

Complete extraction of pigments from macroalgae presents more problems, and an initial extraction with DMSO following by extraction with acetone or methanol has become a method of choice for extracting pigments from recalcitrant species (Duncan and Harrison, 1982).

Plant physiologists have found that N_0N-dimethylformamide (DMF) is an effective solvent for extracting chlorophylls a and b from vascular plants. This solvent may also prove useful for macroalgal samples. Chlorophylls and carotenoids are labile compounds that may decompose when exposed to light, acids, or oxygen. Precautions must be taken to avoid chemical degradation and photooxidation: these include working at low temperature under subdued illumination or darkness and using deoxygenated solvents.

Addition of H_2S to methanol is commonly recommended, and $MgCO_3$ is often added to the sample prior to extraction to neutralize organic acids, which may be released when tissues are disrupted. The principal breakdown products of chlorophylls a and b are pheophytins, chlorophyllides, and pheophorbides.

Acidification of chlorophyll leads to pheophytin production through removal of magnesium from the porphyrin ring. Chlorophyllide is produced by the removal of the phytol chain from chlorophyll a by chlorophyllase. Pheophorbide is produced by the removal of both magnesium and phytol.

Pheophytins and pheophorbides may be present at large concentrations in natural samples as a result of zooplankton grazing, senescence, and/or decomposition.

Chlorophyllide may be produced during sample extraction because chlorophyllase remains active in aqueous organic solvents. In addition, pheophytin or pheophorbide may be produced if organic acids are not neutralized during extraction.

Chlorophyllase is active even in 90% acetone, and extraction in 100% acetone has been recommended to inhibit chlorophyllase activity. Even this may not be sufficient, and Suzuki and Fujita (1986) suggest a brief exposure to heat (65°C) to completely inactivate chlorophyllase.

QUANTIFICATION OF CHLOROPHYLLS AND CAROTENOIDS

Pigments are commonly identified by their absorption spectra, and routine methods for determining pigment concentrations in solvent extracts rely on spectrophotometric measurements. Several different expressions are used to quantitatively describe the absorption characteristics of pigments.

Much of the older data is reported as specific extinction coefficients designated E_{1cm}, where 1 cm refers to the pathlength of the spectrophotometer cell used to measure absorbance. More recently, molar and weight-specific absorption coefficients have become the preferred units. The following relationship can be used to convert among these different expressions:

$$A^* = A_m/M = E_{1cm}10 \qquad (4.1)$$

where: A^* is the $\log_o$ weight-specific absorption coefficient (m^2g^{-1}), A_m is the molar absorption coefficient (m^2 mol^{-1}), E_{1cm} is the specific extinction coefficient ($dm^3 \cdot g^{-1} \cdot cm^{-1}$ $= 0.1\ m^2\ g^{-1}$), and M is the molecular weight ($g \cdot mol^{-1}$) of the pigment.

The weight of pigment in a pure sample (such is would be obtained following separation by thin-layer chromatograDhy) can be calculated from the specific absorption coefficient as follows:

$$W/V = D/(A^*1) \qquad (4.2)$$

where W is the weight of pigment (in grams), V is the volume of solution (in cubic meters), D is the absorbance

Table 6.1: Specific absorption coefficients, molecular weights and absorption maxima of chlorophylls, chlorophylla degradation products and selected carotenoids.

Pigment	*Solvent*	*max* (*nm*)	*A*(max)* ($m^2 \cdot g^{-1}$)	*Molecular Weight* ($g \cdot mol^{-1}$)
Chlorophyll	Diethyl ether	423	12.8	893
Diethyl ether	662	9.85		
Acetone	666	8.90		
90% Acetone	664	8.77		
80% Acetone	664	7.68		
Methanol	664	7.14		
Chlorophyllide	90% Acetone	664	12.7	615
Pheophytin a	90% Acetone	667	5.12	869
Pheophorbide	90% Acetone	667	7.42	591
Chlorophyll	Diethyl ether	453	17.5	907
Diethyl ether	643	6.1		
90% Acetone	647	5.14		
80% Acetone	647	4.70		
Methanol	652	3.86		
Chlorophyll	Acetone/pyridine	447	34.9e	611
Acetone/pyridine	630	3.93		
Acetone	629	3.92		
90% Acetone	630	4.26		
Chlorophyll	Acetone/pyridine	447	32.2	609
Acetone/pyridine	630	3.73		
Acetone	631	3.72		
90% Acetone	631	4.26		
β-carotene	Petroleum ether	453	25.92	537
γ-carotene	Petroleum ether	462	31.00	537
Diadinoxanthin	Acetone	453	23.0	659

(Table 4.1 Contd.)

Pigment	Solvent	max (nm)	A*(max) ($m^2 \cdot g^{-1}$)	Molecular Weight ($g \cdot mol^{-1}$)
Fucoxanthin	Acetone	449	16.0	659
Lutein	Acetone	445	25.0	569
Peridinin	Acetone	466	13.4	630
Violaxanthin	Acetone	442	24.0	601
Zeaxanthin	Acetone	452	23.4	569

measured in a spectrophotometer cell with pathlength 1(in meters), and A^* is the specific-absorption coefficient.

By substituting the specific-absorption coefficient for the red absorption maximum of chlorophyll a into Eq. 4.2, one can calculate the concentration of chlorophyll a in extracts from rhodophytes and cyanobacteria, which lack accessory chlorophylls *b* and *c*.

However, Eq. 4.2 cannot be used where absorption bands of several pigments overlap. Series of equations have been developed to allow estimation of chlorophylls a and *b* or chlorophylls a and c in unialgal samples, as well as for the simultaneous estimation of all three chlorophylls in mixed assemblages.

The trichromatic equations of Jeffrey and Humphrey are based on reliable estimates of specific absorption coefficients and yield satisfactory results when applied to mixed algal assemblages.

Determination of chlorophyll concentrations by spectrophotometry in samples that contain degradation products is problematic. Chlorophyl-lides have nearly identical absorption spectra to undegraded chlorophylls and thus can only be separated by chromatography.

Pheophytins and pheophorbides show reduced absorption when compared to chlorophylls: this is associated with the loss of magnesium from the center of porphyrin ring of chlorophyll. A crude estimation of chlorophyll a and pheop-

Table 6.2: Spectrophotometric equations for estimating chlorophyll concentrations.

Jeffrey and Humphrey's (1975) equations for 90% acetone extracts.

Chlorophylls *a* and *b*

$$\text{Chl}a = 11.93\ D_{664} - 1.93\ D_{647}$$

$$\text{Chl}b = -5.50\ D_{664} + 20.36\ D_{647}$$

Chlorophylls *a* and *c*

$$\text{Chla} = 11.47\ D_{664} - 0.4\ D_{630}$$

$$\text{Chic} = -3.73 D_{664} + 24.36\ D_{630}$$

Chlorophylls *a*, *b* and *c*

$$\text{Chla} = 11.85\ D_{664} - 1.54\ D_{64} - 0.08\ D_{630}$$

$$\text{Chlb} = -5.43\ D_{664} + 21.03\ D_{64} - 2.66 D_{630}$$

$$\text{Chic} = -1.67\ D_{664} - 7.60\ D_{64} + 24.52 D_{630}$$

Lorenzen's (1967) equations for 90% acetone extracts.

Chlorophyll *a* and pheophytin *a*

$$\text{Chla} = 26.7\ [D_{665}(o) - D_{665}(a)]$$

$$\text{Pheoa} = 26.7\ [1.7 D_{665}(a) - D_{665}(o)]$$

where $D_{665(o)}$ is the absorbance of a 90% acetone extract and $D_{665(a)}$ is the absorbance of the 90% acetone extract following acidification to pH 2.7.

Jeffrey and Haxo's (1968) equations for 100% methanol extracts.

Chlorophylls *a* and *c*

$$\text{Chla} = 13.8\ D_{668} - 1.3\ D_{635}$$

$$\text{Chic} = -14.1\ D_{668} - {}^{67.3}\ D_{635}$$

Porra et al. (1989) equations for 100% methanol extracts.

Chlorophylls *a* and *b*

$$\text{Chla} = 16.29\ D_{665} - {}^{8.54}\ D_{652}$$

$$\text{Chlb} = -13.58\ D_{665} + 30.66\ D_{652}$$

horbide a concentrations is possible by measuring the absorption at 665 nm before and after acidification of a 90% acetone extract.

The method does not allow discrimination of chlorophyll *a* from chlorophyllide *a,* nor pheophytin *a* from pheophorbide a. In addition, there is no spectrophotometric technique for simultaneously estimating chlorophylls a, *b,* and c and their degradation products.

Samples for spectrophotometric pigment determination can be readily obtained from macroalgal thalli, which have chlorophyll a concentrations of > 100 mg•m^{-2}.

However, relatively large volumes of natural phytoplankton assemb-lages, in which chlorophyll a concentrations can be < 0.1 µg-dm^{-3}, may need to be concentrated to obtain enough material for spectrophotometric analysis.

A major improvement in routine estimation of chlorophyll concentration in open ocean waters was provided by the introduction of a fluorometric technique that allows up to a 100-fold increased sensitivity over spectrophotometric methods.

A comparison of spectrophotometric and fluorometric determinations of chlorophyll a from ocean waters indicated agreement between the two techniques to within ± 20%.

Measurement of fluorescence before and after acidification of a sample enables the determination of chlorophyll *a* and pheophorbide *a*, but, unfortunately, as routinely employed, the fluorescence technique does not allow the determination of chlorophylls *b* and *c*.

Unlike the spectrophotometric methods, which give an absolute measure of concentration based on the specific absorption coefficients of the pigments under investigation, the fluorescence methods give a relative measure of pigment concentration and must be calibrated with solutions of known composition.

Fluorescence techniques were originally calibrated against acetone extracts of log-phase algal cultures in which chlorophyll a concentration was determined by a spectrophotometric procedure. However, the relationship between chlorophyll a and fluorescence depends on the accessory pigments that are present, and thus the calibration can vary with the algae used to obtain the pigment extract.

To overcome this problem, many investigators prefer calibration against purified chlorophyll a, which provides an objective standard, even though this may lead to a bias in the estimation of chlorophyll a concentration.

Holm-Hansen et al. (1965) recognized that errors in estimating chlorophyll a by the fluorometric technique could result from interference by other pigments that also fluoresce red when excited by blue light. Using data of Lorenzen and Jeffrey (1980), Trees et al. (1985) were able to provide an equation for predicting the effects of other pigments on the concentration of chlorophyll *a* determined by fluorometry.

The equation relating the chlorophyll *a* concentration obtained by the fluorometric technique of Holm-Hansen et al. (1965) to the pigments present is:

$$C_m = 0.974\,(\text{chlorophyll } a) - 0.282\,(\text{chlorophyll } b) + 0.380\,(\text{chlorophyll } c) + 0.0793\,(\text{pheophorbide } a) + 1.392\,(\text{chlorophyllide } a) \quad (5.3)$$

where C_m, is the measured chlorophyll a concentration and the parentheses are used to indicate the true concentrations of the indicated pigments. Thus, the presence of significant chlorophyll *b* in a sample will lead to underestimates of the chlorophyll a concentration, whereas the presence of significant amounts of chlorophyll c or the degradation products chlorophyllide *a* or pheophorbide *a* will lead to overestimates of the chlorophyll a concentration.

Chromatographic Separation of Pigments

To completely characterize the pigment composition of a sample, it is necessary to chromatographically separate

Table 6.3: Spectral characterization of various phycobiliproteins.

Absorption Phycobiliprotein	*Emission* λ_{max}	*Fluorescence Molecular* λ_{max}	*Weight* (*g-mol*$^{-1}$)
C-phycocyanin	620	650	120,000
R-phycocyanin	553, 615	640	130,000
Cryptomonad phycocyanins			
phycocyanin-615	585, 615	—	—
-630	585, 630	—	—
-645	585, 620, 645	—	—
phycoerythrocyanin	568, 590	610	103,000
allophycocyanin B	618, 673	680	98,000
allophycocyanin I	654	680	145,000
allophycocyanin II	650	680	105,000
allophycocyanin 111	650	680	105,000
R-phycoerythrin	498, 542, 565	578	260,000
B-phycoerythrin	498, 545, 563	575	260,000
b-phycoerythrin	545, 563	575	—
C-phycoerythrin	565	578	—
C-phycoerythrin I	555	578	—
C-phycoerythrin II	540, 568	578	—
Cryptomonad phycoerythrins			
Phycoerythrin-544	544, 565	—	—
-555	555	—	—
-568	508	—	—
C-phycoerythrins			
Synechococcus WH7803	500, 545	560	—
Synechococcus WH8018	551	570	—
Trichodesmium	498, 557	—	—
Gloeobacter violacea	501, 564	574, 577	—

Table 6.4: Specific absorption coefficients (a*, with units of $m^2 \bullet g^{-1}$ pigment) of some phycobiliproteins in phosphate buffer.

Biliprotein	λ_{max}	*Molecular Weight*	*a**
C-phycocyanin	618	—	0.724
C-phycocyanin	615	224,000	0.770
C-phycocyanin	620	—	0.650
R-phycocyanin	615	273,000	0.660
allophycocyanin	650	—	0.603
allophycocyanin	650	90,000	0.650
B-phycoerythrin	565	290,000	0.820
B-phycoerythrin	545	—	0.878
C-phycoerythrin	565	226,000	1.250
C-phycoerythrin	550	—	1.250
R-phycoerythrin	565	298,000	0.810
R-phycoerythrin	565	—	0.802
phycoerythrin	545	—	1.260
phycoerythrin	548	—	1.050
phycoerythrin	551	—	0.800
phycoerythrin (M)	492	264,000	1.05
	543	—	0.432

pigments prior to identification and quantification. Quantitative thin-layer chromatography was first used on algal pigments by Jeffrey (1968) and was subsequently improved.

More recently, reverse-phase highperformance liquid chromatography (HPLC) techniques have been developed for routinely separating chlorophylls, chlorophyll degradation products, and carotenoids. Mantoura and Lewellyri s (1983) method required a 20min run to separate pigments using a two-mobile-phase solvent system on a 250 × 5 mm C-18 column (5-µm particle size).

Increasing column diameter and solvent flow rate Trees

et al. (1986) achieved separation of chlorophylls and their degradation products in a 10-min run. Recently, de los Rivas et al. (1989) describe a new three-phase solvent system and a 10 x 8 mm radial compression column, which allows separation of terrestrial vascular plant pigments within a 10-min run.

Widespread application of HPLC and thin-layer chromatography in recent years has led to the identification of previously unknown pigments and to the recognition of the importance of these pigments in various algal groups. A consideration of this research is beyond the scope of this review, and further discussion will be limited to a comparison of HPLC and other methods for measuring chlorophyll *a*.

In general, HPLC and other techniques lead to comparable estimates of chlorophyll concentration, although individual estimates may be greatly at variance. For example, Murray et al. (1986) compared two HPLC techniques, a fluorometric method and a spectrophotometric method for estimating chlorophyll a in 29 plankton samples with chlorophyll a concentrations ranging from 0.02 to 30 $\mu g\text{-}dm^{-3}$.

The chlorophyll a peak accounted for only 57% of the spectrophotometer response and 72% of the fluorescence response. However, including chlorophyll allomers in the comparison led to a one-to-one correspondence of spectrophotometric and HPLC methods.

In sediments with chlorophyll a and pheopigment concentrations of 1-30 $\mu g\text{-}g^{-1}$ dry weight, Riaux-Gobin et al. (1987) found that the fluorescence measurements underestimated chlorophyll a and pheopigments by 30% to 40% relative to the HPLC measurements.

Trees et al. (1985) found that fluorometric determinations of chlorophyll a were in error by from -68% to +53% when compared with values obtained from a HPLC method. They found that errors in the fluorometric determination varied between stations within a given oceanographic region, and between regions.

When data from various oceanographic regions were combined, chlorophyll a determined from HPLC and fluorometric techniques were highly correlated with a correlation coefficient of 0.961. Despite the high correlation obtained when measurements over a large range of chlorophyll a concentrations (< 10-40,000 ng•dm^{-3}) were compared, individual estimates of chlorophyll a by the fluorometric technique were as much as three times lower or 1.5 times greater than the true value.

The increased discrimination available from HPLC analysis of phytoplankton pigments has also proven useful in ecological investigations. Aside from providing qualitative information on the major taxa present, a quantitative estimate of the relative contribution of phytoplankton with different accessory pigments to total chlorophyll a can be obtained from the application of a multiple regression analysis to quantitative pigment determinations.

Changes in the concentrations of accessory pigments can also be used to characterize the growth and loss rates of different phytoplankton taxa in grazing experiments.

EXTRACTION AND QUANTIFICATION OF PHYCOBILIPROTEINS

Phycobiliproteins are water-soluble light-harvesting pigment proteins found in the rhodophytes, cryptomonads, and cyanobacteria. The major classes of phycobiliproteins are phycocyanin (PC), phycoerythrin (PE), allophycocyanin (APC), and phycoerythrocyanin (PEC) (Gantt, 1981). Within each of these classes are phycobiliproteins with several related spectral forms.

The phycobiliproteins consist of open-chain tetrapyrrole chromophores (referred to as bilins or phycobilins) covalently bound to proteins. The main chromophore types are (1) phycocyanobilin, found in PC and APC, (2) phycoerythrobilin found in PE, and (3) phycourobilin found in some PEs.

There is no routine method generally used for determining phycobiliprotein concentrations. However, as in the case of lipophilic pigments, most methods employ extraction of pigment molecules, followed by spectrophotometric or fluorometric determination of chromophore concentration.

Extraction of phycobiliproteins can be achieved by mechanical and/or enzymatic cell disruption, which releases phycobiliproteins into aqueous solution. Laboratory cultures of microalgae and cyanobacteria are commonly disrupted by repeated cycles of freeze-thaw treatment and passage through a French press, or by prolonged sonication.

Phytoplankton can be concentrated onto membrane filters and disrupted by mechanical shearing and lysozyme treatment, although recoveries may not be complete in recalcitrant organisms. Particularly troublesome in this regard are the small coccoid cyanobacteria, which are resistant to mechanical disruption.

Wyman (unpublished) sought to overcome this problem when measuring phycoerythrin in marine *Synechococcus spp.* by measuring in vivo fluorescence of samples resuspended in 50% glycerol.

Glycerol effectively uncouples phycoerythrin from photosynthetic energy transduction enhancing fluorescence by up to 15-fold relative to untreated cells. A constant maximum fluorescence yield under these circumstances allows calibration against extracted phycoerythrin.

The technique is simple, rapid and has been used for routine measurements at sea. Variations in the magnitude of the package effect may preclude a simple quantitative relationship between glycerol enha-nced fluorescence and phycoerythrin in large cyanobacteria, but this effect should be insignificant for the *Synechococcus spp.* examined by Wyman. Although different phycobiliproteins can be identified by characteristic absorbance and/or fluorescence emission spectra, the diversity of these pigments complicates quantification. An indication of the range of specific absorption coefficients that have been obtained is given in Table elsewhere in this chapter.

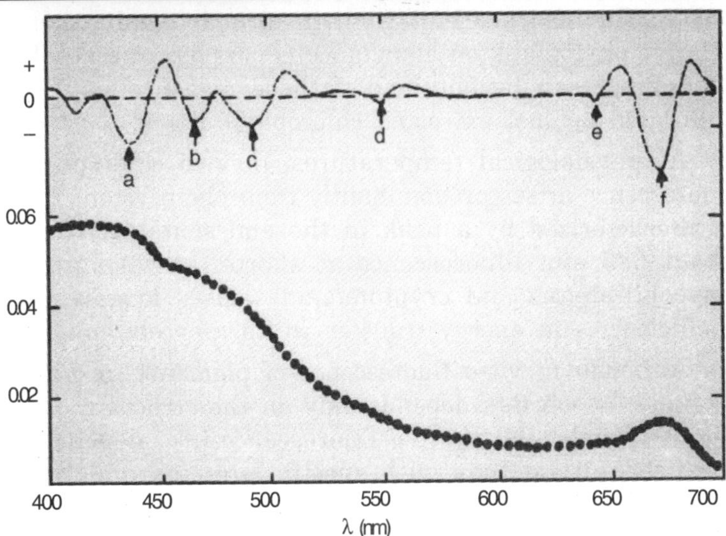

Figure 6.1: Spectral variations in the absorption coefficient of a natural phytoplankton assemblage and their second derivative spectra. The letters a-f denote the derivative positions of the major pigments, chlorophyll a (a) , chlorophyll c (b), phycobiliproteins (c,d), chlorophyll b (e) and the red absorbing form of chlorophyll a (f), which are not clearly identifiable in the original in vivo absorption spectra.

Bennett and Bogorad (1973) and Kursar and Alberte (1983) developed trichromatic equations that account for spectral overlap for estimating phycocyanin, allophycocyanin, and phycoerythrin concentrations from absorption measurements in aqueous extracts.

These equations are specific to the organisms under investigation, and, for maximum accuracy, individual equations need to be derived for each particular application.

In Vivo Fluorescence for Estimating Chlorophyll *a*

Measuring the red fluorescence of chlorophyll a when algae are illuminated with blue light has become a standard method of determining microalgal abundance in natural samples and unialgal cultures.

Although subject to some uncertainty because of variations in fluorescence emission, in situ determination of relative phytoplankton abundance is possible, and absolute abundance can be obtained if these measurements are calibrated against extracted chlorophyll *a*.

At physiological temperatures, in vivo chlorophyll a fluorescence arises predominantly from photosystem 2 and is characterized by a peak in the emission spectrum at about 685 nm. Fluorescence at shorter wavelengths in phycobiliphytes and cryptomonads arises largely from inefficiencies in energy transfer within phycobiliproteins.

Although in vitro fluorescence of pigments in organic or aqueous solvents depends only on the structure of the pigment molecule, in vivo fluorescence also depends on localized interactions with specific proteins and lipids, together with cell structural and metabolic variations.

As a consequence, the ratio of in vivo fluorescence to extracted chlorophyll a can vary by approximately an order of magnitude. The relationship between fluorescence emission and chlorophyll a concentration can be considered as the product of the *in vivo* chlorophyll a-specific absorption coefficient (a*), the photon yield of fluorescence (ϕ_f) and the incident irradiance (E),

$$F_{chl} = a^*\phi_f E/2.303 = a^*\phi_f E \qquad (4.4)$$

where F_{chl} is the chlorophyll-a-specific fluorescence emission. The absorption coefficient, a*, is influenced by factors that affect light absorption, whereas ϕ_f may be affected by a range of physiological variables.

The chlorophyll a-specific fluorescence emission has been shown to have a size dependence in microalgal cultures and natural phytoplankton assemblages. Specifically, F_{chl} is found to vary approximately by a factor of five between picoplankton (2 µm diam) and net plankton (> 20 µm diam), consistent with expectations based on the relationship between a* and cell size that are predicted by the package effect.

In addition to a dependence on cell size, F_{chl} varies by a factor of two to four due to physiological responses to irradiance and nutrient availability. Chloroplast aggregation in response to high irradiances resulted in decreases of both absorption (λ 440 nm) and fluorescence in the large diatom *Lauderia borealis*.

Changes in ϕ_f may also influence F_{chl}. For example, F_{chl} tends to be higher in stationary-phase cultures than in exponential cultures, and is related to a reduction in the photon yield of photosynthesis under nutrient-starved conditions.

Up to an order of magnitude diel variation in F_{chl} in which F_{chl} is highest at night and lowest during the day, may also reflect changes in ϕ_f. Significantly, the diel variation in F_{chl} is opposite to that observed for photosynthesis rates, suggesting complimentary variations in the photon yield of fluorescence and photosynthesis.

FLUORESCENCE MICROSCOPY

Epifluorescence microscopy has only recently become a standard tool for examining microalgal samples despite the introduction of fluorescence techniques to phycological research over 30 years ago. In early applications, Wood (1955) employed transmitted light fluorescence microscopy in plankton studies, and Jones (1974) used epifluorescence microscopy to identify living algae on the surfaces of stones.

Epifluorescence microscopy has many advantages over transmitted-light, phase-contrast, or interference-contrast microscopy for examining plankton samples. Small organisms can be identified as algae by their red fluorescence, whereas cyanobacteria, cryptomonads, and rhodophytes can be characterized by distinctive orange or yellow fluorescence, enabling the separate enumeration of photosynthetic from heterotrophic forms.

Use of this technique indicates that between 10 and 90% of oceanic nanoplankton (approximately 2-20 µm diam) are photosynthetic, with autotrophs typically accounting for 50% of total counts. In another application of fluorescence microscopy, Lessard and Swift (1986) found that approximately 40% of oceanic dinoflagellate taxa lack chlorophyll *a,* indicating a large phagotrophic component in a group traditionally regarded as autotrophic.

Quantitative determinations of the chlorophyll or phycobiliprotein content of single cells may be possible when a fluorescence microscope is used as a microspectro fluorometer. However, variations in the photon yield of fluorescence that hamper the in vivo determinations of chlorophyll concentration of cell suspensions will also influence measurements made with single cells.

USE OF DERIVATIVE SPECTRA IN PIGMENT ANALYSIS

Faust and Norris describe an in vivo spectrophotometric technique for determining chlorophylls *a, b,* and c on intact phytoplankton. The technique rests on the observation that taking the second derivative of the absorption spectrum leads to considerably greater detail than is evident in the original data.

The second derivative yields the rate of change of the slope of the absorption spectrum and so accentuates differences in curvature associated with in vivo absorption peaks. In its original application to microalgae, regression analysis was used to find the optimum wavelengths for determining chlorophylls *a, b,* and c from second derivative absorption spectra of samples concentrated on glass-fiber filters.

The method was calibrated with a mixture of microalgae from major taxonomic groups: that is, the cyanobacterium *Anabaena flos-aquae,* the green *Chlorella sp.,* the cryptomonad *Cryptomonas ovata,* and the dinoflagellate *Prorocentrum mariae-lebouriae.*

As employed by Faust and Norris (1982), the technique is strictly correlative, requiring calibration of the in vivo spectra against chlorophyll a, b, and c concentrations determined in solvent extracts of the same samples.

Optimum wavelengths for determining these chlorophylls from second derivative spectra differed from the wavelengths of peak absorption in vivo, presumably because of overlap of absorption bands of chlorophylls and other pigments and absorption flattening, which causes nonlinearities at wavelengths of maximum absorption.

Bidigare et al. (1989) used second and fourth derivative analysis to locate in vivo absorption peaks of pigments in open ocean phytoplankton. Peaks for chlorophylls a, b, and c, as well as for phycoerythrobilin and phycourobilin were apparent in these spectra, despite the lack of features in the original in vivo absorption spectra, which were dominated by the contribution of detrital material.

In contrast to the empirical approach of Faust and Norris (1982; 1985) described above, Bidigare et al. (1989) chose to examine the relations between the most prominent peaks in the derivative spectra (which corresponded to known in vivo absorption maxima) and the concentrations of these pigments.

PHOTOSYNTHETIC WATER OXIDATION

Photosynthetic water cleavage into dioxygen and metabolically bound hydrogen is of central relevance for the bioenergetics of the exploitation of solar radiation as the unique energy source of the biosphere.

The key step of the overall process is water oxidation which takes place in system II via a four-step univalent redox reaction sequence.

The kinetic pattern of photosynt-hetic water oxidation has been resolved. It can be summarised by the scheme depicted in Figure elsewhere in this chapter.

Basically, three types of events can be distinguished:

1. generation of sufficiently oxidising redox equivalents (holes) by photooxidation of a special chlorophyll-a referred to as P680,
2. transfer of the holes via at least one redox group Z acting as oneelectron component, and
3. stepwise univalent electron abstraction from the manganese-containing catalytic site of water oxidation leading to oxygen evolution after the accumulation of four holes.

The functional groups participating in these reactions are incorp-orated into a protein complex containing at least seven polypeptides.

The exact location has not yet been clarified. In this

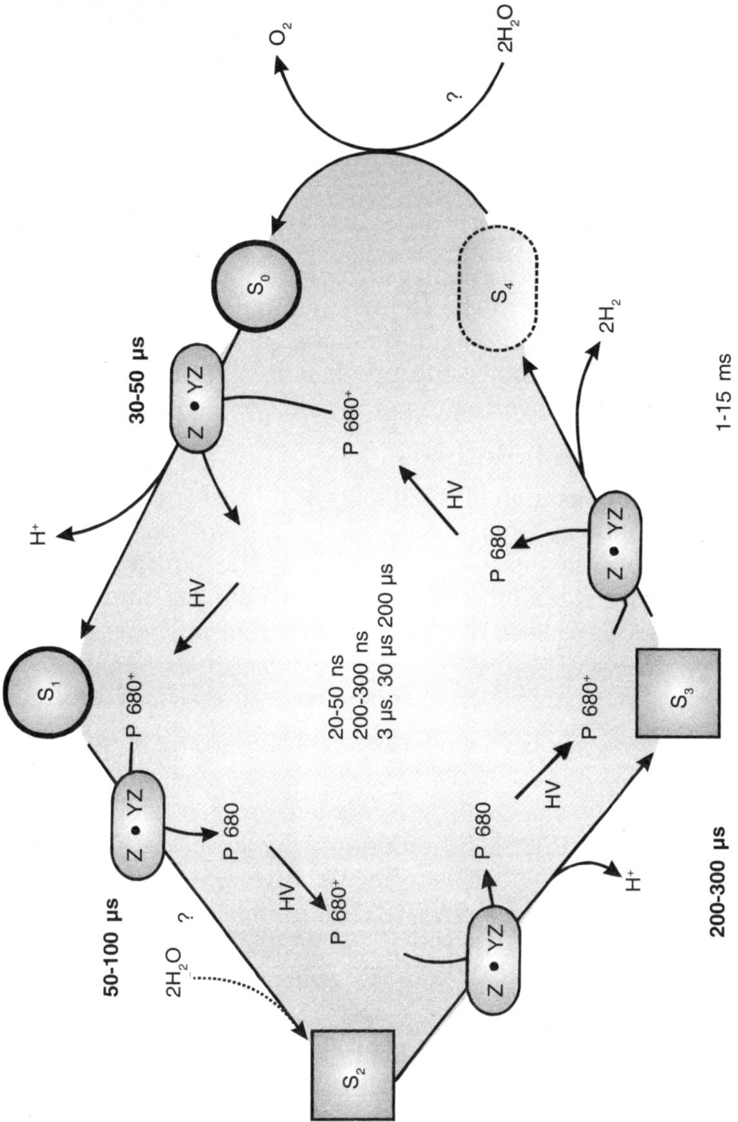

Figure 7.1: Functional scheme of photosynthetic water oxidation to dioxygen. Oxidised redox equivalents are produced by the P680° photoreaction within few picoseconds, typical half transfer times via intermediate redox component Z (predominantly in the ns time domain) to the catalytic site (SO JAB—1.5 me) are denoted inside and at the corners, respectively, of the scheme.

communication, new results are presented about:

(*i*) the functional coupling between the catalytic site of water oxidation and $P680^+$,

(*ii*) the activation parameters of the reactions leading to sequential oxidation of the catalytic site, (ill) the possible role of hydrogen bonds for the functional integrity of the system 11 complex, and

(*iv*) the kinetics and stoichiometry of proton release coupled with the stepwise -oxidation of the catalytic site of water oxidation. Based on these data and taking into account previous results the mechanism of photosynthetic water oxidation is discussed.

Materials and Methods

The preparation of thylakoids and PS II fragments from cyanob-acteria (*Synechococcus vulcanus* Copeland) and higher plants (spinach) as well as the equipments for measuring flashinduced absorption changes and oxygen evolution have been described in detail in previous reports.

RESULTS AND DISCUSSION

(A) *The reduction kinetics of $P680^+$ as an indicator of the functional coupling between the catalytic site and the reaction centre*

In samples with fully competent oxygen evolution the reduction of P680+ is dominated by kinetics in the ns-domain. Based on measurements with the most powerful ADRY-agent, 2-(3-chloro-4-trifluoromethyl) anilino-3, 5-dinitrothiophene (ANT2p), the $P680^+$ reduction kinetics were shown to depend. on the redox state of the catalytic site of water oxidation.

More refined measurements at markedly higher time - resolution confirmed this basic conclusion. The dependence of the ns-kinetics on the redox state S_1 was interpreted by -electrostatic effects on. the redox equilibrium between two components which are assumed to act as primary and secondary donor of $P680^+$.

Alternatively, the data could be also .explained by struc-

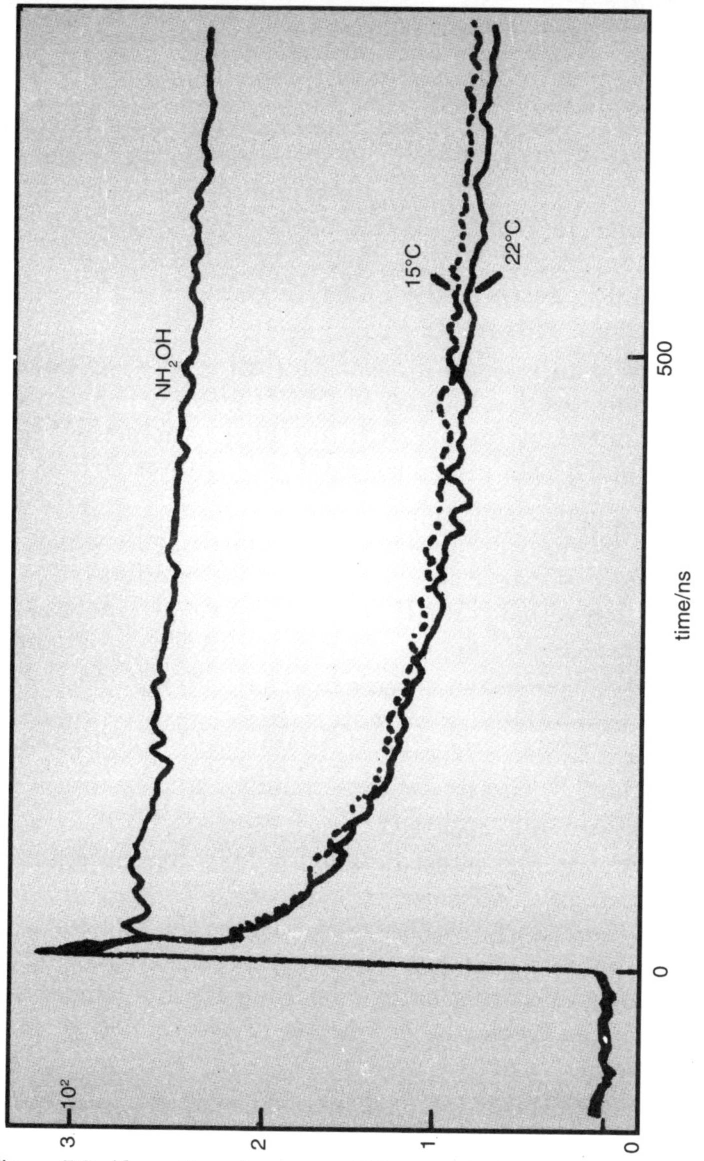

Figure 7.2: Absorption changes at 830 nm as a function of time in O_2, evolving PS II membrane fragments from spinach under repetitive flash excitation (1 Hz) at -1.5°C (dotted trace) and +22°C (full trace). For comparison there is depicted the trace obtained in the presence of 3mM NH_2OH.

tural changes of the states S_2 and S_3 that modify the electronic and nuclear coupling between P680$^+$ and its donor component referred to as Z in the literature.

In order to analyse this coupling more thoroughly, the temperature dependence of P680$^+$ reduction was measured by monitoring laser-flash-induced absorption changes at 830 nm in PS II membrane fragments from spinach. Figure elsewhere in this chapter shows traces obtained at +20°C and –1.5°C, respectively, under repetitive flash excitation on samples with intact oxygen evolution.

The results reveal almost identical relaxation kinetics. This indicates that the overall P680$^+$ reduction is practically independent of temperature in the physiological range under steady state population of redox states S_i (i=0,...3).

For comparison Figure elsewhere in this chapter also shows 830 nm absorption changes in samples which are deprived of their oxygen evolution capacity due to incubation with 3 mM NH_2OH. In this case μs-kinetics arise at the expense of complete disappearance of the ns-kinetics.

This phenomenon is indicative for a strong effect of the functional integrity of water oxidation on the P680$^+$ reduction kinetics. Therefore, it has been speculated that the extent of the ns-kinetics could be a measure of the oxygen evolution -capacity.

However, the latest detailed studies on the effects of *trifluoperazine*, *diisothiocyanostilbene-2. 2-disalfonic acid* (DIDS) and *lauroylcholinechloride* show this not to be the case. The data of Figure elsewhere in this chapter do not provide detailed information about the affect of temperature on P680$^+$ reduction as a function of the individual redox states S_i.

To check this point, dark adapted samples were illuminated with a laser flash train and the absorption changes caused by each flash were separately monitored. The results obtained are summarised in Figure elsewhere in this chapter.

An inspection of the data shows that there is almost no

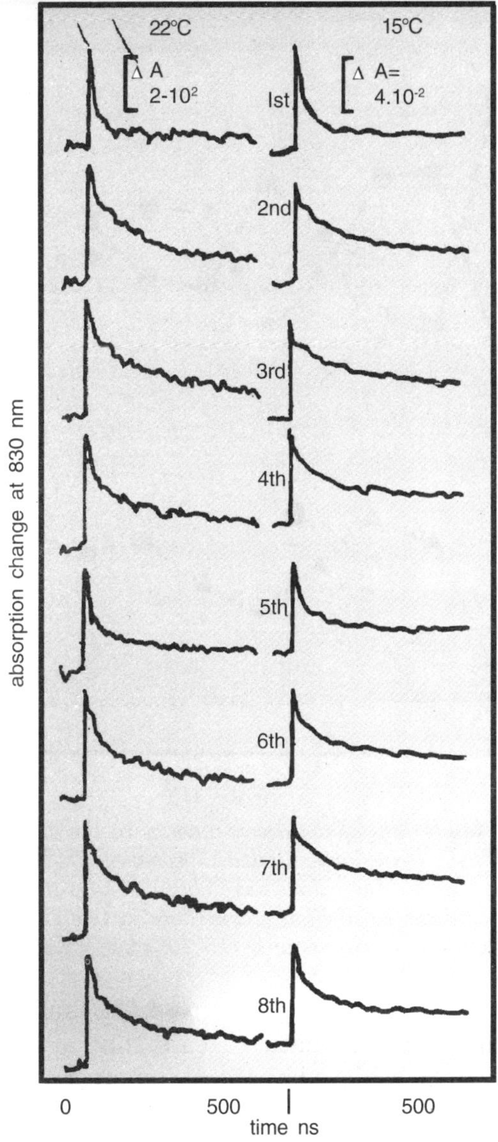

Figure 7.3: Absorption changes at 830 nm as a function of flash N° and time in dark adapted O_2 evolving PS II membrane fragments from spinach at –1.5°C (right side) and +22°C (left side). The measurement at –1.5°C were performed with suspensions of doubled chlorophyll concentrations compared with those used at +22°C.

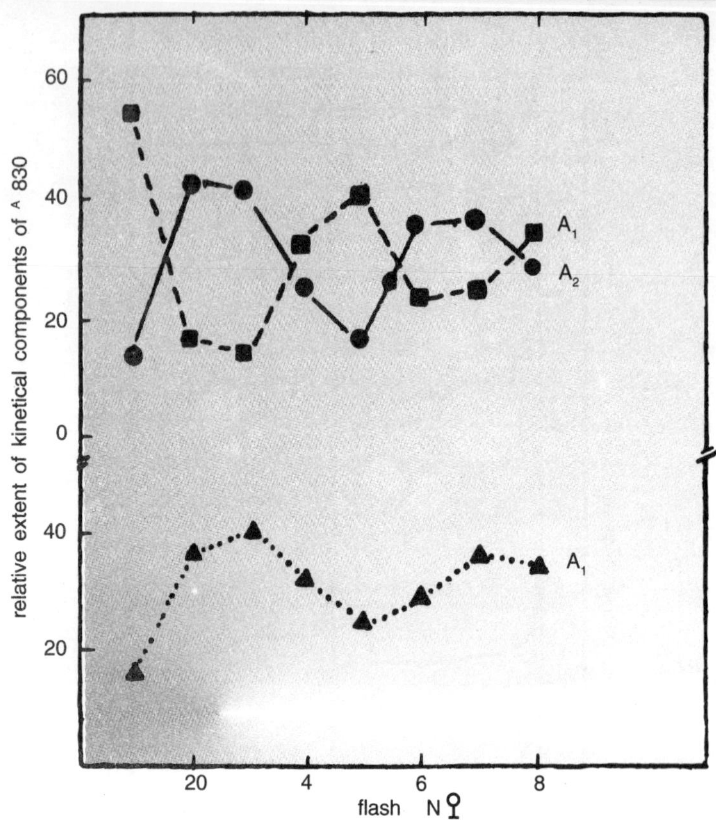

Figure 7.4: Amplitudes of the decay kinetics in the as-range as a function of flash N° in dark-adapted O_2-evolving PS II membrane fragments at –1.5°C. The values were obtained by a triexponential fit of the data depicted in Figure elsewhere in this chapter (right side) with fixed into constants of k_1=1.7.10^7 s^{-1}, k_2 = 3.10^4 s^{-1}, and k_2 < 7.10^5 s^{-1}.

difference between the results at –1.5°C and +20°C. A kinetic analysis of the data reveals that a satisfactory description can be achieved by the assumption of a *triexponential decay* of the form

$$\Delta A_{830}(i)\sum_{\mu=1}^{3} a_\mu (S_i) e^{-k}\mu^{-1} \tag{1}$$

The amplitudes a_μ (S_i) depend on the redox state of the *catalytic* site as is clearly shown in Figure elsewhere in this chapter for the data obtained at –1.5°C. This dependence can be described by:

$a_{\mu}(S_i) = \sum_{i=0}^{3} c_{\mu.i}[S_i]$, where $[S_i]$ is the probability of a catalytic site being in redox state S_i. A reasonable fit can be achieved with the following approximations:

$$c_{1,0} \approx c_{1,1} \text{ and } c_{1,2} \approx c_{1,3}; c_{2,0} \approx c_{2,1} \approx 0 \text{ and } c_{2,2} \approx c_{2,2},$$

$$c_{3,0} \approx c_{3,1} \approx 0 \text{ and } c_{3,2} \approx c_{3,3}$$

These relations are not exactly the same for a_2=(S_i) and $a_2(S_i)$ as reflected by small differences of the corresponding oscillation patterns depicted in Figure elsewhere in this chapter. The origin of this phenomonon will be analyzed in a forthcoming study.

The above mentioned relations tacitly imply that the small contribution, of µs-kinetics to the overall relaxation after the first flash is, caused by a minor fraction of systems II which contain a damaged catalytic site of water oxidation.

The oscillation at -1.5°C closely resembles the pattern at +20°C. The relaxation kinetics at -1.5'C are satisfactorily described by k_1=1.7.10^7 s^{-1}, k_2 = 3.10^4 s^{-1}, and k_2 < 7.10^5 s^{-1}. The same rate constants can be also used for the fit of the data obtained at +20°C, but in this case two different k_1-values of 5.10^7 s^{-1} (relaxation after the first and 5th flash) and of 1.7.10^7 s^{-1} have to be used.

Except for this specific effect which will be analysed else where, the present study shows that neither the kinetics nor the influence of the redox states of the catalytic site exhibit a significant temperature dependence.

The former phenomenon can be explained by a comparatively small activation energy of the electron transfer from Z to $P680^+$. Then oscillation pattern of the P680+ reduction kinetics could be interpreted either by the assumption that the structure of the catalytic site in S_0 and S_1 differs from that in S_2 and S_3, giving rise to markedly different coupling between $P680^+$ and Z, or that redox equilibria between electron transfer components responsible for the S, state dependence of $P680^+$ reduction are only slightly enhanced in the range of –1.5°C and +20°C.

Direct experimental evidence is lacking for these types of equilibria. On the other hand, structural differences of S_2 and S_3 versus S_0 and S_1, respectively, are very likely as reflected. by different Cl^- binding properties. Likewise, water substrate entry into the redox cycle is also discussed to occur at the level of S_2.

Therefore, regulation of $P680^+$ reduction via: structural changes caused by the redox transition $S_1 \rightarrow S_2$ seems to be more attractive than a simple electrostatic point-charge effect.

As a consequence of this idea, the temperature dependence of the oscillation pattern depicted in Figure elsewhere in this chapter indicates that the presumed conformational states regulating $P680^+$ reduction are practically the same at –1.5°C and –1-20°C.

(B) *Temperature dependence of the univalent redox steps at the catalytic site of water oxidation*

The kinetics of the univalent oxidation steps $S_i \rightarrow S_{i+1}$ cam be monitored by measurements of the rise-time of UV absorption changes. The oxidation rate depending on the redox level of the catalytic site of water oxidation kinetically coincides with the reduction of Z^{ox}. As these comprise protolytic reactions and structural modifications, the reaction coordinate of each individual process, $Z^{ox}\ S_i \rightarrow ZS_{i+1} + m_i H^+ + \delta_3 . O_2$ (where i = 0, ..3, with i + 1 = 0 for i = 3), is anticipated to depend on state S_i.

In order to resolve this problem, experiments were performed with PS II fragments from the *thermophilic cyanobacterium Synecho-coccus vulcanus* Copeland which permit covering a broader temperature region. The results obtained are depicted in Figure elsewhere in this chapter.

The data at the left side presenting 330 nm absorption changes induced by repetitive flash excitation at 0°C and 33°C respectively, indicate that in PS II fragments from thermophilic cyanobacteria also the electron transport from

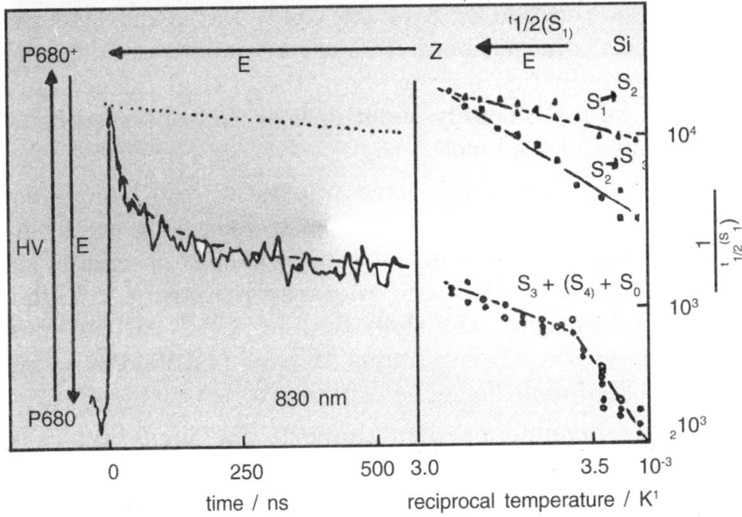

Figure 7.5: Absorption changes at 830 nm (left side) as a function of time and reciprocal half-rise times of S_i oxidation (measured at 350 nm) as a function of reciprocal temperature (right side) in PS II fragments from Synechococcus vulcanus *Copeland. The signal on the left side represents a trace monitored at +33°C, the dashed curve symbolises the data at 0°C. The dotted curve was obtained in the presence of 3 mM N H_2OH. Repetitive excitation (1 Hz) with laser flashes.*

Z to $P680^+$ is almost temperature independent. A markedly different behaviour is observed for the reactions Z^{ox} $S_i \rightarrow ZS_{i+1} + m_i H^+ + \delta_3 . O_2$.

The right side of Figure elsewhere in this chapter shows the reciprocal half-rise times of absorption changes at 350 nm As a function of the reciprocal temperature. As the kinetics of the transition Z^{ox} $S_0 \rightarrow ZS_1 + H^+$ could not be resolved with Sufficient precision, the temperature dependence of this reaction is omitted.

The other three transitions exhibit remarkable differences of the corresponding reaction coordinates. Two 'findings are of special relevance:

(a) the activation energy of to reaction Z^{ox} $S_2 \rightarrow ZS_3 + H^+$ is significantly higher (26.8 kJ/mol) than that of Z^{ox} $S_1 \rightarrow ZS_2$ (9.6 kJ/mol), and

(b) the reaction $Z^{ox} S_3 \rightarrow ZS_0 + O_2 + 2H^+$ is characterized by a break point at about 16°C of its temperature dependence. The activation energy above the critical temperature, T_c (15.5 kJ/mol), is only about 25% of that observed below this point (59.4 kJ/mol).

Bred on these data, some interesting conclusions can be drawn. If one assumes that the transmission coefficient σ of be reaction path is the same for both reactions, the transition state of $S_1 \rightarrow S_2$ requires a markedly higher activation entropy ΔS^* than that of $S_2 \rightarrow S_3$ (in the most simple case of $\sigma = 1$ one obtains $\Delta S^*_{2.1} = -140$ J/mol K versus $\Delta S^*_{2.2} = -80$ J/mol. K).

This phenomenon also supports the idea that S_1 is structrally distinctly different from S_1 although on the basis of EXAFS studies the microenvironment of the catalytic site itself was recently inferred to exhibit almost the same structure in S_1 and S_2.

The latter conclusion is also hardly reconcilable with the assumption that substrate water enters the redox cycle at state S_2 rather than at S_0. Further studies are required to clarify this mechanistically crucial point.

The break point in the temperature dependence of S_3 oxidation leading to dioxygen release probably reflects significant structural changes of S_2 around the critical temperature of 16°C in PS II fragment from thermophilic cyanobacteria. This idea raises questions .about the nature of these changes.

One possible explanation is based on the previous postulation that S_3 already satisfies the energy requirements of dioxygen bond formation at the redox level of a peroxide.

Therefore, the break point could reflect a dramatic shift of the equilibrium between water substrate ligands and the oxidised manganese centre, *i.e.* above T_c the oxidation of S_3 could start at a peroxide-type level with a preformed 0-0 bond, whereas below T_c additional activation energy is required for peroxide formation.

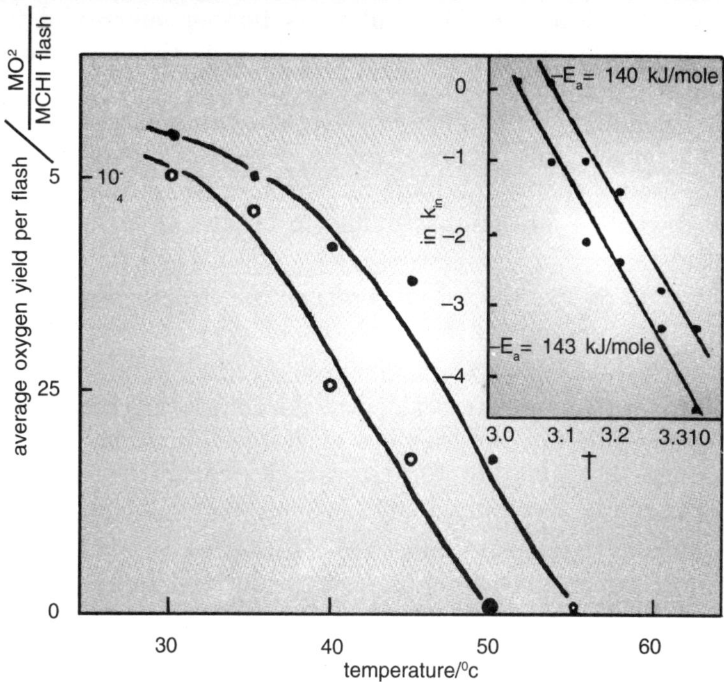

Figure 7.6: Average oxygen yield per flash as a function of the temperature at a 3 min dark incubation.

Alternatively, changes of the protolytic reactions should also be considered. The break point phenomenon at T_c implies a rather sharp and simultaneous change of ΔS^* and ΔH^* in the reaction path of S_2 oxidation.

The origin of this "phase transition type" effect (structural changes of the whole membrane or "all or none" transition in the PS II polypeptide complexes) remains to be" clarified.

The latest thermoluminescence data provide additional (interesting information about the reactivity of S_3 as a functions of temperature. It was shown that in spinach thylakoids at subzero temperatures (between-50°C and –5°C) electron. abstraction from ZS_2 leads to a redox state S* which cannot be further oxidised into S_0 and dioxygen.

If one excludes the trivial possibility of $\boldsymbol{S^*_3}$ being $Z^{ox}S_2$

one could consider this. finding as further support of the idea that 0—0 bond preformation in S_3 is the key step of the reaction n.H_2O + $Z^{ox}S_3$→ ZSo+ O_2 + $2H^+$ (here n = 0 or 2 depending on the stage of water substrate entry into the redox cycle, see figure elsewhere in this chapter. This question of central mechanistic relevance for the mechanism of dioxygen, formation remains to be answered by future studies.

(C) *Effects of hydrogen bonds on the structural integrity of the oxygen evolution capacity*

The oxygen evolution capacity can be selectively eliminate& by a number of protein denaturing conditions. Among different_ interactions of charged and/or polarisable groups responsible for the structural integrity of a polypeptide, hydrogen bonds. are of special interest.

As an attempt to understand this effect in more detail, comparative experiments were performed with spinach thylakoids suspended either in H_2O or D_2O under denaturing conditions. The oxygen evolution capacity of spinach thylakoids was shown to be rather sensitive to a thermal shock.

If this degradation process comprises the break of hydrogen bonds, then suspending of thylakoids in D_2O instead of H_2O is expected to provide some kind of protection. The number of systems II fully competent in oxygen evolution was determined by measurements of the average oxygen yield per flash. Y_{ss}, under repetitive excitation at sufficiently low frequencies (2 Hz) to exclude kinetical limitations.

In order to separate effects of DO on thermal degradation from those of a possible influence on the activity, thylakoids were suspended in either D_2O or HO and subjected to a 3 min incubation of the desired temperature.

After this treatment the samples were injected into a normal aqueous (H_2O) buffer solution and Y_{ss} was measured at 20°C. The data depicted in figure elsewhere in this chapter reveal a significant stabilising effect of D_2O as reflected by the shift of thermal sensitivity by about 5 K

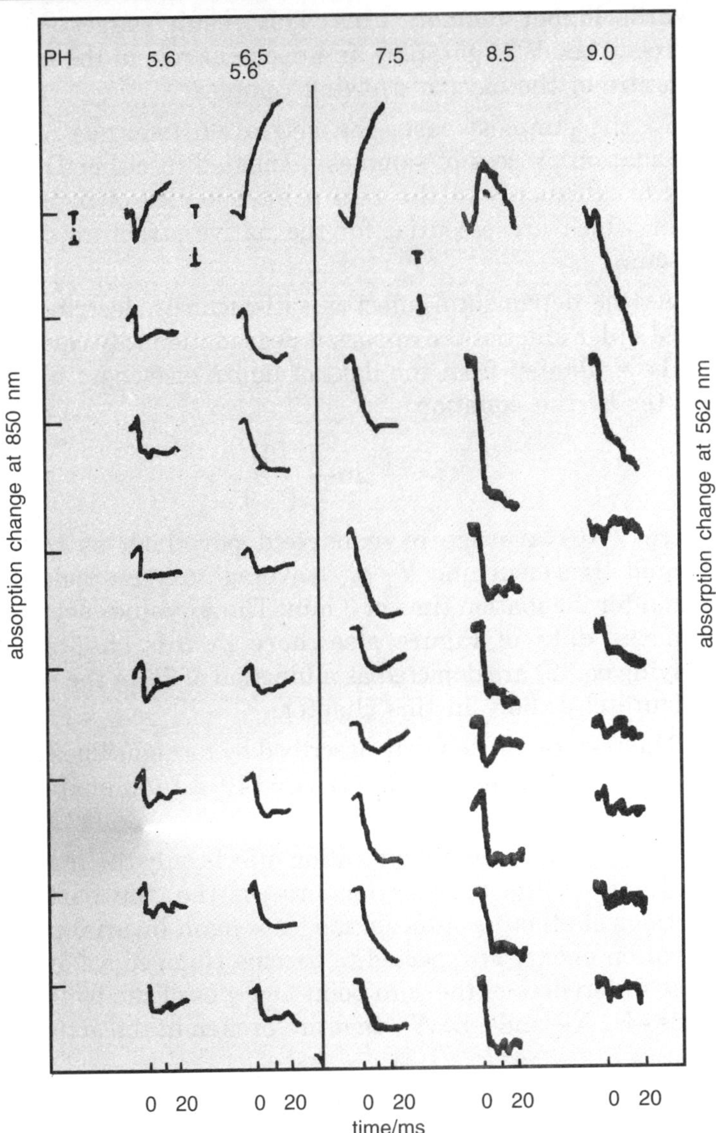

Figure 7.7: Δ pH-indicating absorption changes at 562 and 580 nm as a function of time in O_2 evolving PS II membrane fragments from spinach at room temperature. The traces at the left side were obtained with bromocresol purple, at the right side with phenol red.

towards higher temperatures. This result suggests that hydrogen bonds might: play an important role in the native structure of the oxygen evolving complex.

In the simplest case, the activation energies of the degradation process of samples incubated in either D_2O or or H_2O differ only in the zero point energies of hydrogen bonds which are essential for the native structure of the protein.

As the detrimental effect is satisfactorily described by a first order kinetics the apparent degradation rate constant can be evaluated from the data of figure elsewhere in this chapter by the equation

$$k_{in} = \frac{1}{t_{inc}} .\text{in} \frac{Y_{ss}(0)}{Y_{ss}(t_{inc})} \qquad (2)$$

where $Y_{ss}(0)$=average oxygen yield per flash at t=0 of thermal treatment and $Y_{ss}(t_{inc})$=average oxygen yield per flash after incubation time of 3 min. The k_{in} values obtained from the data of Figure elsewhere in this chapter by applying eq. (2) are depicted as a function of T^{-1} in the insert of figure elsewhere in this chapter.

The results can be fairly described by straight lines with activation energies of E_A (H_2O)=140 kJ/mole and E_A (D_2O)=143 kJ/mole.

If one assumes that deuteration affects only the reaction coordinate of the degradation process (i.e. the partition functions of all other internal modes remain invariant), the activation energy is expected to become changed solely due to the differences of the zero point energies of the hydrogen bonds –H...Y—and—D...Y—that are broken in the activated state.

To calculate the order of magnitude of this effect the number of hydrogen bonds undergoing cleavage and their zero point energies are required. Using 20-25 kJ/mole as data taken from the literature for the average energy of hydrogen bonds in proteins, the experimental activation energy of 140-143 kJ/mole indicates a break of 6-7 hydrogen

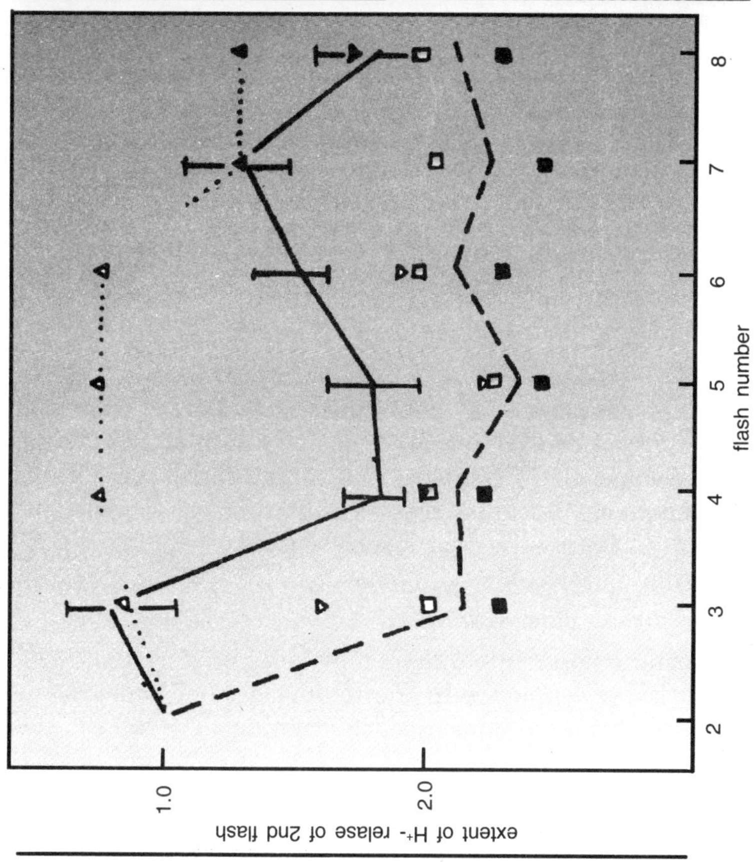

Figure 7.8: Extent of proton release due to the n-th flash normalised to the extent due to the 2nd flash as a function of flash No. (n) in dark-adapted PS II membrane fragments from spinach at different pH.

bonds in the activated state. Likewise, the activation entropy ΔS^* of denaturation is computed to be 190 J/K mole for thylakoids suspended in H_2O or D_2O. These values correspond with data reported for the denaturation of well-characterised isolated enzymes like trypsin or pancreatic proteinase.

The difference of the zero point energy per hydrogen bond is given by $\Delta_{\varepsilon D} = 1/2 h.\upsilon H \, (1—1\sqrt{2})$, where υ_H=frequency of the normal hydrogen bond containing a proton and the difference in the reduced mass is about 2 due to the large mass of the protein compared with that of H and D. respectively.

Typical were numbers of hydrogen bonds are of the order of 200-300 cm^{-1} which gives rise to a difference of the activation energy of (5-10). 10^{-22} J per hydrogen bond. Accordingly, for the cleavage of 6-7 hydrogen bonds, a total difference of the activation energy of ΔE_A = 2—4 kJ/mole iss obtained, in close agreement with the experimental findings.

This supports the idea that some special hydrogen bonds are of crucial relevance for the native structure of the oxygen evolving complex. The localisation of these bonds and a possible functional involvement in protolytic reactions remain to be analysed in future studies.

(D) *Kinetics and stoichiometry of proton release coupled with, water oxidation*

Water oxidation to dioxygen by holes produced at $P680^+$ is inevitably coupled with the total release of four protons into the lumenal space of thylakoids. Therefore, the stoichiometry of H^+ ejection from the catalytic site in each univalent redox step. $S_1 \rightarrow S_{i+1}$, referred to as the *intrinsic* proton release pattern should provide direct information about the deprotonation sequence of substrate water during the redox cycle.

Results. obtained with special pH-sensitive indicators in thylakoids inside-out vesicles and PS II membrane fragments from spinach in the physiological range of 6.0<pH<7.5 can be satisfactorily explained by a stoichiometry of 1.0.1. 2 for the redox transitions $S_1 \rightarrow S_{i+1}$, with 1=0,1,2,3, respectively.

However, it has to be emphasised that, for several reasons, this experimentally detected *extrinsic* stoichiometry cannot be expected to reflect directly the protolytic state of the substrate water coordinated to the catalytic site at redox state S_i. The main source of ambiguity is obviously

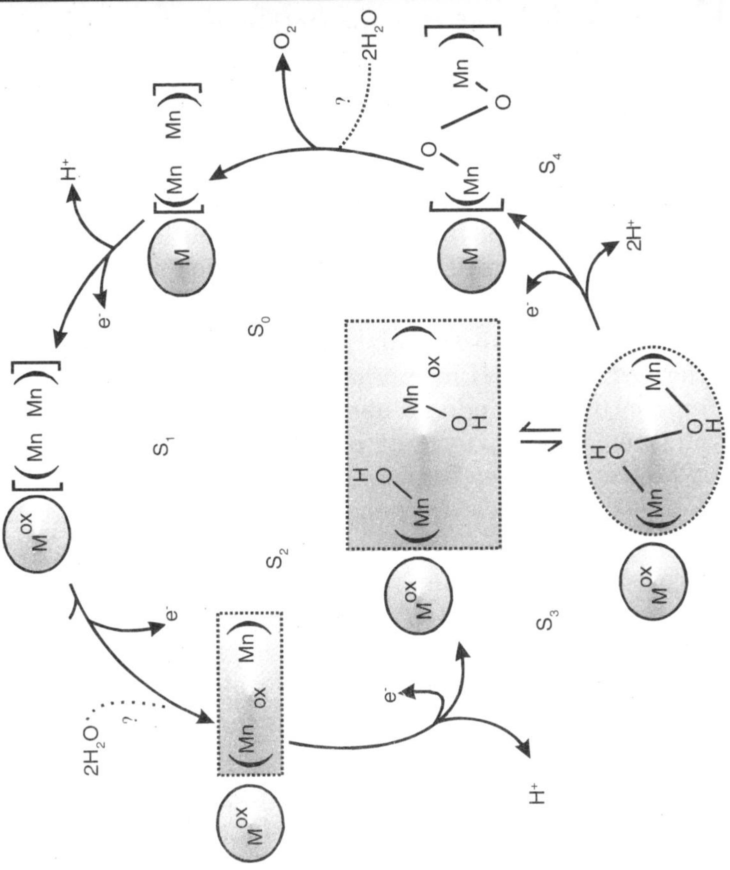

Figure 7.9: Mechanism of photosynthetic water oxidation to dioxygen. Only the manganeses of the binuclear catalytic core are presented, for the nature of M see text. As the stage of water entry into the cycle is not unambiguously clarified substrate ligation is only indicated for S_3 and S_4. The other ligands are symbolised by a half oval around Mn. Oxidised states are represented by grey areas. The possibility of a redox equilibrium between manganese and the water substrate ligands could lead to a peroxidic intermediate in S_3 as indicated in the scheme which tacitly implies that S_3 is oxidisable only in the peroxidic contiguration. For the sake of simplicity, redox equilibria are omitted, which can occur between the binuclear manganese site and redox centres other than the substrate. Likewise, each redox level (except that of S_3) is characterised by only one symbol.

the participation of the apoprotein in the protolytic reactions due to pK-shifts of protonisable groups caused by the turnovers of Z and of the catalytic site itself (Bohr-type effect).

If the apoprotein actually plays a key role for the protolytic reactions coupled with water oxidation, then changes of the stoichiometry and/or kinetics. of proton release are anticipated to occur by variation of the environmental pH.

In order to address this problem, experiments were performed with PS II membrane fragments in the range of $5.5<pH<9.0$. Flash-induced absorption changes of indicator dyes (bromocresol purple at $pH < 7.0$ and phenol red at $pH>7.0$) caused by excitation of dark-adapted samples with a train of µs-flashes are depicted in figure elsewhere in this chapter.

The data obtained reveal a significant dependence of H^* release on Sash No. 0. A Pronounced H^+ uptake after the first Bash is probably due to a single turnover of the high spin Fe^{2+} located between Q_A and Q_S at the PS II acceptor side. This phenomenon will not be discussed here.

The amplitudes of H^+ release exhibit characteristic oscillation patterns that are dependent on the external pH as is shown in figure elsewhere in this chapter. No significant changes (within the limit of experimental error) are observed in the physiological range of $6.0<pH<8.0$, but marked deviations arise outside this region.

The results at alkaline pH are -seriously affected by a decline of the oxygen evolution capacity in PS II membrane fragments and therefore do not permit unequivocal conclusions. The interpretation of the other data within the framework of Kok's model depends significantly on precise knowledge of the probability of misses (a) ands double hits (b) and the apparent dark-state population $\{S_i\}o$.

A detailed analysis however indicates that a 1.0, 1,2 stoichiometry often does not provide the best fit. In many cases, stoichiometries of 0, 0, 2,2 and 0, 0, 1, 3 permit a better description of the data. Regardless of the details, these findings support the idea that the apoprotein seriously affects the extrinsic proton release pattern. This conclusion implies that the intrinsic proton release is still an unresolved problem.

An inspection of the proton release kinetics reveals a multiphasic pattern. Generally, at least a four-exponential kinetics with half-life times of ≤ 100 μs, 200-300 μs, 500-800μs and 1-5 ms is required for a satisfying fit.

We were not able to find an unequivocal correlation between the amplitudes of the different kinetics and individual redox. transitions $S_1 \rightarrow S_{i+1}$, even within the physiological pH range.

The most striking observation is the marked retardation of the proton release with increasing pH in the range of 5.5 up to 7.5. Preliminary studies did not show a clear kinetical correspondence of the rates of H+ release and the $S_1 \rightarrow S_{i+1}$, transitions in the above-mentioned pH range. Experiments. are in progress to analyse this point.

(E) *Mechanism of photosynthetic water oxidation*

The understanding of the molecular mechanism of photosynthetic water oxidation to dioxygen requires detailed knowledge of the electronic structure and the nuclear geometry of the catalytic site in the different redox states S_i for $i = 0...4$.

Different spectroscopic techniques (XANES, EXAFS, UV/VIS, IR, EPR, NMR) were used to resolve this problem but only few pieces of the huge puzzle were found. Despite lack of essential information (e.g. the ligands of the first coordination sphere at the catalytic manganese beyond substrate water, the existence and role of hydrogen bridges between substrate water and the apoprotein, dynamics of the apoenzyme and its effect on the reaction coordinate) an attempt will be made to discuss the mechanism of water oxidation within the framework of our current stage of limited knowledge.

This discussion is. based on two crucial postulates of

our previous model (a) the central step of water oxidation, i.e. the 0—0 bond formation occurs at a binuclear manganese centre at the redox level of a peroxide in S_3 and (b) there exists a special state; or centre symbolised by M that undergoes a redox turnover at the steps $S_o \rightarrow S_1$, and $S_3 \rightarrow (S_4) \rightarrow S_o + O_2$ (protolytic reactions are omitted).

The former part of the first postulate is supported by the remarkable heterogeneity of the four manganeses which are present in each oxygen evolving complex.

Accordingly, twomanganeses are assumed to form the functional core of water oxidation whereas the other two manganeses could act asfurther redox centres (redox buffer or electronic coupling with Z) or as an essential structural element.

The second part of the first postulate appears to be mechanistically attractive because, in case of an intermediary peroxide formation, the electron abstraction from two water molecules takes place via two sequential 2-electron steps rather than by a more complex. single 4-electron step.

This idea has been accepted also for other models but, in contrast to our original postulate, the peroxide level is assumed to occur only as a transient S'_4 state.

However, it has to be emphasised that S_3 already satisfies the energy requirements for the formation of peroxidic state (based on experiments with $H^{18}{}_2O_2$ even S_2 might be considered as a candidate).

Recent mass spectroscopic studies were used as argument against the formation of a peroxidicstate prior to S_4. However, due to the very limited time resolution of this method, the data cannot be used as an unequivocal proof. Furthermore, a nonexchangeable metastable S_3 state does exist in strictly dark-adapted *oscillatoria chalybea*.

The latest results on the reactivity of S_3 as a function of temperature (see section B) might also support our postulate that 0-0 bond preformation occurs prior to S_4. The second postulate was primarily introduced in order to explain the extreme stability of S_1.

Actually, it was later found that, in sufficiently dark-adapted samples, almost all catalytic sites, attain the redox level S_1 M is not yet identified. It could be either a special valence state of the catalytic manganese or another redox-active component.

The latest and very elegant study confirms that the reaction $S_0 \rightarrow S_1$ does not cause significant absorption changes in the range of 290-570 nm, in contrast to the transitions $S_1 \rightarrow S_2$ and $S_2 \rightarrow S_3$. Based on this result, it was concluded that, most likely, no manganese oxidation takes place at the transition $S_0 \rightarrow S_1$.

With respect to the other redox steps, at least a 1-electron abstraction from manganese was inferred to occur for S_2 formation from S_1. On the other hand, it is not clear whether or not S, oxidation to S_3 is also mainly restricted to the manganese core.

The above-mentioned results neatly fit in with the basic conclusions of our previous model. Different lines of evidence support the idea that S_1 contains a [Mn (III) Mn (III)] and S_2 a [Mn (I11) Mn (IV)] core. As a summary of our fragmentary knowledge a molecular mechanism of water oxidation can be proposed which is depicted in figure elsewhere in this chapter.

BIOCHEMISTRY OF SENESCENCE

One problem of biology involves understanding the factors that control the timing of the various periods in the life cycle of a cell. The dramatic events of cell division and cell enlargement have received much attention but the gradual changes during maturation and the on set of cellular senescence are less easily observed and have received less attention.

Nevertheless, all phases of the life cycle of a single cell or a group of cells are of equal intrinsic interest and a knowledge of each is of equal potential practical application.

Starting from the point of view that postharvest fruits and vegetables are merely specific examples of maturing and senescing cells, it is the purpose of this review to consider the general subject of the metabolism of aging cells with particular reference to cells and tissues of higher plants.

GENERAL THEORIES OF AGING

There seems no reason to doubt that senescence is a universal phenomenon in living organisms. The visible changes that occur during senescence in higher plants and animals are easily recognizable although not always readily susceptible to quantitative measurement.

The physical changes occurring at the cellular and subcellular level have been described "only briefly and while observations of the metabolic changes that accompany aging are more numerous, they are disappointing in that ,cause and effect relationships are seldom clear. Lansing has described aging as "a problem of cellular change-of unfavourable change in the ability of protoplasm to maintain itself."

To make this description more explicit it is useful to recall Dixon's definition of living matter as "a system of unstable catalysts being kept in existence by the occurrence of the reactions which they catalyse". The suggestions that the life span of an individual is limited by the loss of optical purity of certain crucial substances by increasing protein immobilization due to progressive crosslinking reactions or by thermal denaturation of irreplaceable molecules are largely speculative and need no further discussion here.

In many respects the loss of cellular vitality in senescence resembles the effects of radiation injury. The similar effects of aging and of ionizing radiations on the ability of mice to withstand stress suggest that, in some respects, ionizing radiation accelerates the normal process of aging.

However, because massive application of nitrogen mustard does not induce premature aging, Curtis and Gebhard believe that mutation in somatic cells does not cause the effects observed. During the germination of wheat and soya bean, maximum sensitivity to ionizing radiation occurs at the time the growth substance in the endosperm is mobilized.

However, the cells of leaves are remarkably resistant to radiation; a dose of 40,000 is without effect. Neary has suggested that there is "some intrinsic process of biological aging, enhanced by radiation, which operates from the start of life and is virtually complete by the time the changes of old age begin to appear."

This theory "assumes that there is a common process at work in natural and radiation-induced aging which is fundamental, inevitable and irreversible." Once aging has been induced its development proceeds autonomously and autocatalytically. Although there is no conclusive evidence to indicate that loss of nuclear function by a cell is a primary event in senescence, there is no doubt that the nucleus of a somatic cell exerts a profound effect on the metabolism of the rest of the cell and that, conversely, events in the cytoplasm have a profound effect on the nucleus.

The accumulation with age of some inhibitor or deleterious substance has frequently been proposed as a cause of senescence. Lansing's elegant experiments on factors affecting the life span of rotifers led him to suggest that a transmissible, cumulative, reversible factor is responsible for aging in this organism. The accumulation and deposition of calcium salts in aging cells of plants and animals is well documented.

That this accumulation of calcium is to some extent a causative agent in the aging of rotifers is shown by the fact that a low level of calcium in the culture medium was associated with an, increased life span ; also, the experimental removal of calcium. from rotifers with sodium citrate increased their life span by 50 per cent.

Because calcium in old cells of *Elodea*, a rotifer, a planarian, and a toad tended to deposit in the cell cortex, Lansing suggested that cell permeability was being adversely affected.

It has often been proposed that permeability changes. are causative factors in the aging of plants and animals, and recently such proposals have been vigorously restated to be of significance in senescent plant cells with auxin exerting a decisive influence.

De Kock and co-workers have studied responses of old and young leaves and of tissues of old and young rats to various metabolic inhibitors and have found that the magnitude of response produced by the various inhibitors was less in the older tissues of both plants and animals.

From these experiments they conclude that "the balance between the various. processes changes with aging of the organism" and "that no metabolic system is lost or new system introduced during the life of the organisms". Over 50 years ago Rubner proposed that an inverse relationship existed between rate of metabolism and duration of life (of animals) and that various mammals during their lifetime used up approximately the same number of calories per unit weight.

This theory gains much support from the many reports demonstrating that the life span of animals can be increased by lowering the body temperature. It is indisputable, of course, that the life span of post harvest plant tissues can be extended by judiciously lowering the temperature.

It is interesting to consider Rubner's theory in terms of what is. now known of the cellular components involved in energy metabolism. One attractively simple hypothesis is that the mitochondria of any cell have a definite total work capacity and senescence is the result of the failure of the mitochondria to be reproduced or repaired.

Development of this hypothesis depends upon gaining.. further knowledge of the biogenesis and life span of mitochondria.

At the moment, any cell component (particulate or soluhle, enzyme or coenzyme) required in the chain of reactions producing energy is a possible candidate for the role of limiting. factor in total energy production. The influence of temperature on a life span can also be cited as support for other theories of aging.

For example, a decrease in temperature would greatly reduce thermal denaturation of macromolecules. Measurement of the temperature coefficients of the induction and development of aging would be most useful as a means for elucidating possible mechanisms.

The foregoing theories and ideas have been presented without regard to their immediate applicability to the specific problems of postharvest physiology. In the following section the discussion will be limited to data and theories that deal almost entirely with plant cells and are more closely related to postharvest prohlems.

RESPIRATION AND CELLULAR WORK DURING SENESCENCE

Biale's contention, in his 1950 review of the postharvest physiology and biochemistry of fruit that emphasis should be placed on respiration as a central process common to all fruits has been amply justified. It now seems satisfactorily established that, up to the time of the climacteric peak, respiration as measured by oxygen up take is a reflection of the work performed by the cells, and most of this work is mediated by ATP.

The individual papers that allow these conclusions have been reviewed recently in several excellent articles. It is also established that the mitochondria of postclimacteric (senescent) cells are still capable of oxidative phosphorylation and are still performing anabolic functions such as the synthesis of proteins and of pigments.

Further, it is certain that normal ripening, in tomatoes at least, requires the expenditure of energy from oxidative phosphorylation because infiltration of whole, green, mature tomato fruit with dinitrophenol prevents the chemical and physical changes associated with ripening.

This requirement for energy for normal ripening is probably a general one because decreased oxygen tension also delays or prevents the climacteric and ripening.

During the pre-climacteric period the cells are not fully utilizing their work capacity as ecidenced by the increased rate of oxygen uptake by whole fruit, slices, and isolated mitochondria after treatment with dinitrophenol.

There is convincing evidence that at least part of the climacteric rise in respiration is caused by a decreased ATP/ADP ratio resulting from increased synthesis utilizing ATP. Prominent examples among these syntheses are the increases in aldolase and carboxylase in bananas observed by Tager and Biale, the increase in malate decarboxylase in apples observed by Neal and Hulme, and the synthesis of lycopene in tomatoes.

Hulme has pointed out that an increased rate of protein turnover would require energy at an increased rate and thereby promote an increased oxygen uptake without any increase in total protein. In considering protein turnover the recent observations that energy is required for protein degradation become of unusual interest.

The synthesis of highly reduced compounds, such as lycopene, from acetate obviously requires energy, as does the synthesis of ethylene, and these syntheses also must contribute slightly to a decreased ATP/ADP ratio.

Until someone devises a means of measuring the work capacity -of cells, one cannot rule out the possibility that a partial uncoupling of oxidative phosphorylation makes a contribution to the decreased ATP/AD" ratio and the increased oxygen ,uptake during the climacteric rise.

It is equally impossible to state the degree of coupling in the post-climacteric period although the electron transport function of the mitochondria is operating at full capacity, as indicated by the lack of effect of dinitrophenol on oxygen uptake of whole fruit, slices, and isolated mitochondria.

However, it is clear that the post-climacteric mitochondria *In vivo* are not completely uncoupled in spite of the appearance of uncoupling agents in the cytoplasm.

There can be little doubt that the cellular respiratory capacity and work capacity decrease during senescence, and it seems likely that this is caused by gradual loss of mitochondrial function with the loss of phosphorylative activity preceding the loss of electron transport capacity. Further development of this approach must center upon the details of mitochondrial metabolism and its control.

At this point it seems appropriate to anticipate the expansion of the discussion to include other senescent tissues-particularly leaves, flowers, and the cotyledons and endosperms of germinating seeds. The changes accompanying the gradual respiratory decline and senescence of these tissues, either attached or detached, are comparable to those that occur in ripening and postharvest fruit. In addition, in many instances, such tissues are easier to obtain and therefore are more amenable to laboratory investigation. The recent thesis of Gindel that an important function of many fruits is to provide the embryo of the germinating seed a supply of nutrients, renders especially apt the comparison between fruits and cotyledons (and endosperms).

Ample evidence now exists that synthesis of specific proteins occurs in the cotyledons and endosperms of germinating seeds, even though there is a simultaneous decline in the total protein content of these structures.

In pea cotyledons one of the proteins synthesized is a phosphatase (another is amylase) with a pH optimum of 7 and a high specificity for ATP and ADP. This enzymes is apparently synthesized by the ribosomes, accumulates in the soluble fraction of the cytoplasm, and is distinctly different from the ATPase activity associated with mitochondria.

Clearly it is a candidate for an important role in controlling the cytoplasmic ATP/ADP ratio and thereby, respiration and the efficiency of utilization of the energy that is conserved as ATP during oxidative phosphorylation.

The synthesis of this phosphatase depends upon the energy supplied by mitochondria. In turn, the functional integrity of the mitochondria depends upon a heat stable organic factor that moves into the pea cotyledons during the first 24 hr. of germination.

In the absence of this factor (that is, when the axis tissue is dissected, away from the dry seed and the cotyledons are incubated under germination conditions) the mitochondria become "leaky" and begin to lose phosphorylative efficiency within 24 hrs. and are completely uncoupled within 38 to 48 hr.

After 72 to 96 hr. the cotyledons no longer take up oxygen. As the oxygen. uptake decreases there is a concomitant rise in R.Q. The factor from the axis tissue has not been identified. Imbibition by the dry cotyledons of solutions containing 10^{-4} to 10^{-10} M kinetin, gibberellic acid indoleacetic acid, napthalepeacetic acid, accorbic acid, glutathione, and many other substances was without effect in simulating the natural agent except in the case of 5×10^{-6} M napthaleneacetic acid.

In this instance the respiratory decline and the increase in R.Q. are delayed until the sixth or seventh day. Cotyledons from which the axis tissue has been dissected after 18 to 48 hr. of normal germination will remain alive and healthy for as long as 4 to 6 weeks.

The axis-free cotyledons could also be maintained in a healthy state (as indicated by their oxygen uptake, R.Q., ability to incorporate labeled glycine into protein, and the fact that active mitochondria could be obtained from them) for at least seven days by allowing them to imbibe $CdCI_2$ (10^{-2} M) or *p*-fluorophenylalanine (1mg/ml) during the first few hours of incubation.

Although all of the present evidence is against the possihility of the factor being an antifungal or antibacterial agent such as that reported by Spencer *et al.* it is necessary to bear in mind the possible effects of the presence of such agents in mature and senescent cells.

A soluble, heat-labile, nondialyzable substance that produces swelling and uncoupling of isolated mitochondria is found in the cotyledons of germinating peas after IC to 18 days and in the axis-free cotyledons after 38 to 72 hr.

This substance is absent from the axis-free cotyledons pretreated with $CdCl_2$ or *p*-fluorophenylalanine. It does not appear to be an RNAase; extraction with iso-octane does not affect its activity, nor is the iso-octane extract active; it is strongly adsorbed by mitochondria; and its action on isolated mitochondria is prevented when it is preincubated with. 10^{-4} M $CdCl_2$.

To resolve the physiological meaning of these results one needs to know:

(a) the source of the uncoupling substance-is it produced by mitochondria, microsomes, or nuclei—is it the cause or the result of *in vivo* mitochondrial inactivation?

(b) what part of the mitochondrial structure is attacked by the substance, and

(c) what is its relation, if any, to mitochrome?

Through teleological spectacles it appears that pea cotyledons are supposed to die gracefully, gradually relinquishing their demand on their own reserves.

Mobilization of these reserves requires the synthesis of new enzymes and at the same time, to insure the selfless participation of the cotyledon cells in the establishment of the growing parts of the seedling, it is their heritage to produce their own slow poison. In castor bean and other oil-bearing seeds, synthesis of enzymes of the glyoxalate cycle is necessary before the triglycerides can be converted to, and mobilized as sucrose.

Mitochondrial uncouplers or inhibitors or both have been reported in ripening avocadoes in rose petals and in animal cells. Further insight into the role of such substances in the respiration of postharvest tissues should be greatly aided by the development of satisfactory methods for isolating mitochondria from such fruits as apples, tomatoes and bananas.

In addition to the specific examples already mentioned of enzymes showing a net increase in activity, there are many independent and more general indications of an active protein metabolism in mature and senesecent tissues.

In mature leaves excision from the plant initiates a rapid decline in total protein content that is not stopped by supplying mineral salts, carbohydrates, or nitrogen compounds, but is slowed by the administration of kinetin benzimidazole and 2, 4-D and is stopped by the formation of adventitious roots.

During this period of decline the leaves retain a reduced capacity to incorporate N's-labeled ammonia and C^{14}-labeled amino acids into protein, and virus synthesis still occurs. Vickery has shown that after the protein of detached leaves falls below certain levels the leaves are no longer able to recover from various stresses, presumably because of the irreversible loss of some necessary enzyme.

Mothes' recent experiments dramatically demonstrate the effective-ness of kinetin and benzimidazole in maintaining the capacity of *Nicotiana* leaves to withstand stress.

These observations that protein turnover occurs in mature cells are consistent with the turnover detected in - resting cells of yeast and of *E. coli.* In starving excised barley leaves, the rate of respiration is limited by available substrates; there is a shift of respiratory substrates from carbohydrates to amino acids derived from protein breakdo-wn; and a marked accumulation of glutamine and asparag-ine is apparent.

Administering glucose to detached wheat leaves causes an increased CO_s output, with part coming from the admi-nistered glucose and part from the endogenous substrates.

There is a general increase with maturity in the level of proteolytic enzymes of root cells and an increase with age of dipeptidase activity in *Elodea.* Likewise, a steady increase of the proteolytic activity of the mycelia of *Penicillium griseofulvun* and other fungi occurs with age.

During the first few hours of nitrogen starvation a several-fold> increase is noted that persists until nitrogen is again supplied. This increase in activity probably repres-ents *de novo* synthesis, and is not accompanied by net protein breakdown.

CHANGES IN SPECIFIC SUB-CELLULAR EXTITIES DURING SENESCENCE

Mitochondria

A central question in the study of senescence is the problem of the biogenesis and life span of mitochondria. Is there replacement of mitochondria in fully expanded nondividing cells or are mitochondria produced only during cell division and cell enlargement?

If the latter, what parts of the mitochondrion are subject to wear and repair and what parts to wear without repair ? The present knowledge of the origin and ontogeny of mitochondria has been discussed hut as yet we have no satisfactory answer to the questions posed.

It is clear that there is a great similarity in the structure and function of plant mitochondria derived from a wide variety of tissues, and that plant mitochondria are closely comparable to animal mitochondria.

There appears to be a definite development of the internal structure of mitochondria in the meristematic cells of both corn roost and pea roots from a more or less homogenous interior to one with well defined cristae. In the mature cells the mitochondrial interior again tends to be disorganized and a loss of respiratory efficiency is evident.

Howard & Yamaguchi have reported a striking increase in the oxidative activity of isolated mitochondria during the maturation of pepper fruit. The mitochondria from immature: fruit, compared to those from mature fruit, contained less succinic dehydrogenase.

Isolated plant mitochondria exhibit characteristic osmotic behaviour together with a change of dimension, structure, and biochemical capacity in hypotonic solution and isolated mitochondria are capable of an energy-dependent salt uptake.

The physiological significance of these properties is unknown. Isolated plant mitochondria incorporate labeled amino acids into mitochondrial protein and synthesis of some specific protein may be expected to occur because of the demonstrated net synthesis of cyto-chrome-c in isolated calf heart mitochondria.

Pertinent to the problem of the cause and nature of the changes in the mitochondria of senescent cells are the studies of Hanson on the effect of ribonuclease on isolated mitochondria.

Hanson found that corn root mitochondria contain about

1 per cent, RNA and concluded that at least a part of this RNA is functional because of the deleterious effects of treatment with RNAase.

Low concentrations of RNAase caused a slight rise in oxygen uptake and a decreased P/O ratio while higher concentrations (1 mg/ml) uncoupled phosphorylation and decreased oxygen uptake.

These effects were not attributable to the action of RNAase products, to adsorption of RNAase on mitochondria, nor to proteolytic contaminants of RNAase. In a later paper Hanson suggests, on the basis of the effects on root tissue of RNAase, ethylenediamine tetracetic acid, and potassium chloride, that RNA associated with various membranes is essential to respiration, ion accumulation, and solute retention.

He proposes that calcium or magnesium, or both ions bound to RNA protect it against RNAase and that the in *view* function of mitochondria is governed by the $K^{+}/Mg^{+++}Ca^{++}$ ratio.

Zinc ions have also heen implicated in the RNAase-RNA-protein relationships of citrus leaves and it should be noted that an enhancement of the nuclease activity of bean hypocotyls by indoleacetic acid and kinetin has been reported.

Cytoplasmic Membrane and Cell Wall

Sacher has recently 'proposed that the changes accompanying senescence of fruits and abscission of leaves and fruits are due to a loss of integrity by the membranes, resulting from insufficient levels of auxin.

This proposal is based on experiments with auxintreated and untreated segments of the pods of Kentucky Wonder pole beans and leaf slices *of Mesembryanthemum sp.* and *Rhoeo discolor.*

The untreated segments *of* bean endocarps became soft and flaccid and water-logged in the intercellular spaces within three days, while the treated (4 to 50 p.p.m. NAA or IAA) segments remained rigid and plump up to 17 days.

A surface exudate appeared on the untreated segments, cellular dissociation occurred, and the leakage of solutes was three times that from the treated segments. Furthermore, endogenous respiration ceased much earlier in the untreated samples. Similar effects of IAA and NAA in preventing degradative changes were obtained with *Mesembryanthemum* and *Rhoea.*

These experiments do not foster the conclusion that the cytoplasmic membrane is the only membrane affected because many of the same effects might be .expected if either the tonoplast or the mitochondrial membranes were impaired.

Nor do the results necessarily indicate that loss of membrane permeability is the primary event in the degradative changes that occur in the absence of added auxin; however, the effects of IAA and NAA in delaying senescence are clearly demonstrated. Osborne has shown that senescence in both attached and detached leaves *of* several deciduous species may be delayed by application *of 2,4-D* or 2,4,5-T.

The treated areas of the leaves remain green, retain both a relatively high rate of oxygen uptake and the ability to fix carbon dioxide photosynthetically, while the surrounding untreated tissue undergoes 'normal senescence.

The aging processes have been arrested in detached leaves of *Xanthium* by treatment with kinetin and in detached wheat leaves by treatment with benzimidazole.

Leaf yellowing and abscission have been delayed in several species by spraying with gibberellic acid and the delay of the onset of senescence by removal of the flowers has recently been re-investigated.

These experiments indicate that senescence, as well as growth and differentiation, is linked to the hormone level of the tissues but they do not yet elucidate the series of events at the molecular level.

The natural fall in the gradient of pectin methylesterase activity that occurs across the abscission zones of petioles of *Phaseolus vulgarls* can be prevented by treatment with 2,4-D or 2,4,5-T and abscission is prevented.

Yager has proposed the existence of other enzymes active in abscission. Pectin methylesterase is present in the exudate of water-logged (low auxin) bean endocarp segments. These observations suggest that a low level of auxin may bring about a change in the distribution and activity of pectin methylesterase (and possibly other enzymes) and thereby cause a change in pectin metabolism that would contribute toward the changes occurring in senescence and abscission.

Glasziou has reported that at least 90 per cent of the pectin methylesterase of intact oat coleoptiles is bound, probably to the cell wall, and that the degree of binding is dependent on the level of IAA. Jansen *et al.* however, found no influence of IAA on the binding of pectin methylesterase by *Avena* coleoptile cell walls.

Whatever the relationships between senescence, auxin, and pectin methylesterase, it is now becoming evident that several enzymes are localized primarily or exclusively in the cell wall. Invertase appears to be located at the surface of cells of *Canna* leaves and in the free space of wheat roots and coleoptiles while an extracellular amylase has been reported encultures of bean stem segments.

Pyrophosphatase, ATPase, and uridine diphosphoglucose pyrophosphorylase activities are associated with corn coleoptile cell wall fragments and ascorbic acid oxidase and hexose phosphatase activities with the wall fraction of sycamore cells in solution culture. It is interesting to note that the hydroxyproline of plant cells is also located in the cell wall proteins.

Therefore we have an increasing scope for ideas on the possible action of auxin in controlling growth and senescence through cell wall metabolism.

Nuclei, Endoplasmic Reticulum, and Ribosomes

It is becoming.. increasingly evident that the various structures of the cell are intimately and subtly interrelated, both structurally and functionally. There is strong evidence that a part of the vesicular network of the endoplasmic reticulum is continuous with the cytoplasmic membrane and extends into and through the walls and that this portion of the reticulum may constitute the limiting membrane between the apparent free space and the remainder of the cell volume.

Another portion of this vesicular network of membranes is apparently continuous with the nuclear membrane. The ribonucleoprotein particles of the microsomal fraction appear to be produced in the nucleus and expelled into the cytoplasm through the nuclear pores.

Within the nucleus the nucleoli are the centers of the most intense RNA metabolism while protein synthesis occurs in particles similar to the ribonucleoprotein particles of the microsomal fraction.

To what extent the cytoplasm of somatic cells is dependent upon a continuous supply of RNA from the nucleus remains to be established. A ready pathway probably exists for the exchange of coenzyme and substrate molecules between the nucleus and the cytoplasm.

In this closely interrelated continuum of structural elements and enzymatic functions it is not surprising that many treatments, e.g., removal of the nucleus, addition of metabolic inhibitors, and starvation, bring about a metabolic decline similar to that of normal senesence, and that a decrease in the levels of many enzymes and cofactors can be correlated with senescence.

Because the bulk of the cellular protein is synthesized by the ribonucleoprotein particles it is of interest to study this synthetic capacity in senescent cells.

The microsomal fraction, isolated from post-climacteric avocado fruit in which the mitochondria have lost the ability to carry out oxidative phosphorylation *in vivo* and *in vitro*, is still capable of an ATP-dependent incorporation of labeled amino acids into protein.

Exactly similar hut more detailed results have been

obtained with the microsomal fraction from pea cotyledons in normal and induced senescence. Within the limits of such a test to indicate the functional integrity of ribonucleoprotein particles, one can conclude that the particles are still capable of functioning *in vivo* but cannot because of the lack of ATP.

Such a conclusion is consistent with the known stability of isolated ribonucleoprotein particles their capacity for dissociation into subunits, and their reassociation to form functional particles.

A conclusion of that nature also draws support from the report of only a slight decline in both RNA content and the amino acid activating enzymes of rat liver during extensive protein deprivation of the rat.

Further evidence that the microsomal fraction is rather stable derives from the observations that anucleate fractions of *Acetabularia* live for several months and during this time bring about a net synthesis of several enzymes.

Intriguing as these experiments are, they do not begin to deal: with the possibility that several (or many) kinds of ribonucleoprotein particles with different stabilities exist in the same cell or that there are different kinds in different cells of the same plant.

However, although we have substantial evidence for the role of the nucleus in controlling metabolic events in the extra nuclear portion of a cell during mitosis, growth, and maturation, there is virtually no information on the functi-onal" state of the nucleus in a senescent cell.

Huang has found no change during senescence in the ability of the nuclei of pea cotyledon cells, either *In vivo* or *in vitro,* to incorporate tritiated thymidine. Again, within the limits of the test to indicate the functional integrity of the nucleus, the results indicate that loss of nuclear activity is not the primary event in the senescence of pea cotyledons.

It is perhaps of interest to recall that the senescence of pea cotyledons can be delayed by napthaleneacetic acid, by a factor from the axis tissue and that Thimann and Beth have shown that anucleate fragments of *Acetabularia* still respond to treatment with indoleacetic acid.

This section can be concluded by noting that these studies will now be greatly faciliated by the availability of adequate methods for the isolation of nuclei and nucleoli from plant tissues.

Chloroplasts

Because senescence is not limited to green cells, chloroplasts obviously are not requisite structures for this phenomenon and they deserve attention from the standpoint of their possible capacity for modifying senescence.

To the well established observations that chloroplasts are self-propagating entities capable of photosynthetic phosphorylation and photosynthetic carbon dioxide fixation we must now add the recent observations that chloroplasts contain amino acid activating enzymes and conduct a light-dependent incorporation of amino acids into protein.

They may therefore synthesize much of their own protein, RNA, and perhaps DNA as well. Although only a small fraction of the total RNA of a green cell is localized in the chloroplasts a close correlation is evident between the total RNA of a green leaf and its capacity for photosynthetic phosphorylation.

Hence the RNA content of a green leaf appears to be a measure of its photosynthetic ability as well as an indication of its capacity for respiration, oxidative phosphorylation, protein synthesis, and cell division. In drought and senescence a more rapid loss of protein takes place from chloroplasts than from the remainder of the cell.

In detached leaves, however, there is a parallel in the rate of protein loss in chloroplasts and cytoplasm. Relevant to the earlier discussion about protein catabolism requiring energy, Wood and Cruickshank have observed that detached leaves in nitrogen showed no loss of protein although there was a decrease in carbohydrates.

It will be interesting to learn whether chloroplasts contain an energy dependent system for protein catabolism.

Apparently we have too little information to allow a decision on the possibility that chloroplasts and mitochondria can serve as alternate and independent sources of ATP for the work requirements of a cell, although Smillie concludes that it is unlikely.

Vacuoles

The vacuoles probably cannot be considered functional entities in the sense that they carry enzymatic apparatus necessary for the synthesis of cell stuff, yet it is clear that the integrity of the tonoplast must be maintained to prevent the release of a flood of noxious substances into the cytoplasm.

The osmotic properties of vacuoles have been clearly demonstrated. The origin of the tonoplast and the means of the maintenance of its permeability properties are highly uncertain.

Probably many events observed in the final stages of senescence result from the leakage of such substances as phenols from the vacuole and their consequent interaction with the remaining functional elements of the cell. It seems likely that this leakage is secondary to the loss of energy necessary to maintain the membranes.

Publication of a method for obtaining isolated vacuoles should permit a more detailed study of their properties.

Cytoplasmic Ground Substance

This fraction is poorly characterised at present and includes the left-overs after clearly recognizable structures have been accounted for. Current indications are that this fraction too possesses a structure not quite resolved by present methods.

This matrix separates and supports the particulate structures of the cell, contains many of the "soluble" enzymes, and absorhs and perhaps produces the shears and stresses accompanying cytoplasmic streaming.

Loss of activity by one or more of the enzymes belonging to this fraction might be sufficient to trigger the onset of senescence and death. It appears, though, that this portion of the cell is not selfreproducing and the enzymes present are synthesized by other cellular structures.

In this view, changes observed in the ground substance, even though correlated with senescence, would be derivative rather than primary.

CHANGES IN METABOLIC PATHWAYS

Studies of the effects of various metabolic inhibitors on young and old plant and animal tissues suggest a gradual shifting of metabolic pathways during aging.

The data of Tager and Biale indicate a shift from the pentose phosphate pathway to the Embden-Meyerhof-Parnas (EMP) pathway in the ripening banana: carboxylase and aldolase activities are very low in the immature banana but increase several-fold during and after the climacteric rise in respiration.

By measuring the relative rates of production of labeled carbon dioxide from glucose-6-C^{14} and glucose-6-C^{14} it is possible to determine the relative contributions of the pentose phosphate pathway and the EMP pathway in the degradation of glucose.

Embryonic plant tissues, especially roots, seem to degrade glucose exclusively by the EMP pathway with an increasing importance of the pentose phosphate pathway as germination proceeds.

Gibbs and Earl have reported changes of sufficient magnitude in the activities of aldolase, 6-phosphoglucose dehydrogenase, ribose5-phosphatase, and fructose 1,6-diphosphatase of developing pea roots to provide a convincing explanation for the change an pathways.

Alternatively, the controlling factor in the proportioning of the contribution of the two pathways might be the TPNH/TPN^4 and DPNH/DPN^+ ratios. In the experiments of Gibbs and Beevers added indoleacetic acid had no influence on the pathway of glucose metabolism. On the other hand, such an influence has been observed by Humphreys and

Dugger and by Shaw *et al.* The work of Wang and his associates demonstrates the presence of the pentose cycle pathway in mature pepper and tomato fruit.

The importance of the synthesis of the enzymes of the glyoxalate cycle in the conversion of fatty acids to carbohydrates in the endosperms of oil-bearing seeds has already been mentioned.

In the petals of cut roses a decrease occurs with age in the malate to citrate conversion, as well as in the dark fixation of $C^{14}O_2$,. The increased malate decarboxylase in apple tissue apparently diverts malate into a decarboxylation pathway that results in an increased R.Q. for the tissue.

Recent reviews have dealt at length with the various possible pathways for the transport to oxygen of hydrogen or electrons from reduced cofactors in a variety of plant tissues including senescent tissues.

The fact that young and old tissues differ in their responses to various respiratory inhibitors suggests at least a change in the rate-limiting reactions, if not a shift in electron transport pathway.

These changes are almost certainly of great significance in the metabolism of plant tissue and Hackett's excellent review should be consulted for a complete discussion of the problem.

It is perhaps useful to be reminded that changes in the intensity of various metabolic pathways can occur without changes in the concentrations of the enzymes involved.

Changes in Chemical Composition

Ulrich's review considered the changes in chemical composition of ripening fruit in detail, and Kefford has reviewed the work on the chemical and enzymatic constituents of citrus fruits.

Since these reviews there has been a painstaking account of the histological and histochemical changes in developing and ripening peaches further delineation of the changes during growth and storage of avocado fruit a detailed analysis of the chemical changes in cut roses and aging maple leaves as well as a heroic documentation of the chemical compo-sition of the leaves and fruit of the banana, and of the influence of various factors on their composition.

BIOGENESIS OF ETHYLENE

Ethylene is a normal metabolic product of plant tissues and the gross effects (epinasty, acceleration of ripening) of its physiological activity are well known. Whether the quantities of ethylene present in plant parts other than the fruit are of any physiological significance under usual growing conditions is still an open question.

Many kinds of ripening fruit, however, accumulate sufficient ethylene to influence the rate of ripening. It is uncertain whether ethylene initiates this ripening or is simply a by-product of it.

Because of the physiological activity of ethylene and because it is produced in fruit only during ripening. both its biogenesis and its further metabolism are of great interest. The development of micromethods for the separation, identification, and estimation of ethylene has resulted in significant progress in the problem of ethylene biogenesis.

Using a gas chromatographic procedure Burg and Thimann studied the conditions affecting ethylene production by plugs of apple tissue. The process was strongly inhibited by low oxygen tensions and ceased entirely under completely anaerobic conditions.

Storage for 1 to 4 hr. in nitrogen and subsequent return to air brought about an increased rate of ethylene production, suggesting that an ethylene precursor accumulates under anaerobiosis. After a 4-hr. exposure to nitrogen, a 5-min. exposure to air allowed ethylene production to continue for about 60 min.

Soaking the plugs in water for one hour greatly decreased ethylene production, while soaking in glycerol, potassium chloride, and a variety of other substances prevented such a decline. Because the decline brought about by soaking in water could be reversed by a subsequent soaking in glycerol, the decline did not result from a loss to solution of ethylene precursors.

Experiments with a range of concentrations of .glycerol and potassium chloride indicated that a certain minimum tonicity of the cell sap must be preserved in order to maintain ethylene production. Higher tonicities were not inhibitory.

The threshold concentration for the inhibition of ethylene production and oxygen uptake was the same for six different metabolic inhibitors and ethylene production and respiration-were closely parallel over a large concentration range of each of the inhibitors.

Also, the responses of the two processes of oxygen tension were nearly identical. These properties of the ethylene-producing system led Burg and Thimann to suggest that (*a*) it is located in a particle, (*b*) it is inactivated by swelling of the particulate structure, (*c*) it is closely linked with a terminal oxidase and (*d*) it is dependent upon the respiratory process for energy. The observation that the inhibitions caused by dinitrophenol and fluoride were partially reversed by ATP (and other energy sources) further indicates that ethylene production requires respiratory energy.

The experiments of Spencer in which whole mature green tomatoes infiltrated with dinitrophenol showed an immediate depression of ethylene evolution, also indicate a requirement of oxidative phosphorylation for ethylene production.

While the observations of Burg and Thimann are strongly indicative of the site of ethylene synthesis, the data of Spencer seem to establish the mitochondrion as this site.

She reported that mitochondria isolated from tomato fruit produce ethylene in quantities equivalent to those produced by the whole fruit and the pattern of ethylene production by mitochondria isolated from tomatoes of different physiological ages closely parallels the evolution of ethylene from whole fruit of comparable ages.

However, Meigh *et al.* observed no ethylene production by isolated apple and tomato mitochondria even though the mitochondrial preparations were capable of oxidative phosphorylation and the crude homogenates from which the mitochondria were prepared produced easily, detectable quantities of ethylene.

The small quantities of ethylene produced in plant tissues make the study of ethylene metabolism difficult even with radioactive tracers. A few such studies have been reported, however, and indicate that the immediate precursors of ethylene are not closely related to any known major metabolic pathway.

No radioactivity could be found in ethylene produced by plugs of apple tissue after treatment with 1,3-C^{14} glycerol and 2-C^{14} glycerol although the label was found in glutamate, aspartate, malate, fructose, glucose, sucrose, alanine, and succinate.

When, labeled sucrose and acetate were used in long term experiments, (22 to 58 hr.) the ethylene produced was labeled. The ratio of the specific activity of ethylene to that of carbon dioxide was much, higher for the labeled sucrose (0.25-0.29) than for the labeled acetate (0.10-0.0025) experiments.

Labeled tyrosine did not give rise to labeled ethylene. These results indicate that the direct precursors of ethylene must be sought among compounds. other than the intermediates of glycolysis, of Kreb's cycle, and of the degradation of aromatic compounds. In apple tissue the tritium of tritiated water is rapidly incorporated into ethylene and reaches complete equilibration in about three minutes. Consideration of both the physiological properties" of their system and the data from the carbon and tritium tracer experiments led Burg and Thimann to propose the following. sequence of steps in the biosynthesis of ethylene.

$$\xrightarrow{}\ A \rightarrow B \underset{+H_2O}{\overset{-H_2O}{\leftrightharpoons}} C \rightarrow \text{ethylene}$$

$$-2H$$

The evidence suggests that compound A is normally present in low concentration but accumulates under nitrogen; the conversion of A to B requires oxygen and is relatively fast; the rate-limiting step under normal conditions is the formation of A; after prolonged exposure to nitrogen, the conversion of B to ethylene is rate-limiting; and one of the final' steps is a reversible dehydration.

The rapid equilibration of the ethylene with tritiated water might be the result of the binding of ethylene to an enzyme in such a way as to enhance the already acidic nature of the ethylene hydrogen.

It is intriguing to speculate further about some of the possible pathways for ethylene biogenesis. The oxygen requirement and energy requirement of the ethylene producing: system and the tracer experiments seem to rule out the synthesis of ethylene by the simple dehydration of ethanol.

The elimination of ammonia from ethylamine by an aspartase-like reaction seems equally improbable. The recent demonstration of the formation of carbon-carbon double bonds by a nonhydrolytic elimination of phosphate raises the possibility that 3-phosphopropionic acid might be an intermediate in analogy with the formation of isopentenylpyrophosphate.

Acrylyl CoA formed in the conversion of P-alanine to propionic acid might also be considered.

6-alanine→β-alanyl-CoA→acrylyl-CoA→acrylic acid→ethylene

Whatever the pathway for the biogenesis of ethylene, the enzymatic apparatus involved is presumably highly specific since there is only a scant production of other olefins.

Huelin and Kennet report that if C_3 to C_6 olefins occur in apples the proportion must be less than 0.1 per cent of the ethylene, while Meigh found acetylene, ethylene, propylene, and propane in the quantities of 20, 27,000, 9 and 7 mpg/kg/hr produced by apples in air at 20°C. Meigh also reported that potatoes produce a variety of hydrocarbons.

Not only is the rate of production of ethylene slow and the biosynthetic pathway obscure, but the further metabolism is slow and the pathway unknown. After exposing avocadoes, pears, oranges limes, papayas, apples, tomatoes and grapes to one part per thousand ethylene-C^{14} (1.4×10^6 counts per minute per millimole) for several days, only avocadoes and pears showed any measurable incorporation of radioactivity and this was mainly in the organic acid fraction.

Degradation of the succinic and fumaric acids from the avocado fruits showed 77 per cent of the label in the carboxyl groups in both cases. The respired carbon dioxide was inactive in all experiments.

Buhler et al. concluded that ethylene is probably an end product of plant metabolism and the small incorporation that is observed results from exchange reactions in the biosynthetic sequence of ethylene.

Meager as these results as, they do demonstrate that experiments with labeled ethylene are feasible. Further work along these lines, using ethylene of the highest possible specific activity so that the kinetics of the up ,take and distribution of the label might be followed should be rewarding.

PHYSIOLOGICAL CHEMISTRY OF FUNGITOXINS

As is the case of almost any discussion of chemical properties relating to biological action, there will be considerable simplification. Killing of living cells by a chemical compound is not a simple process, but rather the total observable response to a single or multiple chain reaction.

Whether or not a specific property of a compound will result in the death of a specific cell or tissue very often depends on an exquisite interaction between the physical-chemical properties of the compound and those of the cell affected.

For example, fluoroacetic acid is produced in the poisonous plant *Dichapetalum* without harm to the plant. Peters has found that when mammals ingest the plant, the fluoroacetate is mistaken for acetate in the Krebs cycle and fluoroacetate is produced which inhibits aconitase.

This causes citrate to accumulate. Peters feels that the excess citrate is the toxicant. Here is a delicate change with a profound effect. Fluoroacetate is not a direct poison, but may be changed by mammalian tissue into another compound, fluorocitrate, which causes the accumulation of the toxicant.

It would indeed be an oversimplification to ascribe 'to. one property of *fluoroacetate* the ability to kill directly. What must a compound be able to do in order to poison a cell? Simply stated, a poisonous compound must be able to get to a site of action, resist changes in transit, and exert a -deleterious effect when it arrives.

Requirements for poisonous molecules will, therefore, differ according to where they exert their effect. If they act outside the cell or at its surface, they will have no need to penetrate the intricate cellular membranes.

In this case, the requirements for toxicants would be much simpler and less specific than for compounds which must penetrate. Most organic molecules enter living cells most efficiently in the nonionized state.

Organic toxicants, therefore, are usually ,most toxic in their nonionized form. Are molecules always most toxic in their nonionized form? Albert (1951) and his group have found that the bactericidal effectiveness of the acridines and related series depends on their .ability to ionize.

Also the addition of an aliphatic side chain, which usually aids permeation and attendant toxicity, actually, reduces the bacteritoxicity of these compounds. Albert has deduced that acridine must act at the surface of the bacterial cells.

The 8-quinolinol derivatives, on the other hand, must be nonionized for maximum effect. If, as in the case of 8-quinolinols, the toxic molecule must enter the turbulent laboratory of the living cell, the molecule must resist destruction before it reaches its site of action.

Rich and have demonstrated correlation between the detoxifying enzymes present in fungi and the resistance of these fungi to poisoning. What does this mean in terms of comparative reactivity?

A toxic molecule which is highly reactive and relatively unstable would be most likely to act in the outer portions of the cell. Great reactivity might serve to destroy and detoxify such a molecule before it moved very deeply into the cell.

This property may, in fact, destroy a compound in the ambient fluid before it reaches the cell. For example, the presence of cysteine in the ambient fluid destroys captan before it can poison yeast cells. Lukens and Rich find that if yeast cells are treated with cobalt and then washed free of excess cobalt they are more susceptible to captan than cells not treated with cobalt.

Assuming that cobalt ties up surface sulphydryl groups the cobalt pretreatment presumably prevents the partial breakdown of captan on its way to its site of action within the cell. A more stable, relatively unreactive molecule would have a greater chance of penetrating unchanged to a site of action deeper githin the cell.

It will be seen that compounds considered chemically inert may be toxic. Not only the relative site of the action, but also the mode of action dictates requirements for a toxic molecule. For example, a competitive antimetabolite has more and subtler requirements than those of a non-specific poison, such as phenol.

Sulfanilamide must not only be able to penetrate to. a site of action and be resistant to detoxication, but in addition its molecular configuration must very closely approximate the metabolite p-aminobenzoic acid with which it competes within the cell.

The distances between atoms in the molecule and their spatial relations are critical to the action of sulfanilamide. Much has been said of the solubility of toxicants in relation to their toxicity. Does a compound have to be water-soluble to be toxic? How else can it be reactive in the water-flooded interior of the cell?

Actually, such materials as copper oxide, sulphur, and dichlone, highly insoluble in water, are toxic. Very often water solubility is inversely related to toxicity as in the analogues of metallic 8-quinolinolates. This does not imply that good solubility in water precludes toxicity. The organic mercury salts, highly water-soluble, are excellent fungicides.

Usually those toxicants which are water-soluble, are very reactive compounds exerting general nonspecific toxicity. Why this wide variation in the relation between toxicity and' water solubility? As the sites of action may be in polar or nonpolar milieu, or in a medium with both polar and nonpolar groups, e.g., proteins, toxic compounds must and do vary in their solubilities depending on where they must go to become toxic.

Most often in the case of organic toxicants, of primary importance is not water solubility or lipid (nonpolar) solubility, but rather the partitioning of the compound between the two phases. Rich and Horsfall (1952) state the case for the importance of this relationship in the action of fungicides.

Working with a series of nitrosopyrazole analogues, they showed that. increasing the oil-water partition coefficient from 0.48 to 6.66 increases fungitoxicity ten thousandfold with no appreciable change in the dosage response slopes of the analogues.

They interpret this to mean that the change in the direction of high oil-water partition has greatly increased the penetration of the compound into the cell without altering the mode of action.

This solubility balance may be so critical that it may decide whether a compound will be toxic to one plant species and not to another.

Well man and McCallan (1946) working with 2-substituted imidazoline derivatives found that the tridecyl derivative was fourteen times more phytotoxic than the hepta decyl derivative. The heptadecyl homologue, however, was twice as toxic to fungi as the tridecyl homologue.

A more complicated relationship between toxicity and comparative solubilities exists in the 8-quinolinol derivatives. Albert and Hampton (1954) and Albert *et. al.* (1954) showed that the antibacterial action of oxine derivatives is directly and closely correlated with oil-water partition.

Albert *et. al.* (1953), with bacteria, and Block (1956) and Sijpesteijn *et. al.* (1957), with fungi, have demonstrated by various indirect biological methods that the toxic species of oxine and its derivative is the watersoluble half chelate.

When the system is flooded with oxine well in excess of

that needed for full chelation, there is no toxicity. Excess oxine would maintain the full chelate within the cell, preventing it from going to the half chelate.

Thus, high oil-water partition is essential for movement of the molecule to a site of action, but, once there, the water soluble half chelate must be present for toxicity. This does not imply that water solubility per se is essential to the toxicity of the half chelate but merely that high oil-water partition is essential to movement, and once inside the cell this condition is not essential to toxicity.

The toxicity of another group of compounds appears to be completely correlated with oil-water partition, with no evidence that any other property is involved. These are the so-called inert, nonspecific toxicants which follow the Ferguson effect, to be discussed later.

The properties aiding direct permeation into a cell may not be the only ones of importance in moving a damaging number -of toxic molecules to the site of action. Sussman (1954) showed that dormant ascospores of *Neurospora* adsorb ethylenediamine tetraacetic acid to their surface.

The adsorption takes place liven if the spores are first killed by boiling. If the ethylenediamine tetraacetic acid is removed from the spores before their dormancy is broken, there is no toxicity, but ethylenediamine tetraacetic acid is toxic if present when germination processes begin.

Sussman interprets this to mean that the ethylenediamine tetraacetic acid cannot enter the dormant spore. Not until the permeability properties of the spores change by the onset of germination can the toxic molecules enter. Lowry *.et. al (1957)* presented evidence that metallic cations such as Ag^{+}, Cu^{++}, and UO_2^{++}, follow this same course.

Here, then, is an example of adsorptive forces concentrating a toxicant at the surface of a cell, ready to enter when the permeability properties of the cell change. The work of Sussman and his colleagues should not be taken to mean that metallic ions enter only in the fashion they describe.

Miller *et. al. (1953)* have shown that fungus spores take

up silver and cerium extremely rapidly and greatly concentrate the toxicants in so doing.

With silver, for example, as high as 2124 p.p.m. of spore weight may be taken up by *Monilinia fracticola* spores in the first 30 seconds of exposure to a maximum possible dose of 4160 p.p.m.

Cerium entered *Aspergillus niger* spores at the rate of 7625 p.p.m. of spore weight in the first 30 seconds of exposure to a maximum possible-dose of 10,000 p.p.m. Miller *et. al.* (1953) point out that if doses of this magnitude were the result of simple adsorption, then the spore surface would have to be covered with multimolecular layers of toxicant.

This does not appear likely. Owens and Miller (1957) later studied the distribution of cerium and silver toxicants in spores. These workers disintegrated toxicantreated spores by sonic vibration, then fractionated the spore fragments by centrifugation.

They found that only 4% of the total amount of cerium or silver taken up was—associated with the cell walls. Owens and Miller feel that adsorption of cerium or silver on spore walls or plasma membranes plays little or no role in the movement of these toxic ions into the conidia of their two test organisms, *Neurospora sitophila* and *Aspergillus niger*.

Having the properties necessary to move to site of action without being detoxified, how many compounds poison? The following two sections discuss specific inorganic and organic toxicants in detail. The last section will deal with fashioning fungicides and with the future of fungicides.

Destructive Properties of Fungitoxicants

Very few fungitoxic mechanisms are fully understood. Possession of one of the properties discussed below does not necessarily make the molecule toxic, nor does it explain why the molecule is toxic. Rather, this is a discussion of chemical and physical properties by which molecules may disrupt essential life processes.

DIRECT CHEMICAL INTERACTIONS

Toxicants may undergo direct chemical interactions with vital constituents of the cell. For example, irreversible addition or substitution reactions with important enzymes or substrates would effectively poison a cell. Even reversible reactions will inhibit manifestations of life, and eventually cause death if a continuing supply of the toxicant is fed to the cell.

These reversible reactions, inhibiting only as long as the toxicant is present, exemplify fungistasis or bacteriostasis. Whether or not a toxic reaction is reversible, will depend =largely on the type of bonds formed between toxicant and vital -component. Albert (1951) summarizes bonds of importance -in biology and gives their usual bond strengths.

The *van der Waal's bond* is a weak bond (about 0.5 kilocalories) which may occur when any two atoms or two different molecules approach each other. Atoms must be able to approach each other very closely if they are to be firmly bound by van der Waals' bonds.

Although a single one of these bonds is weak, there may be many of them between molecules of toxicants and vital constituents. The formation of many van der Waals' bonds is more likely to occur between molecules which can fit close together because of their molecular configurations.

The hydrogen bond, with a strength of 2 to 5 kilocalories, is fairly common in biology. In biological systems the hydrogen bond donors are usually the groups $\equiv N^{+}$ —H, =N—H, or—O—H. The hydrogen bond accepts oxygen or nitrogen, atoms, or sometimes chloride ions.

The hydrogen bond is apparently made by resonance between two structures where hydrogen is attached to one or the other of the atoms which it joins. There is supposedly no actual oscillation, but the distribution of electrons is intermediate between the two forms [A—H B] and [AH—B] and is represented by [A—B].

The hydrogen bond is stable, because the energy of the mesomeric state is less than that of either of the other structures. *Ionic bonds*, with a usual strength of about 5 kilocalories, form between oppositely charged ions. This is the bond of salt formation.

By far the strongest is the *covalent bond* with bond strengths of from 40 to 100 kilocalories. This bond, in which combining atoms each contribute one shared electron, makes for essentially irreversible combinations between toxic molecules and vital components.

Such reactions as alkylation, acylation, or halogenation are most likely to cause irreversihle poisoning. For example, Burchfield and Storrs (1956) suggest that 2, 4dichloro-6 (o-chloroanilino)-s-triazine may be so effective as a fungitoxicant because it alkylates amino acids.

Factors other than bond strength are also important in toxicity by direct chemical interaction. One of these factors is reaction rate. Burchfield and Storrs (1957) studied the importance of reaction rate in the activity of toxicants.

Specifically, they investigated the kinetics of reaction ***in*** *vitro* between toxicants and vital constituents of cells. Although two toxicants may possibly react with the same group of a vital constituent, the ease and speed with which the reaction occurs may well decide whether the reaction is important to the toxicity of one compound and not the other.

Some of the factors discussed were energies of activation, frequency factors, degree of solvation of a reactive halogen, and the degree of dissociation of the substrate. l-Fluoro-2, 4-dinitro-benzene was found to be a more highly specific reagent for sulfhydryl groups than is 2, 4-dichloro-6 (o-chloroanilino)-s-triazine.

Conversely, the s-triazine is highly reactive with organic amines and phenols, while the 1-fluoro-2, 4-dinitrobenzene is not. This latter difference is apparently related to the low dissociation constants of organic amines and phenols important to the growth of the organism.

Lukens and Sisler (1958) suggest that the toxicity of captan is related to double decomposition reaction of captan with sulphydryl containing components of the cell. Here again, whether or not a compound will react in a certain way is not enough to make it a toxicant.

The rate of reaction must be sufficiently fast to be effective. For example, if captan is toxic because of the reaction of —S—C(Cl)$_s$ with essential sulphydryl groups, then the rest of the molecule may decide the toxicity of the compound as, a whole.

The phthalimide moiety of captan bas carbonyl groups on each side of the N. These electron attracting groups weaken the N - S bond. If these electronegative groups were not present, or not in conjugation with the N, the resulting N-S linkage would be much more stable.

The reaction rates would be slowed down and toxicity would be lessened. For example, our data show that N-trichloromethylthiocarbazole is much more stable than captan and also practically nonfungitoxic.

The heavy metals, such as silver and mercury, combine readily and firmly with sulphydryl groups. Without question, $_{tt}$his property contributes to their toxicity. Certain well-known specific reagents for sulphydryl groups, such as iodoacetamide, are also toxic.

Not only are metals toxic because they may combine readily and firmly with cellular constituents, but also other molecules, may be toxic because they combine with metals which are necessary to life. This latter mechanism has been proposed for chelating agents.

Binding metals is presumably the action of azide and cyanide. Bisulfite, toxic to many organisms, is known to combine with pyruvate. This combination would inhibit the decarboxylation of pyruvate, essential to organic acid metabolism.

The α, β-unsaturated ketones, including quinones, form addition products with thiols and amino compounds. This pro perty has been suggested as a basis for toxicity. There are, then, a number of direct reactions between, foreign molecules and cellular components which may lead to toxicity.

EFFECTS ON ENZYME SYSTEMS

One of the most popular areas of research on toxicants has been the study of their effects on enzyme systems. The primary reason for this has been the need to explain the profound effects produced by the application of extremely low dosages of toxicants.

A most reasonable explanation is the assumption that the toxicants hit the organisms in a vital link in their metabolic chain. The many enzymes needed by organisms to change raw food materials into energy and living substance loom large as potential targets.

These organic catalysts are not only themselves susceptible to inactivation, but also the processes they perform may be so altered as to result in toxicity. When these effects are described, therefore, they are presented in terms of effects on enzyme systems.

Enzyme Inhihition

The three principal kinds of inhibition of enzyme systems are termed competitive, noncompetitive, and uncompetitive. Competitive inhibitors presumably poison by so closely resembling vital substrate that they are taken up by the enzymes which normally work on these substrates.

The inhibitor molecules, however, differ sufficiently from the normal suhstrate molecules so that they cannot be changed by the enzymes into nutrilites needed by the cell to survive. The insertion of these ill-fitting keys into the active sites on the enzyme exclude the required substrate. The competition between the essential molecules and the imposter molecules for enzyme sites is in proportion to the ratio of the two competing molecules in the system.

In other words, the degree of enzyme inhibition is proportional to the ratio of substrate to inhibitor. The more substrate, the more inhibitor required for the same degree of inhibition, and *vice versa.*

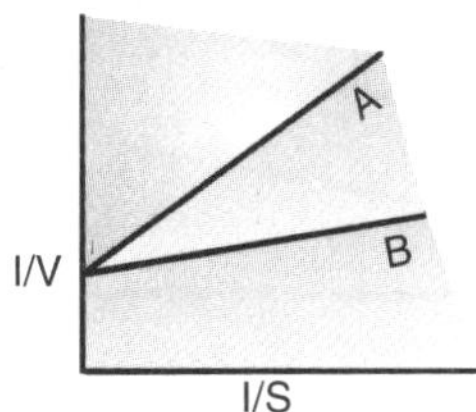

Figure 9.1: Lineweaver-Burk plot for competitive inhibition.

The classic Lineweaver-Burk (1934) plots of enzyme kinetics compare the reciprocal of substrate concentration S to the reciprocal of the observed reaction rate *v*. Figure elsewhere in this chapter represents a typical plot for a case of competitive inhibition.

The slope V of the inhibited line (a) is much steeper than the slope of the noninbibited line (b). The intercepts with the ordinate, however, are identical.

Equation 1 describes the steady state for competitive inhibition. At steady state V= maximum velocity when the enzymesubstrate combination is maximum.

$$\mathrm{v} = \frac{V}{I + K_s\left[I + (I)/K_i\right]/S} \tag{1}$$

K_s= Michaelis constant, which is the substrate concentration at which half maximum velocity is reached.

I = Concentration of inhibitor.

S = Concentration of substrate.

K_i= Constant for dissociation of enzyme-inhibitor combination into enzyme and inhibitor.

As S is increased it affects both K, and V. When S is sufficiently large, inhibition is completely overcome, and the intercept at sufficient value of S becomes identical with that of no inhibitor.

The slopes of the two systems, one with and the other without inhibitor, differ by the function (I+(I)/K_i]. Nonco-

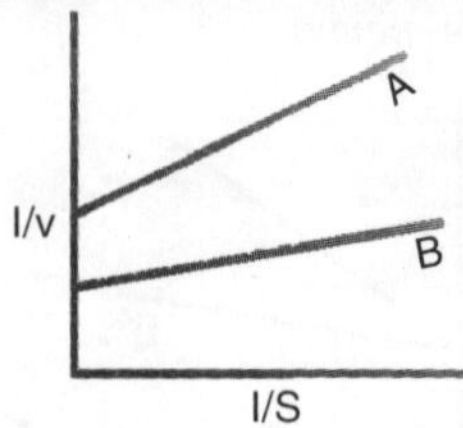

Figure 9.2: Lineweaver-Bark plot for noncompetitive inhibition.

mpetitive inhibition applies to the case where the inhibitor combines with the enzyme at a point other than the site at which the substrate attaches.

There are two other requirements for this type of inhibition: (a) the inhibitor exerts a total inhibitory effect; and (b) the binding of inhibitor to enzyme is independent of substrate. Under these conditions, the Lineweaver-Burk plot shows lines differing in both slope and intercept.

Equation 2 describes such a system.

$$\mathrm{v} = \frac{V}{[I + K_s/S][I + (I)/K_i]} \tag{2}$$

Here, as **in** the preceding equation, the slope of V is still influenced by the inhibitor function, so that the slope of the inhibited system varies from the slope of the noninhibited system by $[I+(I)/K_i]$. It differs, however, by not having, the inhibitor function modified by substrate concentration.

Hence, at the intercept, the lines are separated by $[I+(I)/K_i]$. In other words, the reaction rate of a system noncompetitively inhibited can never attain the rate of the noninhibited system, regardless of the amount of substrate added.

Uncompetitive inhibition requires that the inhibitor combine only with the enzyme-substrate complex. In these circumstances, the Lineweaver-Burk plot shows parallel slopes for the two systems, and of necessity, different intercepts.

Equation 3 describes uncompetitive inhibition,

$$v = \frac{V/\left[I+(I)/K_{\mathrm{i}}\right]}{I+K_{\mathrm{s}}\left[I+(I)/K_{\mathrm{i}}\right]/S} \tag{3}$$

Other special cases include inhibition by a partial inhibitor, and inhibition by one of the products of the normal substrate with enzyme.

What does all this mean in terms of in vivo toxic effects? The great interest in competitive inhibitors as a toxic mechanism stems from the classic research of Woods (1940), who demonstrated that sulphanilamide is a competitive inhibitor of *p*-aminobenzoic acid.

Not until after Woods report was *p*-aminobenzoic acid found to be an essential metabolite. Since that time, whenever a toxicant is found which bears a structural resemblance to a vital substrate, competitive inhibition is invoked.

Actually, proven cases of competitive inhibition as a fungitoxio mechanism are not too common. West and Wolf (1955) present strong evidence that 2-beptadecyl-2-imidazoline is a competitive antagonist for guanine and xanthine in *Sclerotinia fructicola*.

Because a compound may act as a competitive inhibitor on one organism is no reason to believe that it acts as such in another. Usually, competitive inhibition is most striking in those cases where the organism is heterotrophic for the particular metabolite being antagonized.

A very striking example of the complexity of enzyme inhibition as a toxic mechanism is described by Woolley and Shaw (1951). They found that 2-azaadenine is particularly lethal to *Lactobacillus* species.

They tested the purines, hypoxanthine, adenine, and xanthine as possible metabolites being antagonized, with the following results. 2-Azaadenine competitively inhibits hypoxanthine.

Its toxicity is largely overcome by trace amounts of adenine, but is not appreciably alleviated by large amounts of xanthine. Without the inhibitors, xanthine is as effective as hypoxanthine in the purine nutrition of these bacteria.

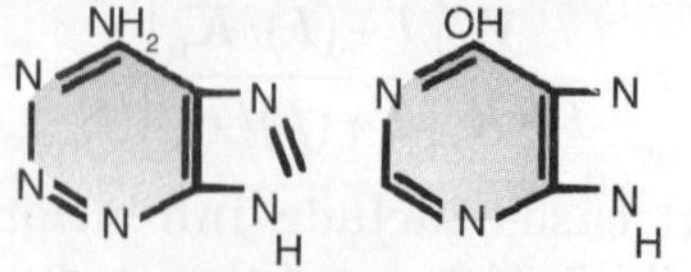

2-azaadenine–hypoxanthine

Figure 9.3: Hypoxanthine (right) and its antimetabolite, 2-Azaadenine (left).

From their results, it becomes obvious that 2-azaadenine is highly specific in its effects on *Ladobacilli.* It is not simply a competitive inhibitor of parines as a class, but of one purine in particular, hypoxanthine.

Their experiment again serves to illustrate the physiological implications that may result from toxicological studies. Their results indicate that the chain of nucleoside synthesis in *Lactobacillus* goes from xanthine → hypoxanthine → adenine.

If 2-azaadenine breaks the chain at hypoxanthine, the addition of more xanthine could have little effect. The addition of adenine, however, would be beyond the block and nucleic acid synthesis could continue. Noncompetitive inhibition as a toxic mechanism may be postulated for almost any toxicant which can denature proteins.

For example. picric acid, a protein precipitant, is quite fungi—toxic and may act by denaturing proteins. The same may be-said for formaldehyde. Any of the amino acid reagents shown to be fungitoxic by Horsfall and Zentmyer (1944) may be acting, as noncompetitive inhibitors. Uncompetitive inhibition has not been postulated as a toxic mechanism for any one particular known toxicant.

This type of inhibition must surely contribute to the toxicity of some, poisons. Many known fungitoxicants probably act as nonspecific enzyme inhibitors. The enzyme proteins may lose their activity if the attacking toxic molecule has a particular avidity for, or ability to react with any of the reactive groups on the protein.

The susceptibility of enzymes may be realized when we consider the number of reactive sites possessed by amino acids which make up the proteins. Some of these reactive sites are primary, amino groups (—NH_2), alcohol groups intermediate between aliphatic and aromatic (the —OH of hydroxyproline), the imino group (=NH), the acid amide group (—$CONH_2$), the sulphydryl group (—SH), the a-hydrogen of tryptophan, and the guanidine nucleus.

The —OH groups of hydroxy amino acids may be of particular importance as susceptible sites because they combine with phosphoric acid to bridge polypeptide chains. There are other toxic mechanisms closely related to enzyme inhibition which may well be discussed here.

One of these, a variation on the theme of competitive inhibition, is a phenomenon classified by Markham (1958) as a type of "lethal synthesis." In this particular mechanism, the imposter molecules are so like the normal substrate molecules that the toxicants move along the chain of synthesis and are actually incorporated into the final building blocks of living substance.

Thebuilding blocks containing these imposter molecules are defective and cannot be utilized in a normal fashion by the organism. The organism shows toxic effects as a consequence.

Heinrich *et al.* (1952) found that the protozoan *Tetrahymena gelen*, which is readily poisoned by 8-azaguanine, incorporates this aminopurine into its ribonucleic acid when grown on sublethal doses of the toxicant. The toxic effect of 8-azaguanine is readily overcome by the simultaneous addition of the nucleo side, guanosine.

Another example of this type is reported by Dunn and Smith (1957). They found that *Escherichia cola* made sensitive to poisoning by 5-bromouracil incorporates this halogenated pyrimidine into its deoxy-ribonucleic acid.

The toxic effect of this compound cannot be overcome by the addition of thymine for which it is known to be an antimetabolite. *E. colt* is not inhibited by 5-bromouracil nor does it incorporate it unless the bacteria are made to require thymine by treatment with *sulphanil-amide*.

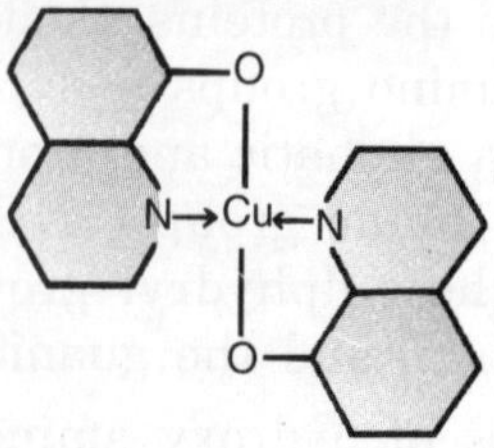

Figure 9.4: 8-Quinolinol combining with copper. An example of bidentate ligands.

To call this type of toxicity a form of competitive inhibition may not be strictly proper, as it may or may not be reversible. It is quite apparent, however, that in these cases there must be competition between normal substrate and imposter.

Once the imposter molecules become incorporated into the nucleic acids the toxic molecules may or may not be replaceable.

Enzyme Stimulation

Not only may toxicants act by inhibiting enzymes, but they may also act by overstimulating enzymes. Such overstimulation may throw the normal cellular physiology completely out of balance. This abnormal unbalance may be analogous to an overdose of insulin in humans.

Byrde *et al.* (1956), with *in vitro* studies of enzymes from *Monilinia laxa,* showed that -copper greatly stimulates the activity of DPN oxidase, while o-phenylpheaol greatly stimulates cytochrome c oxidase.

Mahler *et al.* (1955) suggest a plan to explain the burst of molecular oxygen released from systems containing metalloflavoprotein enzymes (EF-Fe) when they are acted upon by quinones. Normally the electron transfer goes DPNH→EF-Fe→Cytochrome c.

With quinone in the system, the electrons may be diverted completely from EF-Fe to molecular oxygen rather than cytochrome c, thus uncoupling all subsequent phosphorylations.

CHELATION

Before presenting chelation as, a toxic mechanism it would]be well to know something about chelates. Chelates are cyclic structures formed by the union of metallic atoms with inorganic or organic molecules or ions.

The term comes from *chela,* the Greek name for crab's claw. One molecule of the nonmetallic portion of the complex is called a ligand. Compounds which chelate must be able to combine at more than one point with metals. A simple 2 point, orbidentate, ligand is pictured in Figure elsewhere in this chapter. Each 8-quinolinol. molecule is a ligand.

Note that the metal is combined with each ligand by two bonds : (a) an ionic bond, and (b) a coordinate bond. In a coordinate bond, both of the electrons shared by the combining atoms come from only one of the atoms, nitrogen in this case.

Other chelates are known in which all the bonds between ligands and metal are coordinate, without any ionic bonding. It is the multiple bonding feature of chelation which gives chelators their most interesting property.

This property is the formation of an extremely stable complex which can holdmetals so tightly that they are released or exchanged only with great difficulty. The formation of chelate compounds is usually accompanied by colour formation and the loss of polar properties by the ligand molecules.

As the atoms on the ligand which combine with metals are usually nitrogen, oxygen, or sulphur, it is quite apparent why polar properties are lost. Whether or not the complex remains water-soluble depends on whether or not theligand has polar groups not involved in chelation. For example, copper 8-quinolinolate is quite insoluble in water, while copper 8-quinolinol-5-sulphonate is water-soluble.

The smaller chelated cyclic structures are considered to be coplanar. According to the Baeyer strain theory, these, like other organic cyclic compounds, would be most stable when there are 5 or 6 atoms in each ring. Chelate cycles with less than 4 atoms or more than 7 atoms are known, but they are uncommon and usually unstable.

Because of certain peculiarities of chelate rings, 4-membered structures are more common and more stable than 4-membered carbon rings. The probability of a compound being a chelator is highest if it has 2 electron-sharing atoms separated by 2 or 3 other atoms.

In the union of ligand with metal, the ligand is considered to be the electron-pair donor, or base, while the metal is the acceptor, or acid. All other things being equal, the greater the basic strength of the ligand, the more stable the chelate complexes it can form.

What properties of the metal influence the stability of the .complex? Irving and Williams (1953) present the following three features as being the most important metallic properties in chelation: (a) valence, (b) the ionic radius, and (c) the degree of ionization.

The higher the cationic valence the more stable the complex. For example, Fe^{+++} complexes are much more stable than Fe^{++} complexes.

The larger the ionic radius the less stable the complex. Mn^{++} has a much larger ionic radius than Cu^{++} and usually forms less stable chelates.

Other things being equal, chelate stability is directly correlated with the second ionization potentials of the metals.

Chelating compounds are both common and important in biology. Among them are organic acids, amino acids, enzymes, vitamins, hemoglobin, and chlorophyll.

Chelation as a toxic mechanism has been a subject of active research and debate since it was first proposed by Zentmyer .for fungi (1943) and by Albert for bacteria (1944).

Zentmyer (1944) showed that the toxicity of the powerful chelator 8-quinolinol (oxine) to the fungus can be overcome by the addition of excess zinc to the growth medium.

Furthermore, reducing the pH of the medium to an acidity at which oxine cannot chelate, also destroyed its fungitoxicity.

On this evidence, Zentmyer related the fungitoxicity of oxine to its ability to chelate, and proposed that oxine poisons by robbing the organism of required trace metals. Albert and his group were also able to destroy the antibacterial action of oxine by the addition of excess metal, iron in this case.

In addition, they found that isomers or analogues of oxine able to chelate, were also antibacterial. Those related compounds unable to helate, e.g., 2-quinolinol, were not antibacterial. Soon, however, the metal-robbing theory was seriously questioned by Mason (1948) who showed that copper oxinate is more fungitoxic than the unchelated oxine.

This was particularly damaging to the theory of metal-robbing. Since the -copper chelate is one of the most stable of oxinates, it would not be expected to chelate other trace metals. Albert and his group found that oxine is not antibacterial unless iron is present in trace amounts. It must be made clear here that chelation as a toxic mechanism was not questioned.

In doubt was only the theory that the toxicity of oxine derives from metal-robbing. It is ironic that the metal robbing theory of toxicity should have been based on oxine which may or may not work in that way.

There is not much doubt that chelators may exert their toxicity by metal-robbing. For example, Rich .and Horsfall (1948) have shown that dimethylglyoxime will produce trace

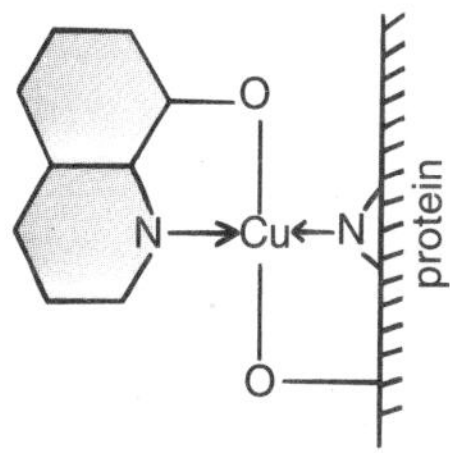

Figure 9.5: Half chelate blocking functional groups.

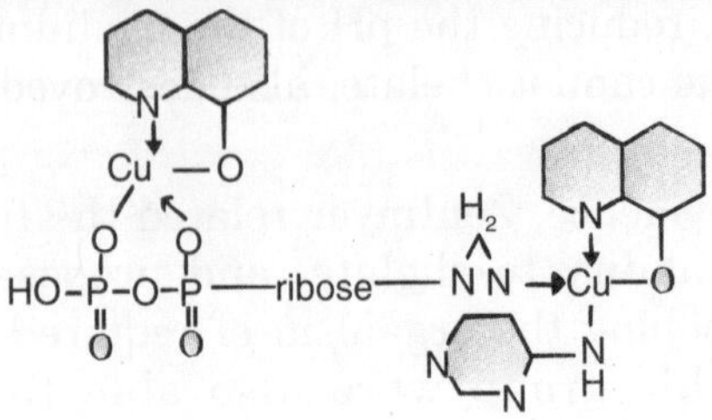

Figure 9.6: Half chelate blocking ADP.

metal deficiency symptoms in *Aspergillus niger*. On dimethylglyoxime, the fungus grows in curds, rather than .in a normal mat, and sporulation is poor or absent.

In what other way may chelators or chelate compounds ;poison ? Albert and others have suggested that the poisonous Form of oxine is the half chelate. Goksoyr (1955) also proposes the half chelate as the toxic species of dithiocarbamates.

If this is so, then the half chelates may be poisoning by blocking functional groups. For example, an amino group and hydroxyl group properly spaced on the surface of an enzyme protein would form a mixed chelate with the half chelated toxicants.

This is illustrated in Figure elsewhere in this chapter. The same effect could be had with a sulphydryl group in. place of the amino or hydroxyl group. Another type of functional group blocking would be the formation of mixed chelates with the phosphoric acid or nitrogen base portions of nucleotides.

This may be illustrated with copper oxinate and adenosine-5'-diphosphate (ADP). So much for chelators and their possible toxic mechanisms. The fascinating stories of oxine and dithiocarbamates as toxicants will be described in detail in a later section.

SELECTIVE SOLUBILITY

Toxic compounds may act by selective solubility. Ferguson (1939) has shown that the insecticidal value of many chemically "inert" materials, such as saturated hydrocarbons, is. correlated with their relative solubility in the medium in which they are applied.

He pointed out that the partition of these compounds between the ambient medium and the biophase will be proportional to the degree of saturation of the ambient medium.

In other words, the less soluble the toxicant in the applying medium, the greater the saturation of that medium and the greater the proportion entering the biophase. The degree of toxicity of these structurally nonspecific compounds is directly proportional to their saturation of the medium in which they are applied.

For example, nonspecific compounds X, Y, and Z may require respectively 1000 p.p.m.,. 100 p.p.m., and I p.p.m. to half-saturate the medium in which they are applied, whether it be water or air. These dosages should approximate half the maximum toxicity possible for treating organisms with compounds X, Y, and Z.

Ferguson was able to use this effect to explain another situation common in toxicity studies. Very often in comparing homologues of a toxic molecule, toxicity increases as the alkyl side chain lengthens. This continues until the addition of one more methyl group makes that homologue almost nontoxic.

Ferguson suggests that the final methyl group would make the compound so insoluble in the applying fluid, that the amount required for complete saturation would partition less than a toxic dose into the biophase. This cut-off point will vary with compounds, applying medium, and tissue poisoned.

Ross and Ludwig (1957) have presented evidence that thefungi-toxicity of the N-n-alkylethylenethioureas follows the Ferguson effect. All this is interesting and useful, but does not explain how supposedly "inert, non-specific" compounds can poison. There are at least two possibilities.

The first is a solvent effect. If the inert molecules partially replace and force apart the biophase molecules, metabolic reaction rates could be altered enormously. Taking a test-tube .example from organic chemistry, the reaction of ethyl iodide with triethylamine is only 1/1000 times as fast in hexane ass it, is in benzyl alcohol.

The nonspecific toxicants could slow down vital reaction rates by reducing the frequency with which substrate Molecules must collide with enzyme molecules essential for continuing normal, processes.

The second way in which nonspecific toxicants may act is by altering the colloidal structure of the semipermeable membanes of the cell.

Many of these, toxicants, have a particular avidity for the lipoproteins of the cellular membranes. They are also known to exert, cellular narcosis, allowing cellular contents to leak from the cell.

The most likely way that these compounds could do this is by affecting the structure of the hydrophilic colloids making up; the semipermeable memnes.

DISSOLUTION

Toxicants may act by dissolving cellular components necessary to the physical structure of the cell. A good example is lysozyme, an antibiotic enzyme discovered by Fleming (1922) in mucous secretions. Lysozyme is a mucopolysaecharide depolymerase.

It is capable of completely dissolving the cell walls off bacteria. Commercial lysozyme, prepared from egg whites, is assayed by its ability to dissolve suspensions of the bacterium *Micrococcus lysodeikricus.* The end-product of lysozyme activity is N-acetylglucosamine.

There is no increase in reducing groups. Lysozyme has been found in many bacteria, including those susceptible to its activity. It also occurs in *Ficus latex* and in commercial papain.

Rich has found that lysozyme, with no apparent effect on spore walls, will lyse the germ tubes of *Stemphylium sarcinaeforme,* allowing the cellular contents to escape. Rich also found that sodium hypochlorite causes the separation of the cells of this multicelled spore.

Carter and Lockwood (1957) described the lysis of the mycelium of *Glomerella cingulata* by a diffusate from *Streptomyces* sp. They also report the lysis of *G. cingulata* mycelium by antibiotics such as mycostatin and thiolutin, and by fungi—tides such as ferbam, thiram, and zineb. The latter effect they ascribe to a hastening of autolysis of the poisoned mycelium, rather than a direct dissolution of the mycelium by the fungicide.

A material may not cause a complete dissolution of cell wall, but may in cad have a partial effect on its rigidity. Griscofulvim may sat in this fashion.

This antibiotic was found to be the "curling factor" produced by Penicillium *janczewskii.* It causes a spiral growth of. the germ tubes of *Botrytis ails*and other fungi. This abnormality of the germ tubes apparently prevents the organismifrom developing mycelium.

PRECIPITATION

Precipitation, the opposite of dissolution, may poison either '·by making metabolites unavailable or by destroying colloidal structure. Polysulfides, present in lime sulphur, may produce their poisonous effect by precipitating essential metals and so making them unavailable. *Aspergillus niger,* grown in the presence of potassium sulfide, will produce yellow, rather than black, spores.

This is a symptom of metal deficiency. Hydroxides or carbonates may also produce this effect. Precipitation or coagulation of hydrophobic colloids, such as proteins, would also have a profound effect on normal cellular processes. The ability of a compound to bring about coagulation will depend on two things.

First, the power to neutralize the charge on the dispersed phase, or the lowering of the zeta potential and, second, the ability of the coagulant to take the stabilizing hydration water from the dispersed particles.

The ability to neutralize charges will depend on the valency of the ion charge oppositely to that of the dispersed phase. For example, if a protein so] is at a pH on the alkaline side of its isoelectric point, the dispersed phase will be negatively charged.

The ability of the coagulant to reduce the charge on the protein micelle will be directly related to the valency of the cation of the coagulant. Actually, very small amounts of oppositely charged ions may cause a large drop in the zeta potential.

The hydrophilic colloid map increase in viscosity as its charge is neutralized, but coagulation is prevented by the - stabilizing effect of the hydrated shells around each micelle.

The final phase of coagulation depends on the ability of the toxicant to dehydrate. This ability to take water from the particles usually follows the lyotropic series. For the effect of anions to precipitate proteins, this series is usually shown as follows : citrate > tartrate > SO_4 > acetate > CI > NO_3 > Br > I > CNS. Citrate shows the greatest effect and thiocyanate the least. This series for cations is, Th > Al > H > Sr > Ca > K > Na > Li. Ethanol and formaldehyde are two other toxicants which may act as protein coagulants.

HYDROLYSIS

Acids or bases may poison by hydrolysis. Hydrolysis is the breaking of the reacting molecule and the combination of the pieces with H^- and OH^- from water.

From the viewpoint of toxicity, proteins are probably the most important biological compounds which may be hydrolyzed. Hydrolysis would, of course, be a denaturing process,. particularly disruptive to enzymes.

When enzymes are hydrolyzed, the most profound effect is the breaking of peptide linkages which join amino acids to make the peptide chains of which proteins are built (Equation 4).

$$H_2N-R-\overset{\overset{O}{||}}{C}-N-R'-\overset{\overset{O}{||}}{C}-OH + H_2O \xrightarrow[\text{base}]{\text{acid cr}} H_2N-R-\overset{\overset{O}{||}}{C}-OH + H_2N-R'-\overset{\overset{O}{||}}{C}-OH \quad (4)$$

Mandels (1953) used weak acid treatment to destroy the .activity of enzymes presumably located at or near the surface of *Myrothecium* spores. Blood (1937) suggested that the acid production by fermen·ting tomato pulp is responsible for the elimination of *Corny-bacterium michiganense* from tomato seed. He showed that soaking infested seed in acetic or lactic acid does as well as the fermentation process.

Tyner (1951) made the surprising discovery that merely soaking barley seed in water for a period of time can control loose smut. An investigation of this phenomenon by Leben *et. al.* (1956), and Jacquet *et. al.* (1957) showed that the control is achieved by organic acids. These organic acids, acetic, 'butyric, and formic, produced by bacteria operating during the water soaking, are the actual toxicants.

OXIDATION-REDUCTION

Oxidation-reduction changes, in order to cause any real damage to cells, must be drastic rather than mild. Living cells usually have too large a capacity to equilibrate changes in oxidation-reduction to expect any lasting toxicity from mild changes. Calcium hypochlorite, a strong oxidant, is very toxic. Whether or not it acts on a specific system is not important.

It is probably nonspecific by virtue of its capacity to oxidize strongly many vital components within the cell. Ozone, another strong oxidant, is toxic to many types of cells. Its production by ultraviolet radiation may account in part for the deleterious effects of UV light.

Such systems as $Cu^{++} \rightleftharpoons Cu^{+}$ may be poisonous by virtue of their oxidant action. For example, Albert (1952) reported that Cu^{++} reacts rapidly with cysteine to give cystine and cuprous cysteinate. Other toxic oxidizing agents are SO_S, H_2O_2, potassium permanganate, sodium perborate, and sodium dichromate. As will be discussed later, elemental sulphur may poison by acting as an oxidant.

Horsfall (1945) suggested that the dinitrophenols are toxic because they can oxidize and so split unsaturated fatty acids.

Dinitrophenols are very effective against powdery mildews. Horsfall later (1956) proposed that these compounds kill conidia of powdery mildew by destroying the fatty envelope that retains the water these spores need to survive. The spores then die by desiccation.

Hydrogen sulfide is a powerful reducing agent particularly toxic to cells. It may act not only by precipitating metals, but also by holding them in a reduced state.

Oxidation-reduction systems may show definite antibacterial action not shown by either component of the system. Guest and Salle (1942) found that a combination of Fe Cl_2 with either Fe Cl_2 or Fe_2 $(SO_4)_3$ is much more antibacterial than any of these compounds used separately.

This was also true of $SnCl_2$with Sn Cl_4, Fe $C1_2$ with Sn Cl_4, Sn $Cl_2$with Fe Cl_2, Mn SO_4 with Sn Cl_4, and Mn SO_4 with Fe_2 $(SO_4)_3$. These heavy metal salts were most toxic when mixed in certain proportions. The increase in toxicity required that the mixture had one metal at a higher oxidation state than the other. Only the salts of heavy metals gave this effect.

SURFACE ACTIVITY

Surface activity is a property of any substance whose presence in small amounts greatly alters the surface behaviour of a given system. "Greatly alters" is rather a loose term, as most solutes will alter the surface behaviour of the solvent to some extent. Although there are water insoluble surfactants, we will be concerned with water-soluble organic compounds that markedly lower the surface tension of the liquid system in which they are dissolved.

The most common of these surfactants is, of course, soap. A burgeoning chemical industry has produced a great number of synthetic surfactants that have found uses in all phases of our daily life. What are the molecular properties that make a surfactant ? Basically, a surfactant molecule is a long molecule, one end polar and the other end nonpolar.

The polar end has an affinity for polar substances, such as water, while the nonpolar end has an affinity for nonpolar substances, such as grease, fats, and oils.

When surfactant-containing water is applied to grease particles, the nonpolar end of the surfactant molecules is adsorbed by the grease. Since the polar end will not dissolve in the grease, the surfactant molecules stay at the surface.

The surface-located polar ends having an affinity for water give the grease particle a miscibility with water. This allows the grease particles to become suspended in water, or emulsified, and so removed.

Surfactants lower the surface tension of water because the nonpolar ends of the surfactant molecules are forced out of water, and are concentrated and arranged linearly at right angles to the surface of the liquid, the polar end toward the liquid and the nonpolar end forced away from the liquid.

Thesurface then acquires primarily the nonpolar properties of the surfactant. As the attraction between surfactant molecules is. much less than the attraction of one water molecale for another water molecule, the surface tension is lowered.

The reason, why only a small amount of surfactant is required is that it is forced to the liquidair or aid-solid interface and all that is requiredfor maximum effect is a unimolecular layer of the surfactant molecules at the “interface.

There are three kinds of surfactants, anionic, cationic, and nonionic. The ionic surfactants ionize or dissociate into two parts, a large fatty radical and a small salt radical. If the charge in the fatty radical is negative, the compound is anionic.

For example, a soap dissociates into $C_{17}H_{25}COO$ and Na^+, typical, of an anionic-surfactant. If the charge on the large radical is positive, the compound is classed as cationic. *Cetylpyridinium chloride* ionizes into making it a cationic surfactant. Nonionic, or ampholyticsurfactants form zwitterions in solution. An example is cety-laninoacetic acid: $H_{32}C_{16}NH^+—COO^-$.

Soap is a weak germicide. Its primary value as a sanitizer is to remove germs physically rather than to kill them. The real interest in the toxic and germicidal effects of surfactants dates from the work of Domagk (1935) who found that some cationic surfactants are powerful antibacterial compounds.

Since then a number of quaternary ammonium compounds have been developed both as bactericides and fungicides. These have been principally alkylpyridinium halides and alkyl trimethylammonium halides. These cationic compounds are effective against both gram-positive and gram-negative bacteria and against fungi.

Schwartz *et. al.* (1958) list 43 different types of cationic surfactant germicides. Anionic surfactants are primarily active against grampositive bacteria. Examples of anionic surfactant toxicants are soaps and certain aliphatic carboxylic acids.

Nonionic surfactants usually have little or no germicidal action. Schwartz *et. al.* (1958) list the salts of *dioctylaminoethylglycine* as examples of nonionic germicidal *surfactants*. Surfactants appear to exert their toxic effects by breaking cross-links between polypeptide chains, or by disrupting colloidal structures.

The effect on polypeptide structures is evident in the report of Sreenivasaya and Pirie (1938) who found that the protein of tobacco mosaic virus is disintegrated by surfactants. Anson (1939) also found that surfactants could split proteins into much smaller molecular units.

The profound effect of surfactants on colloidal structure is noted in toxicity studies by a disruption of the semipermeable membranes allowing the leaking materials from the cell.

Horsfall (1956) discusses the importance of this as a toxic mechanism in both bacteria and fungi. Salton *et. al.* (1951) have taken electron micrographs of bacteria treated with cetyltrimethylam monium bromide and have observed *morphological* changes correlated with cell death.

Bacteria treated with 45 mg. of cetyltrimethylamm-onium bromide per 1.5 mg. dry weight of bacteria for 5 minutes show a pulling away of the cytoplasmic membrane from the cell wall.

This dosage of *cetyltrimethylam-monium* bromide just initiates leaking. The proportion of cells (30%) killed by this treatment is the same as the number of treated cells showing contracted cytoplasm. Treating the cells with 900 mg. *cetyltrimethylammonium bromide* per 1.5 mg. of bacteria for 30 minutes strips off the cell walls.

OSMOTIC PRESSURE CHANGES

Probably the oldest means of killing microorganisms is the preservation of foods with compounds that produce high osmotic pressures. Salting and sugaring are ancient means of preventing the growth of molds and bacteria on foods.

Although the effective dosages of these materials are very high, salt and sugar were usually close at hand. On a dosage basis, this toxic mechanism is very inefficient, and will probably not be of importance in the development of future fungicides.

There are probably other toxic mechanisms of importance, 'but those listed here undoubtedly include those of principal interest. It is entirely possible for a single toxicant to have more than one mode of action, one of which will be effective on one organism and another mode on a second organism.

One can picture highly reactive molecules, such as captan, passing into the cell and reacting with metabolites *en route*. Toxicity or death of the cell results when any vital link is broken.

METALS

Inorganic Fungitoxicants

The most widely used inorganic toxicants are metallic compounds. Of the metals used as fungitoxicants, copper, specifically Bordeaux mixture, has been used in the largest amounts.

Actually, in terms of minimum toxic dosages, inorganic metallic compounds are not nearly so toxic as a multitude of organic, nonmetallic toxicants. Even the organic metal complexes are more potent than the inorganic compounds containing the same metals.

According to Horsfall (1956), the descending order of fungitoxicity for the metal cations is approximately Ag>Hg> Cu > Cd > Cr>Ni>Pb>Co>Zn>Fe>Ca.

McCallan and Wilcoxon (1934) found also that osmium and ruthenium arequite fungitoxic. Aluminium and palladium are only slightly toxic, and rhodium and iridium are essentially nonfungitoxic.

McCallan and Wilcoxon (1934) studied the fungitoxicity of the elements in relation to their position on the periodic table. They generalized that toxicity within a group usually increased with increasing atomic weight.

The principal exceptions arc silver, much more toxic than gold, and chromium, usually more toxic than molybdenum and tungsten. A study of the periodic table shows that most toxic metals fall in groups I, II, and VIII. Horsfall (1956) pointed out the good correlation between the toxicity of metals and their ability to form stable chelate compounds. His comparison of chelate stability with the toxicity of the metals is given below.

Toxicity: Hg > Cu > Cd > Ni > Pb > Co > Za > Fe > Ca.

Chelate stability: Hg>Cu>Ni>Pb>Co>Zn>Cd>Fe>Mg.

Horsfall regards this as evidence that the primary toxic mechanisms of metals is their ability to combine with meta=bolites, enzymes, and proteins. Palladium and silver are two glaring exceptions to Horsfall's generalization. Palladium, only weakly toxic, forms very stable chelates, while silver, highly toxic, forms only weak chelates.

Shaw (1954) correlated toxicity with the insolubility of the metal sulphide. His diagrams show excellent correlations between the negative logarithm of lethal dose and the solubility product constants of the various metallic sulphides.

This correlation was. fairly consistent for the poisoning of diastase, urease, the para-mecium, a planarium *(Polycelis nigra),* or a fish (the stickleback). Shaw believes this is the result of the "thermodynamic affinity of the inhibitor [metallic cations] for key functional group in the enzyme's catalytically active site [sulphydryl] groups]."

Shaw, of course, was preceded by Fildes(1940) who showed that mercury toxicity could be alleviated by *suiphydryl*—containing compounds. Fildes suggested that mercury at low concentration acts by inactivating sulphydryl groups without other permanent injury to the cell.

British anti-Lewisite (2, 4-dimercaptopropanol) was developed specifically as an antidote for the arsenical war-gas Lewisite (Cl CH=CH.As Cl_2). The development of BAL was based on the discovery that arsenic poisons by knocking out sulphydryl groups.

Sulphydryl compounds will also reverse copper toxicity of peas and of fungus spores. Foster showed that three kinds of seeds susceptible to copper injury contain sulphydryl groups detectable with nitroprusside. Four kinds of seeds tolerant to copper contain no detectable sulphydryl groups.

Copper seed-treatments eliminated the detectable sulphydryl groups of the copper-sensitive seeds. Both Yoderand

Foster concluded that the sulphydryl groups poisoned were essential to the functioning of the respiratory enzymes.

Metallic compounds are often used as astringents in medicine. Astringency is the precipitation of proteins by high concentrations of metallic compounds. An obvious question is the relation of toxicity to the oxidation state of the metal. Apparently no generalization can be made concerning this point.

Cupric ions are fungitoxic, but cuprous oxide is more toxic than cupric oxide. Mercuric ions are usually more toxic than mercurous ions. No discussion of the toxicity of cations would be complete without including something about sorption. Are cations adsorbed at the periphery of the cell or are they absorbed freely into the interior?

Bodnar and Terenyi (1930) found that the uptake of copper by *Tilletta tritici* followed the Langmuir adsorption isotherm. Sussman and Lowry (1955)have strong evidence that dormant ascospores of *Neurospora* also adsorb cations.

McCallan (194x), working with copper sulfate on spores of *Alternaria oleraceae* and *Monilinia frueticola,* could not fit his data to Langmuir's isotherm. Miller *et al.* (1953) do not believe that silver and cerium are merely adsorbed. As evidence, they cite the enormous quantities of cations taken up by their fungus spores.

The number of cationic molecules taken up, if merely adsorbed, would form layers several molecules thick on the spore surface. In addition, a pretreatment with silver does not interfere with the uptake of cerium and *vice versa.*

Interference would be expected if uptake of these cations were strictly by adsorption. The work of Owens and Miller (1957) also points to penetration of cations into spores with practically no concentration on the cell walls. Rothstein and Hayes (1956), however, find that yeast cells bind both univalent and bivalent cations at the cell periphery.

The binding is rapid and reversible, with the bivalent ions being held more firmly than the univalent ions. They tentatively identify the binding sites as phosphoryl and carboxyl groups. These sites are apparently separated from the interior of the cell by a permeability barrier.

Rothstein and Hayes suggest that certain cations will have special affinities for specific binding groups on the cell surface : UO_2^{++} for carboxyl groups, Hg^{++} for sulfhydryl groups, and Zn^{++} for imidazole groups. The evidence, then, is contradictory, but can be resolved.

In organisms where there is a permeability barrier, adsorption is readily demonstrated. Where no permeability barrier exists or is destroyed by the toxicant, adsorption may play a role but is obscured by the free passage of cations into and out of the cell. Another factor which confounds the sorption picture is the effect of metabolites leaking from the cell. Miller and McCallan (1957) have shown that treating spores of *M. fructicola* with toxic doses of Ag r for as little as 1.2 minutes increases their outward loss of phosphorous compounds.

The loss of phosphorous compounds from these silver treated cells is 20 times that of the untreated spores. This mass of organic material capable of complexing will undoubtedly have a profound influence on the final location of cations on or in the spore.

NONMETALS

Sulphur

Of the nonmetals, elemental sulphur is the most important fungi-toxicant. In spite of its use as a pesticide for centuries, its method of toxic action is still a question for debate. Pollacci (1875) suggested that H_2S produced from sulphur is actually responsible for the fungitoxic action of sulphur.

Young (1922) proposed pentathionie acid as the toxic product from sulphur. Pentathionic acid results from the interaction of H2S and SO_2. The importance of pentathionic acid, SO_2, and SO_2 was largely discounted by Roach and Glynne and Wilcoxon and McCallan.

These workers found that the toxicity of these compounds is no more than could be accounted for by their hydrogen ion concentrations. McCallan and Wilcoxon found that sulphur-sensitive spores produced large amounts of H_2S from sulphur.

They reverted to Pollaccis idea that H2S, which they found to be enzymatically produced, was the cause of sulphur toxicity. When they again tested the HS theory, Miller *et al.* (1953) found that colloidal sulphur is as much as 50 times as toxic as H_2S to sulphur-sensitive fungi.

H_2S, they now believe, cannot be the toxic agent responsible for the toxicity of sulphur. They concluded that sulphur poisons because it is an active hydrogen acceptor and so interferes in normal hydrogenation reactions of the cell.

The intensity of HS production is a measure of the intensity of the hydrogenation process within the cell. The theory of sulphur poisoning by competing for hydrogen seems plausible, but is still open to question.

For example, methylene blue and ascorbic acid, both excellent hydrogen acceptors, are only weakly fungi-toxic Miller *et al.* (1953) use as supporting evidence the work of Sciarini and Nord (1943) who concluded that, in *Fusaria,* elemental sulphur competes for hydrogen freed by dehydrogenases.

Although Sciarini and. Nord present such a conclusion, it is not supported by their data. All of these ideas are possible. What Miller *et al.* (1953) Dave actually shown is that H_IS produced within the spore is more toxic than H_IS in the ambient fluid. This is not sufficient evidence to discard H_IS as the source of sulphur toxicity.

H_IS which. ionizes primarily as, HS^- may well. poison metal-activated compounds just as metals poison sulphydry1-activated compounds. Miller *et al.* (1953), also discount %S as a factor because they find the H_2S given off pretty well accounts for all the sulphur added to the system.

However, the amount of H_IS bound *in situ* by the microquantities of metals in the spore would be. so small, that it would be praetically undetectable. McCallan, and Miller: (1956), made the significant discovery that fungi in reducing sulphur release one mole of extra CO_2 for each mole of H_IS produced.

This contradicts Horsfall's (l955) suggestion tjat sulphur replaces oxygen in Krebs cycle intermediates. If. this were so, then there should be less CO_2 than, normal, rather than more.

The production of CO_2 also indicates that elemental sulphur is not Just cosseting for hydrogen. but appears to be acting as a strong oxidizing agent yin the process of being reduced.

Halogens

Halogenated inorganic compounds are another group of useful toxicants. The commonest inorganic halogen compounds used as germicides are calcium or sodium hypochlorite.

The toxicity of these compounds is directly correlated to the oxidizing power of their solutions. For example, Ridea land Evans (1921) showed that alkalinity which reduces the germicidal effect of hypochlorites also reduces their oxidizing power.

The strength of the hypochlorites is expressed as available chlorine, a measure of oxidizing power.

CaOCl reacts with water and CO_2 from the air as in Equation 5.

$$\begin{aligned} CaOCl + HCO_3^- &\rightarrow Ca \ \ HCO_3 \_ ClO^- \\ ClO^- &\rightarrow Cl^- + O \qquad \uparrow \end{aligned} \tag{5}$$

Chlorine evolved from acidification of CaOCI, will also oxidize -as in Equation 6.

$$\begin{aligned} Cl_2 + H_2O &\rightarrow HCl + HOCl \\ ClO^- &\rightarrow HCl + O \uparrow \end{aligned} \tag{6}$$

This is the method by which chlorine gas purifies water. Halogens may also act by halogenating metabolites, thus produc-ing antimetabolites *in situ*.

Formaldehyde

Formaldehyde (ECHO) is widely used as a soil fumigant. Its action is, primarily .as a protein denaturant. The combination of formaldehyde with amino acids, as in the classic Sorenson formal titration (Equation 7), is representative of the way formaldehyde may combine with and denature proteins.

$$\underset{\text{(Zwitterion)}}{+NH_3CH(R)COO^-} + HCHO \rightarrow CH_2O, NH_2CH(R)COO^- + H^+ \quad (7)$$

Ammonia Gas

Ammonia fumigation has recently been used successfully in -citrus storages for reducing fruit rots. Ammonia, highly soluble in water with which it forms NH_4OH, probably poisons fungi by drastic tic changes in, their internal pH.

ORGANIC FUNGITOXICANTS

Dithlocurbamates

The greatest number of useful organic fungitoxicants has come from the dithiocarbametes. These compounds all have in common the grouping.

```
       S
  |   ||
(—N—C—S—)
```

One series, based on the patent issued to Tisdale and Williams (1934), is made from the alkaline interaction of CS_2 and simple amines. These compounds are the dialkyldithiocarbamates and thiuram sulphides.

The second series, based on Hester's patent (1943), is made from the alkaline interaction of CS_2 and. ethylenediamine. These are the ethylene bisdithiocarbamates.

Dialkyldithiocarbamates and Thiuram Sulphides

The most widely used of these materials are zinc dimethyl *dithiocarbamate* (*ziram*), ferric *dimethyldithiocarbamate* (*ferbam*), and *tetramethyithiuram disulphide*

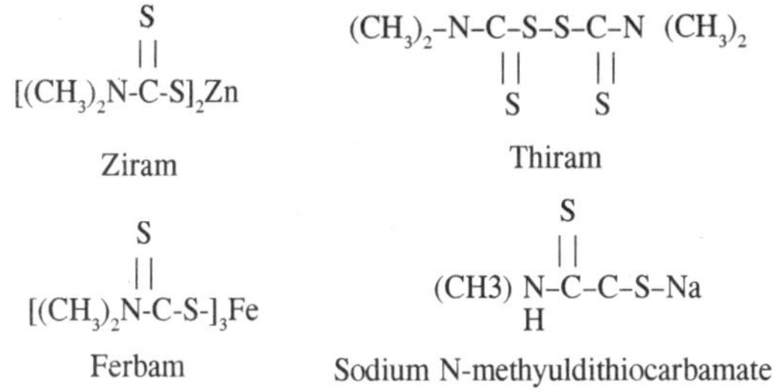

$$\begin{array}{c} S \\ || \\ [(CH_3)_2N\text{-}C\text{-}S]_2Zn \end{array} \qquad \begin{array}{c} (CH_3)_2\text{-}N\text{-}C\text{-}S\text{-}S\text{-}C\text{-}N\ (CH_3)_2 \\ ||\qquad || \\ S\qquad S \end{array}$$

Ziram Thiram

$$\begin{array}{c} S \\ || \\ [(CH_3)_2N\text{-}C\text{-}S\text{-}]_3Fe \end{array} \qquad \begin{array}{c} S \\ || \\ (CH3)\ N\text{-}C\text{-}C\text{-}S\text{-}Na \\ H \end{array}$$

Ferbam Sodium N-methyuldithiocarbamate

Figure 9.7: Structures of ziram, thiram, ferbam, and sodium-N.methyl—dithiocarbamate.

(thiram). Recently, another member of the family sodium N-methyldithio carbamate, has been finding use as a soil fungicide. The structures of these compounds are given in Figure elsewhere in this chapter.

The history of the development of these compounds and& their performance in the laboratory has been reviewed thoroughly by Mopping (1951), Horsfall (1956), and McCallan (1957).

The two most important clues to the toxic action of the dialkyl dithiocarbamates and the thiuram disulphides are (a) their formation of metal chelates and (b) their polymodal dosage response.

The first property is a well-known one, commonly used in analytical chemistry. The second was first reported by Dimond *et at.* (1941), for thiram. This latter effect, also called "inversion" and "quenching," is described in detail and logically explained by Goksoyr (1955). Inversion of toxicity is pictured in Figure elsewhere in this chapter.

The zone of inversion, where increasing dosage actually depresses toxicity, has been particularly band to explain. Goksoyr's explanation is as follows. The dimethyldithiocarbamate ion,

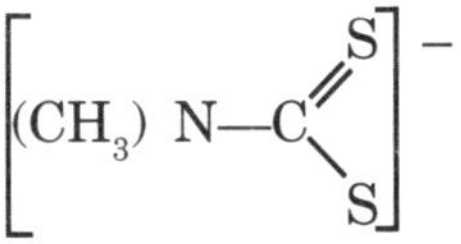

$$\left[(CH_3)\ N\text{—}C \begin{array}{l} /\!\!/ S \\ \backslash S \end{array} \right]^-$$

combines with minute traces of copper in the media to give the highly toxic 1 : 1, or half chelate,

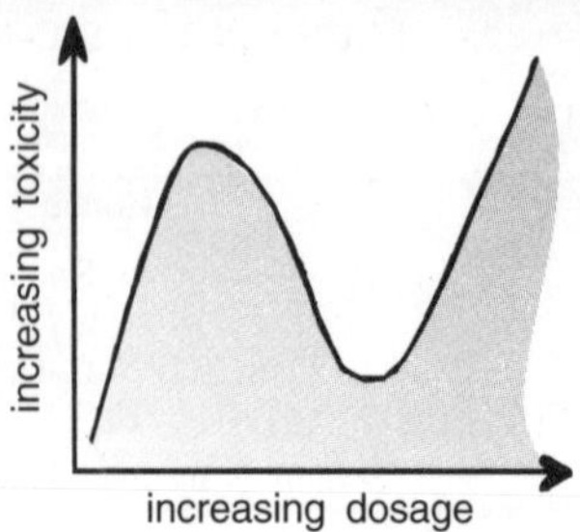

Figure 9.8: Polymodal dosage response curve, or inversion of toxicity.

$$\left[(CH_3)\ N{-}C{\genfrac{}{}{0pt}{}{\nearrow S}{\searrow S}}\right] Cu^+$$

This is the toxic species. As the amount of copper in the media is constant, the addition of more dithiocarbamate forms the less toxic 1 : 2, or full chelate,

$$\left[(CH_3)N{-}C{\genfrac{}{}{0pt}{}{\nearrow S}{\searrow S}}\right] Cu$$

Toxicity falls. As more dithiocarbamate is added, the intrinsic toxicity of the *dimethyldithiocarbamyl* ion exerts itself, acting perhaps by binding essential *metallic micronutrients*. Thus toxicity increases again. Goksoyr demonstrated that yeast cells reduce thiram to dimethyldithiocarbamyl ions.

Hence, thiram activity and its polymodal dosage response curve is identical to those of the dialkyldithiocarbamates. As will be seen later, *N-methyldithiocarbamate* has an action more like the *ethylenebisdithio carbamates* than like the *dialkyldithiocarbamates*.

Bisdithiocarbamates

This group of compounds arose around disodium ethylemebis (*dithiocarbamate*), now called nabam.

The history of their development and the laboratory results -of structure-activity studies are given in Barratt

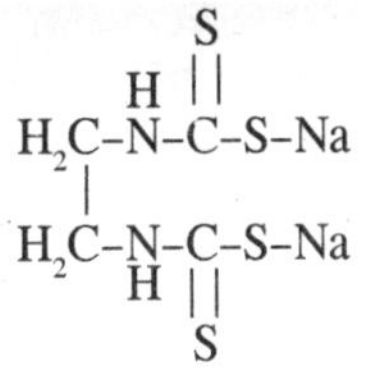

```
        S
      H ||
H2C–N–C–S–Na
  |
H2C–N–C–S–Na
      H ||
        S
```

Figure 9.9: Nabam.

and Horsfall (1947), and Klopping (1951). What is the basis for their activity? Barratt and Horsfall (1947) proposed that since these compounds readily release H_2S, they poison by means of the H_2S evolved. Rich and Horsfall (1950) demonstrated that H_2S could not account for the toxicity of nabam.

The clue to the currently accepted mechanism was noted in the title of the paper by Dimond *et al.* (1943), in the first report on nabam. They called it a "water-soluble fungicide with tenacity."

This anomaly puzzled them. In the data of Barratt and Horsfall appeared another clue. Zineb, the zinc salt of nabam, becomes more toxic upon aging. Klopping (1951) blazed the trail which led to the present theory.

Realizing that diisothiocyanates could form from bisdithiocarbamates, he tested the fungitoxicity of the diisothiocyanates. Klopping's biological tests showed that the *diisothiocyanates* have the same *biological spectrum* as the *bisdithiocarbamates*. By "*biological spectrum*" he meant that different fungi have the same relative susceptibility to both types of compounds.

In addition, the diisothiocyanates are much more toxic than the corresponding bisdithiocarbamates.

Klopping concluded that the ethylenebisdithiocarbamates act by releasing diisothiocyanates, which do the poisoning. The diisothiocyanates being extremely reactive and unstable, are hard to detect as breakdown products.

Shortly after, Ludwig and Thorn (1953) looking for insoluble (*tenacious*) compounds from the oxidation of nabam, found that *ethylenethiurammonosulphide* is a mojor

Table 9.1: Fungitoxicity Data from Klopping Illustrating Similarity between the "Biological Spectra" of Nabam and Ethylene Diisotbiocyanate.

	Minimum p p.m. completely inhibiting growth			
Compound	*B. cinerea*	*P. italicum*	*A. niger*	*R. nigricans*
Nabam	0.1	0.1	0.5	20.0
Ethylenediis-othiocyanate	0.05	0.02	0.05	10.0

product of nabam oxidation. They found that ethylenethiuram monosulphide is highly fungitoxic.

Ethylenethiuram monosulphide they concluded to be the toxic breakdown product accounting for both the tenacity and toxicity of nabam.

In a later paper, Ludwig *et al.* (1955) reported that metallic ions catalyze the formation of isothiocyanates from ethylenethiuram monosulphide. They could demonstrate this only in a nonaqueous medium (chloroform). In return, Sijpesteijn and van der Kerk (1954) confirmed the production of ethylenethiuram monosulphide from nabam.

The present theory of nabam action may be summarized from the literature. Freshly prepared, unoxidized' nabam is presumed to be essentially nontoxic.

Ethylenethiuram monosulphide in turn breaks down torelease ethylene-diisothiocyanate (Equation 10).

The diisothiocyanates, highly reactive and unstable, apparently combine with sulphydryl groups to act as nonspecific poisons.

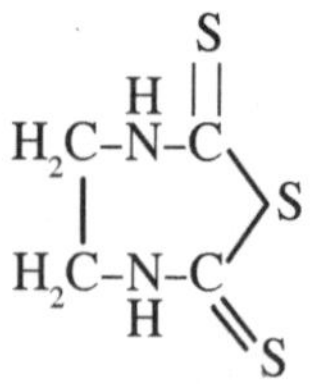

```
         S
       H ||
  H2C-N-C\
  |        >S
  H2C-N-C/
       H  \\
           S
```

Figure 9.10: Ethylenethiuram monosulphide.

The acidic breakdown of nabam proceeds as in Equation 8.

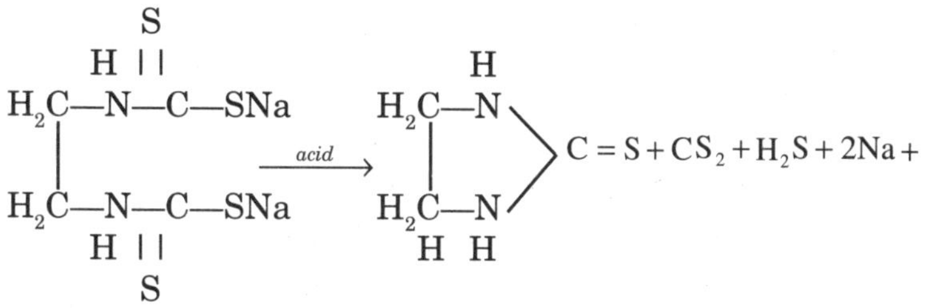

S
H ||
H_2C—N—C—SNa
|
H_2C—N—C—SNa
H ||
S

Nabam

$\xrightarrow{acid}$

H
H_2C—N
| > $C = S + CS_2 + H_2S + 2Na +$
H_2C—N
H H

Ethylenethiourea (nontoxic)

Basic hydrolysis and oxidation of nabam proceeds in another fashion (Equation 9).

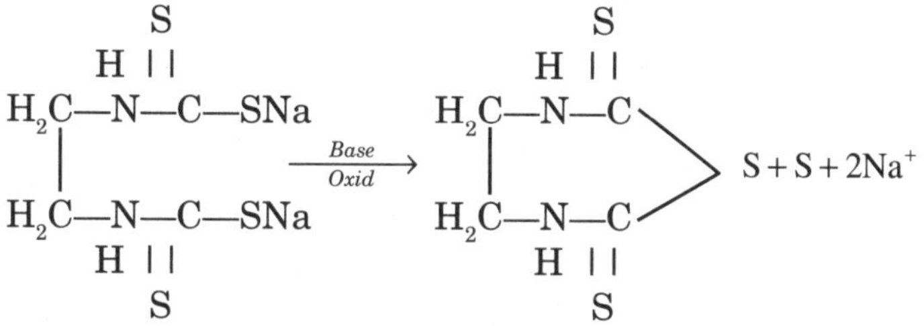

S
H ||
H_2C—N—C—SNa
|
H_2C—N—C—SNa
H ||
S

Nabam

$\xrightarrow[Oxid]{Base}$

S
H ||
H_2C—N—C
| > $S + S + 2Na^+$
H_2C—N—C
H ||
S

Ethylenethiuram monosulfide (Monomer or polymer)

One of the unresolved problems of nabam toxicity is the nature of the gaseous toxicant which it evolves. This unidentifled gas was first detected by Rich and Horsfall (1950), who demonstrated that the gas could not be H_2S or SO_2.

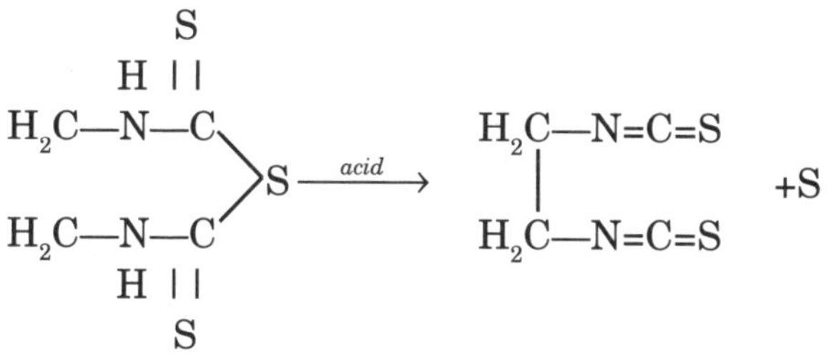

S
H ||
H_2C—N—C
         >S $\xrightarrow{acid}$
H_2C—N—C
H ||
S

H_2C—N=C=S
|
H_2C—N=C=S   +S

EthylenethiurammonosulfideEthylenedisothiocyanate

They did not consider CS_2 as a possibility because it is a relatively weak toxicant. In 1951, Cox *et al.* showed that CS, and ethylenediamine evolve from nabam hydrolysis.

They proposed that these two gases are the toxic vapours, recombining within the spore to give nabam. Lopatecki and Newton (1952) argued that the toxic vapours are simply CS, evolved from nabam.

Later work on the problem by Weed *et al.* (1953) practically ruled out CS_2 or ethylenediamine as factors. These workers also doubted the possibility of the toxic gases being a diisothiocyanate.

Weed *et al.* (1953) conclude that "an unidentified volatile constituent is involved" in the toxicity of nabam.

There the problem stands. Two other types of compounds must be included here although they are not ethylenebisdithiocarbamates.

These are -sodium N-methyldithioc-arbamates and the rhodanines.

Sodium N-methyldithiocarbamate, in spite of structural .similarity to the dialkyldithiocarbamates, is also a source of methylisothiocyanate, as in Equation 11.

$$H_2C{-}\overset{\displaystyle H \atop |}{N}{-}\underset{\| \atop \displaystyle S}{C}{-}S^{(-)} \rightarrow HS^{(-)} + CH_3N{=}C{=}S \qquad (11)$$

N-Methyldithiocarbamate ion *Methylisothiocyanate*

Sodium N-methyldithiocarbamate is used as a soil fungicide under the trade names of "Vapam" or "VPM."

3,5-Dimethyltetrahydro-1,3-5,2H-thiadiazine-2-thione, the active ingredient of the soil fumigant "*Mylone*," also breaks down to give methylisothiocyanate as in Equation 12. Another group of related fungitoxicants, the rhodanines, was described by van der Kerk *et Al.* (1953).

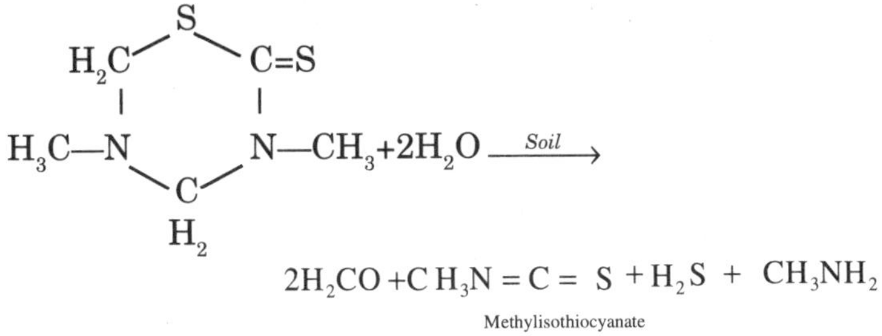

$$\begin{array}{c} \quad S \\ H_2C \diagup \quad \diagdown C{=}S \\ | \qquad\qquad | \\ H_3C{-}N \qquad N{-}CH_3 + 2H_2O \xrightarrow{Soil} \\ \diagdown C \diagup \\ H_2 \end{array}$$

$$2H_2CO + CH_3N = C = S + H_2S + CH_3NH_2$$

Methylisothiocyanate

(12)

The structureactivity of the rhodanines was also reported in 1953 by Brown and her co-workers. Van der Kerk reports (1956)that the rhodanines also are isothiocyanate fungicides and act according to Equation 13.

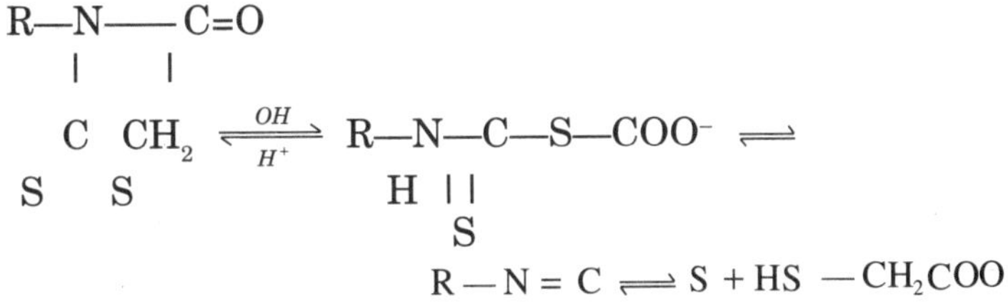

$$\begin{array}{l} R{-}N{-}C{=}O \\ \quad | \quad\;\; | \\ \quad C \;\; CH_2 \underset{H^+}{\overset{OH}{\rightleftharpoons}} R{-}N{-}C{-}S{-}COO^- \rightleftharpoons \\ S \quad S \qquad\qquad\quad H \; \| \\ \qquad\qquad\qquad\qquad\quad S \end{array}$$

$$R - N = C \rightleftharpoons S + HS - CH_2COO$$

(13)

OTHER ORGANIC SULPHUR COMPOUNDS

Although the dithiocarbamates have been the most useful and interesting of the organic sulphur fungicides, others also have been found to be *fungitoxic*.

Some of these are the *ethylenethioureas*, the *xanthates*, 2-*mercapt-obenzothiazole*, the *thiobisphenols*, and those toxicants having a trichloromethylthio group.

Rich and Horsfall (1954) noted that the N-alkylethylenethioureas increased in fungitoxicity with increasing length of alkyl chain. Fungitoxicity is maximal at the 8 carbon homologue and decreased as the chain lengthens beyond 8 carbons.

Ross and Ludwig (1957) demonstrated that this series probably acts as physical toxicants exhibiting the Ferguson effect. The xanthates, long used as disinfectants, were thoroughly investigated by Davies and Sexton (1946). They concluded that sulphur atoms on the C=S groups were not essential to the toxicity of xanthates.

This conclusion was based on the essentially equal fungitoxicity of the following three compounds:

$$(C_2H_5O{-}\overset{\overset{\Large S}{||}}{C})_3S \; ; \; (C_2H_5O{-}\overset{\overset{\Large O}{||}}{C})_2S;$$

$$\text{and } C_2H_5O{-}\overset{\overset{\Large S}{||}}{C}{-}S{-}\overset{\overset{\Large O}{||}}{C}{-}OC{-}H_5.$$

2-Mercaptobenzothiazole, although it is somewhat fungi cidal has found its principal **use** as a synergist with dialkyldi-thiocarbamates in proprietary mixtures sold as "*Vancides*".

The *thiobisphenols* will be discussed under *phenolic fungicides*. The *trichloromethylthio* compounds will be discussed under heterocyclic nitrogen compounds because of the interest in captan, the *tetrahydrop-hthalimide* derivative.

HETEROCYCLIC NITROGEN COMPOUNDS

Horsfall and Rich (1951) reported on the structureactivity relationships in a large group of heterocyclic nitrogen compounds. Many of these compounds are extremely fungitoxic. Their toxic mechanisms, however, differ widely.

Certain of them, such as the ethylenethioureas just discussed, the nitrosopyrazoles, and the tetrahydropyrimidines, probably act as physical toxicants Others, such as the 2-imidazolines have been reported to be competitive inhibitors of enzymes.

The action of acridine was discussed in an earlier section. Two other mechanisms may also be important to the fungitoxicity of' heterocyclic nitrogen compounds. These latter two mechanisms may best be presented by discussing two compounds for which& these mechanisms have been proposed.

The compounds are 8-quinolinol (oxine), and N-(trichlor-omethylthio)-4-cyclo-hexene-1,2-dicarboximide (captan). Oxine has been introduced in the previous section on chelation, and will be discussed first.

Oxine is the cornerstone for the theories of toxic mechanisms involving chelation. As mentioned earlier, the idea. that oxine takes needed metals from organisms was called into doubt by evidence that the metal oxinates, particularly cupric oxinate, is more toxic than oxine itself.

This evidence was further supported by Anderson and Swaby (1951), who found that oxine is a copper-deficient medium is only $^1/_{48}$ as toxic as it is in a copper-sufficient medium. Copper must be present, therefore, for maximum fungitoxicity of oxine. Not only must there be copper present but the oxine must be able to form a chelate with it.

For example, at a pH below which oxine chelates, it is no longer toxic, regardless of the presence of copper. The formation of a copper nate, then, appears to be essential to the fungitoxicity of oxine. Complic-ations arose. Block (1957) showed that the fungitoxicity of copper oxinate can be reserved not only with excess copper but also with excess oxine.

Albert *et al.* (1953) had reported earlier that the antibacterial action of oxine can be quenched by an excess of oxine-the polymodal dosage response again. They proposed that excess oxine inhibited the formation within the cell of the 1 : 1, or half chelate which they suggested as the toxic form of oxine.

Reversal by excess metal, they argued, was caused by inhibiting the 3 : 2 or full chelate in the ambient fluid. They pictured the process as follows. Oxine, because of water solubility, penetrates into cells best as the fully chelated metal complex which is less polar. Once inside the cell, the half chelated complex is required for toxicity.

This half chelate may arise from the full chelate either

by dissociation, or by the action of a hypothetical enzyme. Their theory is illustrated by Equation 14.

Excess metal in the ambient fluid would drive the last equation to the left, reducing the amount of fully chelated oxine needed for penetration. Excess oxine within the cell would drive the last equation to the right, reducing the concentration of the toxic species, the half chelate.

Other chelators in excess will also cause reversal of oxine, ostensibly by competing for metals. Block (1955) demonstrated that in addition to the ability to chelate, analogues of oxine must also be lipoid-soluble to be fungitoxic.

$$\text{Oxine}^- + \text{Metal}^{++}\text{s} \rightleftharpoons \underset{\substack{\text{Half chelate} \\ \text{(Toxic within cell)}}}{\text{(Oxine) Metal}^+} \qquad (14)$$

$$\text{(Oxine) Metal}^+ + \text{Oxiner} \rightleftharpoons \underset{\substack{\text{Full chelate} \\ \text{(Needed for permeation)}}}{\text{(Oxine)}_3 \text{ Metal}}$$

There are at least two discrepancies in the theory that should be noted. The first is that unchelated oxine enters cells quite readily. In fact, the theory for the reversal of toxicity by excess oxine depends on its entry into the cell.

The second discrepancy is that washing with water will revive spores poisoned with oxine in a metal-deficient medium, but will not revive copper oxinate-treated spores. Washing with 0.1 N HCl is needed to revive the latter.

These anomalies imply that unchelated oxine, which is toxic, acts in an area of the cell which does not require high lipoid-solubility to be entered.

This action of oxine may well be metal-robbing. The chelated oxine acts at a site which requires high lipoid-solubility.

This deeper site may well be within a microsome or the nucleus. The action of the half chelate may be the blocking of functional sites as suggested earlier. Other workers have different views about the toxicity of oxine.

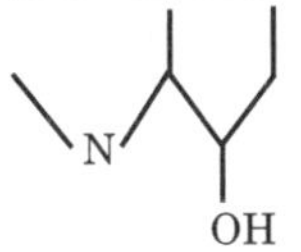

N OH

Sexton (1953) considers it likely that oxine is fungitoxic because of its *phenolic* properties. Gale and Folkes (1957) find that oxine is one of the best inhibitors of the incorporation of *glycine* in disrupted *staphylococcal cells*.

They consider that the portion of oxine structurally resembles, and completes with natural compouents of the system they were studying. They base this conclusion on two observations:

(a) their system is stimulated by 6-amino-4-hydroxy derivatives of benzimidazole or benzotriazole; and

(b) their system is not inhibited by the chelator ethylenediamine tetraacetic acid.

The next heterocyclic nitrogen compound to be discussed is captan. The discussion of captan toxicity has centered on the importance of the -$SC(Cl)_3$ group. Included here, then, will be some analogues of captan that are not heterocyclic nitrogen compounds, but do have the —$SC(Cl)_3$ group.

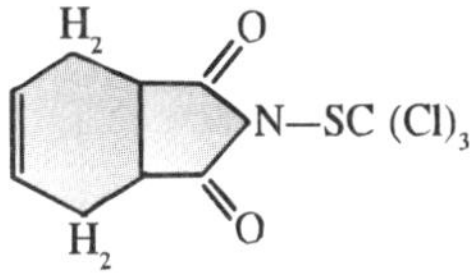

H_2 O N—SC $(Cl)_3$ O H_2

Figure 9.11: Captan.

The fungitoxicity of captan was first reported by Kittleson (1952). He considered the fungitoxic group to be

$$>N—S—(C(Cl)_3).$$

Horsfall and Rich (1953) presented evidence that —CO—NR—CO— could be the toxic grouping of captan. They based their conclusion on the similarity of the dosage-response slopes of captan and the highly fungitoxic antibiotic cycloheximide.

Cycloheximide has the —CO—NH—CO— group but not —$SC(Cl)_3$. Horsfall and Rich assigned to the trichloromethylthio group the function of getting the tetrahydrophtbalimideportion of captan into the cell.

N-nitrosophthalimidine Ladd (1945) is another highly fungitoxic compound with the —CO—NR—CO— group but no —$SC(Cl)_3$. The fungitoxicity of this compound was also used by Horsfall and Rich to support theirtheory.

Horsfall and Rich (1^{0}54) pointed out that electronegative groups adjacent to a sulphur atom enhance activity. heelectronegative carbonyl groups in captan would draw electrons, from the nitrogen atom, making the N-S bond less stable.

Uhlenbroek and Koopmans (1957) found that —$SC(Cl)_3$ alone did not make a compound fungitoxic. They reported that $H_3CSSC(Cl)_3$ is *nonfungitoxic*, $C_6H_5SCC(Cl)_3$ is slightly fungitoxic, while 2-$NO_2C_6H_4SSC(Cl)_3$ is very *fungitoxic*.

In addition, they found that —$C(Cl)_3$ could be replaced without destroying fungitoxicity completely. For example, the ED50 of $H_3CC_6H_4SO_2SC(Cl)_3$ to *Fusarium culmorum* is in the range of 0.315 to 1.0 mg/liter, very fungitoxic.

Replacing the —$C(Cl)_3$ with a —CH_3 results in a compound with an ED50 in the range 1.0-3.1 mg./liter, still quite fungitoxic. Uhlenbroek and Koopmans found that the more electronegative groups on R in $RSSC(Cl)_3$, the more fungitoxic the analogue. In $RSO_2SC(Cl)_3$, however the analogues are quite fungitoxic, regardless of the electroneg-ativity of R.

They concluded that the hypothesis of increased fungitoxicity by electronegative groups adjacent to an S atom may apply for $RSSC(Cl)_3$ but not for $RSO_2SC(Cl)_3$.

According to Ingold (1953), however, —SO_2R is a very strong electronegative group in itself. Changes in R, therefore, may not give good evidence for or against the *electronegativity* theory, when —SO_2R is adjacent to a sulphur atom.

Another theory of captan action was presented by Lukens and Sisler (1958). They found that captan interacts with sulfhydryl compounds, such as cysteine, to give thiophosgene

$$[Cl{-}C({=}S){-}Cl]$$

as in Equation 15.

$$\text{(tetrahydrophthalimide)}\; N{-}S{-}C(Cl)_3 + 2RSH \rightarrow \text{(tetrahydrophthalimide)}\; NH + Cl{-}C({=}S){-}Cl + R{\cdot}S{\cdot}S{\cdot}R + HCl \qquad (15)$$

A clue to this breakdown is in the odor of formulated captan which is that of thiophosgene.

The thiophosgene formed may react with water (Equation 16).

$$\underset{\text{Thiophosgene}}{Cl{-}C({=}S){-}Cl} + 2H_2O \rightarrow H_2S + CO_2 + 2HCl \qquad (16)$$

Thiophosgene also polymerizes to give dithiophosgene which in turn may react with water (Equation 17).

$$\underset{\text{Dithiophosgene}}{Cl{-}C({=}S){-}S{-}C(Cl)_3} + 2H_2O \rightarrow CS_2 + CO_2 + 4HCl \qquad (17)$$

Lukens and Sisler proposed that the toxicity of captan is. produced by the highly reactive thiophosgene resulting from the breakdown of captan by sulphydryl groups.

They were also able to demonstrate this breakdown by reacting captan with yeast cells. They concluded that essentially all of the toxicity of captan to yeast can be accounted for by then —S—$C(Cl)_3$ group.

Thiophosgene produced *in situ* would ostenthly poison

by combining with free sulphydryl, amino, hydroxyl, and perhaps carboxyl groups. In addition, thiophosgene could form

ledges between properly spaced groups within the cell. The production of thiophosgene is undoubtedly of importance to captan activity. Whether or not the captan acts simply as a thiophosgene producer remains doubtful.

If, as Uhlenbroek and Koopmans (1957) reported, some —S—$C(Cl)_3$ compounds are nontoxic, and if replacing —$C(Cl)_3$ does not destroy fungitoxicity, then thiophosgene production may not be the whole story of —S—$C(Cl)_3$ compounds.

Captan, which loses its chlorine atoms readily, may well form the N-chloroetrahydrophthalimide as a transitory intermediate, analogous to diisothiocyanates formed in nabam breakdown. That the N-chloro derivative may form is supported by Orwoll (1954).

He presented the following possibility (Equation 18) for the breakdown of a captan-type molecule.

$$Ar—SCCl_3 \rightarrow CS\ Cl_2 + Ar\ Cl \qquad (18)$$

Although N-chlorotetrahydrophthalimide is too unstable to test, its analogue, N-chlorosuccinimide, is a well known and -highly active germicide. The phthalimide itself could be very fungitoxic when released *in situ.*

The breaking of the N-S bond would leave the N position free to combine with any reactive grouping within the cell. Captan, then may poison by releasing highly reactive *tetrahydrophthalimide radicals*, *thiophosgene*, and *chlorine*. So much for the heterocyclic nitrogen compounds, a particularly rich source of *fungitoxicants.*

QUINONES

Quinones are among the most powerful of the agricultural fungicides. The two most commonly used in practice are bothchlorinated compounds. These are 1, 4-tetrachlor-benzoquinone (chloranil), and 2, 3-dichloro-1, 4napthoquinone (dichlone).

Chloranil has found its use primarily as a seed protectant. As a foliage fungicide it usually fails to protect, being readily photolysed to nontoxic products.

Dichlone, much less readily photolysed, is widely used as a foliage spray. It has been particularly successful against applc scab. The potency of the quinones may be illustrated by the usage of dichlone for controlling apple scab.

Most protective fungicides for apple scab control require 1 to 3 lb. of formulation per 100 gallons. Dichlone is used successfully at a dosage of 1/8 to 1/4 lb. per 100 gallons.

Owens (1953a) points out a number of ways by which quinones may poison spores. As a, (i-unsaturated compounds they may combine with sulphydryl groups (Equation 19). They may also interact with amino groups.

Quinones may also poison by rerouting electron transfer systems as described in an earlier section. McNew and Burchfield (1951) found the following order of increasing fungitoxicity: anthraquinone < benzoquinone < phenanthraquinone < naphthoquinone.

$$\text{(quinone)} + HS-R \xrightarrow{1/2OX} \text{(quinone)}\,SR + H_2O$$

Halogenation, while decreasing water solubility and phytotoxicity, increases fungitoxicity. Chlorination improves fungitoxicity the most, bromination next, and iodination least.

Alkylation ortho to carbonyl groups reduces fungitoxicity, presumably by steric-hindrance. A point of interest is that the quinonoid structure may not be necessary to the activity of these compounds.

For example, Owens (1953) reports that 2, 5-dichlorohydroquinone is almost as toxic as ehloranil. Of course, data of Rich and Horsfall (1954) suggest that the hydroquinone may be oxidized to the quinone by fungi.

PHENOLIC COMPOUNDS

Phenolic compounds have been of interest as germicides since the introduction of carbolic acid into surgery by Lister in the last century. Phenols as fungitoxicants or germicides have been particularly useful in medicine and industry rather than in agriculture.

One of the most widely used germicides in medicinal preparations is hexylresorcinol. Various derivatives of cresol and phenylphenol are used as wood preservatives.

Sodium dinitro-o-cresylate has been used as a spray on orchard floors to kill overwintering forms of fungi which cause fruit diseases. One of the significant contributions to the structure-fungitoxicity relationships of phenols was made by Shirk (194).

He found that alkylating both positions ortho to the phenolic -OH greatly reduced fungitoxicity. In addition, o-chloro-6alkylphenols are less fungitoxic than the corresponding 6-alkyl phenols. Shirk explains this effect as steric hindrance.

He bases his suggestion on the report of Stilison *et al.* (1945) who found that phenols substituted 2, 6 with large alkyl groups gave reactions not at all like typical phenols.

These they called hindered phenols. Interfering with the reactivity of the phenolic —OH, then, profoundly affects fungitoxicity. Another group of phetkolic fungicides of interest are the *bisphenols*.

The germicidal action of these compounds was first reported by Bechold and Ehrlich (1906), Marsh *et. al.* .(1945), and Marsh and Butler (1946) found bisphenols to be highly effective mildew preventives on cloth.

Their best material was 2, 2'-methylenebis (4-chlorophenol) also known as -G-4, preventol GD and dichlorophene.

Goldsworthy and Gertler (1949) reported this compound to te an excellent foliage fungicide for peach trees.

The corresponding thiobisphenols are also effective fungicides. Here, the methane bridge is replaced by a sulphur atom. Pfleger *et. al.* (1949), found that the thiobisphenols are highly toxic *in vitro* to fungi causing human diseases.

Schraufstatter *et. al.* (1949) reported 2, 2-thiobis (4-chlorophenol) as a particularly good antimycotic. Horsfall and Rich (1950) showed Schraufstatter's compound to bc an excellent foliage protectant against apple scab. Unfortunately, it damaged the fruit.

Cade and Gump (1954) summarized the results of structure,activity research with bisphenols. Activity is increased by halogenation of each ring in the 4-positons. Any more halogenation decreases activity.

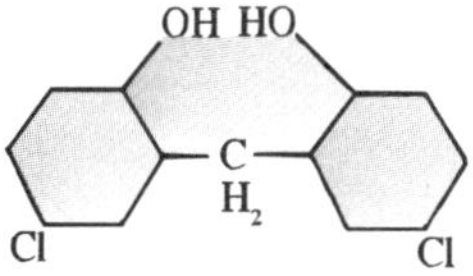

OH HO
C
H_2
Cl Cl

Figure 9.12: 2, 2'-Methylenebis (4-chlorophenol).

The phenolic OH's are most effective ortho to the bridge linking the rings. The type of bridge between the two rings is not too important. The bridge must be small enough, however, to prevent spreading the hydroxyls too far apart.

This latter evidence indicates that chelation may play a part in the toxicity of the bisphenols. There are many other kinds of fungicides, such as salicylates .and benzoates, that have been considered phenolic toxicants. The large group of phenolic toxicants are usually considered as nonspecific, protoplasmic poisons.

HALOGENATED AND NITRATED AROMATIC COMPOUNDS

The halogenated aromatic compounds are usually toxic because they readily release nascent halogens. This is un.doubtedly the mechanism of action of such compounds as chloramine-T and N-chlorosuccinimide. The freed chlorinemay act to form oxidizing $HClO^-$ as in the case of the bypo-chlorites.

Another kind of action may be a direct halogenation of a metabolite to form an antimetabolite. Nitrated aromatic compounds most potent as fungicides are usually either halogenated or they are phenols.

One of these compounds, 2, 4-dinitro-o-cresol was mentioned in the previous. section. Another is 2, 4-dinitrophenol, a powerful uncoupler of phosphorylation. Of the halogenated nitro-aromatics, one of the most powerful fungicides is 1-fluoro-3-bromo-4, 6-dinitrobenzene.

The chlorinated nitrobenzenes have been of continuing interest since they were first described as fungitoxicants. Pentachloronitrobenzene and tetrachloronitrobenzene have found use both as soil fungicides and for the control of *Botrytfs* sp. on plant parts.

These compounds prevent sporulation, and are vapour-phase fungistats which do not prevent spores from germinating but do stop hyphal growth. Horsfall' (1956) suggests that compounds of this type are antimitotics.

It may be that pentachloronitrobenzene and tetrachloronitro benzene act specifically as competitive inhibitors for inositol, a required growth substance for many fungi.

OTHER ORGANIC FUNGITOXICANTS

The list of fungitoxic organic compounds is a long one. They cannot all be mentioned in one short chapter. Such fungitoxicants as quaternary ammonium compounds were mentioned in the section as surfactants. These have been tried for the control of plant diseases.

Not yet mentioned are the aliphatic fungitoxicants. These are of not too much importance and most probably act as nonspecific, physical toxicants. The organometallic fungicides have been of particular interest, so should not be omitted.

Suffice it to say that many organometallic compounds, such as the organic mercurials, are more powerful than the inorganic compounds of the same metals. Of interest in this regard is tin, not very fungitoxic in inorganic combinations, but producing some highly fungitoxic organic compounds.

SUCCESS OF PROGRAMS

The artistry of the synthesizing chemists combined with the carefully designed screening programs of the biologists has given us a wealth of new and highly effective fungicides in recent years.

The methods used for screening are as various as the laboratories so engaged. Although the selection of compounds to be screened is usually empirical, the tests to which the compounds are subjected are based on knowledge of plantdiseases.

Regardless of the method, there is very little question that most of the commercial fungicides now in use would have been selected by any of the presently operating screening programs. The screens work.

Concomitant with the selection of candidate fungicides, the screening programs have resulted in masses of structure-activity data. These data have been carefully scrutinized for "*philosopher's stones*" which will predict fungitoxic configurations.

The literature abounds with such studies. These have been of use in predicting the activity of closely related compounds, and in a few cases have predicted the activity of untested configurations.

PRESENT HOLES IN SCREENING PROGRAMS

One of the main problems plaguing searchers for fungicides is the field failure of compounds which look promising in the laboratory. The present laboratory programs will pick all the winners, but in the process, they also pick too many losers. Field testing is expensive. Why do compounds look good in the laboratory and yet often are of no value for protecting plants in the field ? Some of these factors involve the physical form of the fungicide. One of these physical factors of primary importance is particle size.

A great number of studies have demonstrated the relationship between particle size and both fungitozicity and tenacity. In order for fungitoxic compounds to succeed in the field, they must not only be in a proper physical form but also they must be carefully formulated.

Burchfield and Goenaga (1957) have recently shown that even such an old and widely used fungicide as Bordeaux can be made more effective by formulation with certain wetting agents.

Copper oxide succeeded as a foliage fungicide only after each particle was coated with gum arabic. The gum arabic coating prevented the agglomeration and consequent poor performance of the copper oxide particles. This made the difference between success and failure.

Very often candidate fungicides fail because they have not been subjected in the laboratory to the extremes of weathering encountered in the field.

Although laboratory testing ordinarily includes a washing or rain test, the compounds are not usually subjected to other weathering factors. Some of these additional factors are wind whipping of leaves, leaf expansion, high intensities of actinic light, long periods of continuous high humidity with attendant carbonation and oxidation, and periodic wetting and drying which would tend to increase hydrolysis.

These factors, any of which may be critically important to field performance, are seldom or never tested in the laboratory. Fungitoxic compounds passing the rain test should be subjected to other weathering factors before being field tested.

Fungitoxicants may be lost not only by physical action but also through biological activity. The compounds may be degraded either by leaf emanations or by microbiological activity. Antibiotics are notoriously subject to degradation by soil microorganisms. It is interesting to note that biological ·degradation may actually make a compound more toxic. Byrde .and Woodcock (1953) report such a case.

They found that 1 : 4-diacetoxy-2: 3-dichloronaphthalene, weakly toxic, becomes highly toxic when mixed with an enzyme preparation of .high acetyl-esterase activity. Byrde and Woodcock suggest .that the esterase changes this compound into the corresponding hydroquinone.

Horsf all (1956) suggested that a phenol oxidase .converts the hydroquinone to the quinone. The pitfalls of a candidate fungicide are many and varied. It should be possible, however, to devise laboratory tests to eliminate many of the compounds which now use up time, space, and money, failing in the field.

FUTURE OF FUNGICIDES

What is the future of fungicides? The future of fungicides is excellent. We become discouraged and go through periods of "*agonizing reappraisal*" only because our ignorance is so profound. We cannot make sense of the rapidly accumulating data.

This chapter and others like it were written with the hope of illuminating signposts. Only by extrapolation from existing knowledge can we expect to find a "*field theory*" of fungicide action, if such exists. Without question, the many pathways pointed out by structure-activity studies eventually will become usable roads.

Should we continue to search for better *fungicides*? We need only to look to the history of insecticides for an affirmative answer. The discovery of the insecticidal properties of DDT, the *chlorinated hydrocarbons*, and the *phosphates*, has given us insecticides many times more powerful than the old. So it will be with fungicides.

BIOCHEMISTRY OF NEMATOCIDES

The science of plant pathology was concerned primarily with the fungi during the first 60 years. Then the bacteria had a short period of prominence. This did not last long, however, because fungi were still more numerous as pathogens.

Bacteria were pushed into the background, too, by the viruses which have been demanding increasingly more attention. The nematodes are not "*newcomers*" as plant pathogens, the wheat nematode was known as a plant pathogen in 1744 and other important species were described in the 19th century.

Present-day general acceptance of nematodes as important plant pathogens was arrived at slowly. Numerous reasons could be advanced to account for the seeming reluctance of plant scientists to embrace nematodes as plant pathogens.

Perhaps the fact that they are animals and have been the concern of the zoologist, particularly the parasitologist, has tended to place the plant pathogenic nematodes in the unique position of being unclaimed, until recently, by any organized scientific discipline.

However, throughout this long period of general apathy toward the plant parasitic nematodes, their cause was proclaimed far and wide by a handful of devoted specialists inn nematology who were concerned primarily with the importance of nematodes as destroyers of cultivated plants. As the importance of many types of nematodes as plant pathogens was recognized, plant pathologists became more concerned with them. The result is that we have a new race of plant pathologists those—concerned with animals that are plant pathogenic.

Moreover, we still have the zoologist specializing in nematology and contributing much of the fundamental information concerning systematic, morphology, physiology, and ecology of the soil inhabiting nematodes.

The problem is of great magnitude and presently requires the additional knowledge that will result from the cooperation of these animal and plant scientists.

THE PROBLEM OF PROVING PATHOGENICITY

Nematologists have struggled again over the same old rough ground traversed by the mycologists, bacteriologists, and virologists. How can one prove that a nematode is a pathogen?

Nematologists inherited agar techniques ‘and petri plates from their predecessors but little else that was significant in their search for the clusive proof. The extreme difficulty of obtaining pure cultures of nematodes has made the proof most difficult.

Without proof, many plant pathologists have been loath to accept the pathogenicity of many, species.

They have accepted constant association as sufficient evidence for pathogencity of such obvious nematodes as the root know nematode and the golden nematode. Nematocides have contributed enormously to the proof needed by the nematologists, who were not able, at least until recently, to culture the nematodes, add them to plants, produce the disease, and reisolate the original nematode.

The use of nematocides to kill them has given a type of inverted proof. Constant association made this reasonably easy. Nematocides killed off the nematode and, thus, interrupted the constant association. This was nearly as good proof as Koch demanded.

At least it was good enough to set many men baying down the A rail of nematodes as plant pathogens. The subject grows apace.

WHAT A NEMATOCIDE IS

The term nematocide is restricted in this discussion to chemicals with nematode-killing properties that have been used., or are currently used to redure populations of plant pathogenic nematodes. In addition to nematocidal activity, useful nematocides must possess special properties with regard to phytotoxicity, diffusion in soil, water solubility, vapor pressure, and cost.

The chemicals that are here considered as nematocides are not specific in their toxic action. They usually kill all of the nematodes that are present in the area of their activity.

Some nematocides are fungicidal, insecticidal, and herbicidal as well, and could equally well be referred to as biocides since they partially or completely sterilize the soil. In disease complexes involving nematodes and fungi or bacteria there maybe secondary benefits from the application of nematocides.

Generally, too, the benefits of treatments with, nematocides are measureable in terms of increased crop yield, quality, and better plant growth. In practice, it is expected that the use of nematocides will increase the profit to the user.

Some investigators suggest that a soil fumigation treatment with a nematocide should increase yield or quality of the product sufficiently to return to the grower an amount equal to twice the cost of the treatment.

Taylor (1951) says that it is not economical to fumigate soil for nematode control unless. the gross value of the crop is at least 8375 per acre. These are matters that can only be decided by individual growers, since there are many economic factors that determine whether or not a nematocide is prolitable.

There are situations where a nematocide is not profitable even though it more than doubles the yield of the crop as in California when sugar beet yields have been doubled but the yield on treated land is still not at an economic level.

In other situations there may be no significant increase in total yield, but the quality is increased to profitable levels. This has been evident in such crops as carrots and potatoes.

One of the attractive features of nematode control by nematocides is that the benefits of the treatment are immediately obvious to growers in terms of net profit. This is no doubt responsible for the fairly rapid adoption of nematocides once they ecame available at relatively low cost.

HISTORICAL

The application, of chemicals to the soil to control plant parasitic nematodes was undertaken by a number of investigators because crop failures were associated with the presence of these pests. Kuhn (1881) attempted control of the sugar beet nematode, *Heterodera schachtil* Schmidt, 1871, with a number of chemicals and concluded that the most promising was carbon bisulphide. However, this chemical was not entirely satisfactory because of the high cost of the treatment and the relatively unsatisfactory results.

It is likely that Kuhn used carbon bisulfide because of its then widespread use against grape *Phylloxera.* Neal (1889) applied carbon bisulphide to the soil as well as numerous combinations of tobacco dust, potassium sulphatte, polassium sulphide, sodium hyposulphite, sulphur, and caustic lime in experiments to control root knot nematode in Florida.

He also applied carbon bisulfide to living plants which were killed by the chemical because it is highly phytotoxic. Neal did not obtain satisfactory results with carbon bisulphide probably because he allowed an iterval of only one day between treatment of the soil and planting.

He did, however, indicate that tobacco dust was the most satisfactory of the treatments he tried. It is apparent from the literature that until 1940 numerous chemicals were investigated as possible nematocides for the control of nematodes.

Chloropicrin appears to have been the only satisfactory chemical tested prior to 1940 for the treatment of nematode infested soils on a commercial scale. Chloropicrin was first reported to be an effective nematocidal chemical for use in soil by Matthews (1919).

Subsequently, Johnson and Godfrey (1932) reported excellent control' of root knot nematode in pineapple soils. This chemical is now widely recognized for its nematocidal, fungicidal, and herbicidal properties. As a nematocide, it was once widely used in pineapple soils in Hawaii where satisfactory increases in yield were obtained.

Chloropicrin has a fairly high vapour pressure and it is most effective when confined to the soil by impervious covers, by a water seal, or by the use of high dosages. The high cost of soil treatments with chloropicrin (approximately $150 to $ 200 per acre) has tended to restrict its use to crops of high value per acre.

Taylor and McBeth (1941) developed the spot treatment method of applying chloropicrin and this made it economically feasible to treat large acreages of melons where treatment of the planting site reduced the cost to approximately $5 per acre.

Methyl bromide is sometimes used as a soil fumigant to control nematodes. Richardson and Johnson (1935) reported it to be an effective nematocide and subsequent workers have reported the conditions for its most effective use.

The chemical has had rather restricted use as a nematocide except for special crops of high value but is very effective in situations where fungicidal and herbicidal

Table 10.1: Physical properties of Nematocides.

Nematocide	*Boiling point (°C.)*	*Vapor pressure (25° C.)*	*Specific gravity*	*Solubility (gm./100 ml. water)*	*Physical state*
Chloropicrin	112	24.0	1.65	0.20	Liquid
Methyl bromide	45	1824	1.73	0.09	Gas
D-D Mixture	<95-150>	40.4	1.2	0.27	Liquid
Ethylene dibromide	131.6	12.0	2.17	0.43	Liquid
1, 2-dibromo-3 chloropropane	196	0.9	2.08	0.15	Liquid.
Sodium N-methyl dithocarbamate	—	—	—	72.2	Solid
VC-13	124-130 (0.25 mm.)	—	—	0.245 (mg/1.)	Liquid

qualities are desirable. Methyl bromide has a high vapour pressure and a low boiling point, it can be effectively used only if the vapours are confined to the soil by gas impervious covers.

The chemical is highly toxic to man and extreme care must be exercise to avoid breathing the vapours. A small amount of chloropicrin is frequently added to methyl bromide so that it will be m re easily detected by persons using it as a fumigant.

The era of modern nematocides had its beginning with the discovery by Carter (1943) of the nematocidal properties of 1, 3-dichloropropene-I, 2-dichloropropane mixture (D-D mixture).

This was the first relatively cheap nematocide that could be used to control nematodes in soil at a cost that permitted large-scale commercial treatments. Unlike chloropicrin and methyl bromide, D-D mixture, because of its lower vapour pressure, does not require the use of impervious covers or water seals.

In 1945, Christie reported that ethylene dibromide had given excellent control of root knot nematode in the soil in preliminary tests. Subsequently, this chemical and D-D mixture have been widely used to control nematodes in the soil.

Unlike many of the previous chemicals that were used to control nematodes, D—D mixture and ethylene dibromide have very little effect on soil fungi at the dosage rates ordinarily employed to control nematodes in the field. Both chemicals do, however, kill soil animals and both have been used as soil insecticides.

Ethylene dibromide was widely used to control wireworms until the advent of the chlorinated hydrocarbon insecticides. Since the discovery of D—D mixture and ethylene dibromide, one additional chemical has been developed that is now widely used, this is 1,2 dibromo-3-chloropiopane reported by McBeth and Bergeson (1955).

Later in 1955 Allen *et al.* reported the chemical to be an effective nematocide based on experiments conducted in 1953 and 1954. This material presents a new aspect, low phytotoxicity.

Thus, it can be safely applied to living plants. Historically, the discovery of D-D mixture and ethylene dibromide and their subsequent wide use as low cost effective > nematocides has had a very profound influence on our knowledge of plant pathogenic nematodes.

Many nematodes ectoparasitic on roots have been discovered by the use of one or the other of these nematocides in fields where crop growth and yields were reduced from unknown causes.

In addition, the use of these materials has made possible a more accurateappraisal of the damage that should be attributable to nematodes. The spectacular increases in yield that have frequently resulted when nematodes are controlled have served to make growers aware of the necessity of employing nematode control procedures.

The net result of the use of these materials has been

the awakening of a widespread interest in nematodes as plant pathogens, recognition that nematodes are frequently important in certain disease complexes, and renewed activity in the study of nematodes.

THE EFFECT OF NEMATODE CONTROL ON THE CROP

Nematocides are usually applied in situations where control of nematodes will result in increased quantity or quality of yield of the harvested portion of the crop.

It is not possible to cite all instances of increased yields that have been reported in the literature. The fact that the use of nematocides has, increased many fold during the past 15 years is ample testimony to the effectiveness of nematocides in increasing crop yields.

Thorne and Jensen (1946); Raski *et al.* (1953); Allen *et al.* (1955); Lear and Thomason (1956); Stark *et al.* (1944) and numerous other investigators have reported the increased yields resulting from the use of nematocides.

There is no method, aside from experience, that permits any accurate forecast of the yield increases that can be obtained from nematode control treatments.

Over a period of 10 years when all plots were carefully selected on the basis of previous nematode damage from root knot nematode and for soil types favourable to nematocidal treatments, the yield of lint cotton in California tests has varied from no significant increase to more than one bale per acre with both hroadcast and row placement treatments.

The percentage increase does not appear to be correlated with the yield obtained on untreated soils. Forexample, Allen and Raski (1950) obtained yield increases of 0.6 to 1.0 bale of lint cotton when the yields on untreated plots were only slightly more than one bale per acre.

In 1957 preplanting row placement treatments with 9 gallons of D-Dmixture per acre resulted in a yield of 3.50 bales of lint cotton per acre on land. that produced 2.57

bales of lintcotton without treatment. Although satisfactory yields are sometimes obtained on land which is heavily infested with nematodes, this should not necessarily be the final criterion in determining the necessity of controlling nematodes.

This is so,. because of the variety of soils, and cultural practices that are encountered in the field. If it is known that nematodes are present, then exploratory treatments should be undertaken to determine the advisability of applying a nematocide.

Nematocides applied for the express purpose of securing the maximum reduction in populations and maximum yield that are possible are applied as area treatments. In these treatments, an attempt is made to kill all of the nematodes in the upper layers of the soil.

Conventional treatments of this. type involve the injection of the volatile nematocides by shanks. spaced 12 inches apart and to a depth of 8 inches in the soil. D—D mixture at 20 gallons per acre, 83% ethylene dibromide at 4-6 gallons per acre, or 1,2-dibromo-3-chloropropane at 1 to 2 gallons per acre are the dosage rates ordinarily used to control root knot nematode in sandy or sandy loam soils.

Because of the extreme range of soil types it is not possible to predict the exact results that can be obtained from a specific treatment. However, the application of 20 gallons of D-D mixture per acre to a cotton field in California in 1946 resulted in, nearly 100% control of root knot nematode larvae to a depth of 5 feet.

Examination of the roots of cotton grown subsequently in this field also indicated a high degree of control. This treatment satisfactorily controlled the nematodes for two crops. of cotton. However, this is an exceptional circumstance as. indicated by Allen *et al.* (1955).

Row treatments with 9 gallons of D-D mixture per acre increased cotton yields by 0.3 bale of lint cotton per acre on plots treated the previous year with 20 gallons of D-D mixture per acre. More striking results ,have been obtained in tests on sugar beet nematode by Thorne -(1952) where there was complete crop failure of beets planted on soil that had been treated and had grown a crop of beets the previous year.

There are nematocidal treatments that are directed toward eliminating all of the plant pathogenic nematodes in the soil. Such is the case in the preplanting treatments of soils for perennial crops such as citrus, walnut, apple, cherry, peach, grape.

Here it is necessary to apply high dosages so that kills are obtained to considerable depths in the soil. However, even in sandy soils kills are only obtained to a depth of about 8 feet.

Row placement treatments are a variation of the spot treatments suggested by Taylor and MacBeth (1941). They are applied to protect the root system of the plant from early attack by large numbers of nematodes.

The degree of control is not as high as is obtained with area treatments, and usually the increases in yield are not as great. However, a lesser amount of the fumigant is applied so that the net profits obtained from row treatments are usually about equal to those from area treatments.

The amount of nematocide required for row placement treatments varies with the row spacing. In cotton where row spacings are 38 to 40 inches, satisfactory control of root knot nematode can be obtained by the application of 7 to 9 gallons per acre of the dichloropropene nematocides, 2.5 to 3 gallons per acre of 83% ethylene dibromide or 0.5 to 0.75 gallons per acre of 1, 2, dibromo3-chloropropane.

The amount required is less if row spacings are greater than those indicated. Row placement treatments may be applied with one, two, or three chisels spaced at 1[1]2 inches depending on the crop to be grown.

Nutritional Effects

Plants injured by nematode infestations exhibit symptoms that are characteristic of nutritional deficiencies.

The poor growth and symptoms of sugar beets infested with sugar beet nematode were once thought to be caused by a potassium deficiency.

However, such plants failed to respond to soil applications of potassium, or other fertilizers and it was later found that the primary cause of the trouble was sugar beet nematode.

Nematode infested plants are frequently deficient in certain essential elements and it is not surprising that control of nematodes sometimes results in the correction of deficiency symptoms.

One of the corrective measures that is first used by growers on crops that exhibit poor growth and yellowing of the foliage is the application of additional amounts of fertilizer.

This procedure has been undertaken with little success in many problems that involved nematodes. When the problem has been corrected by the control of nematodes, the plants grown on treated soil appear to be greatly stimulated and symptoms of nutritional deficiency have been alleviated.

This situation has caused some investigators to postulate that nernatocides applied to the soil cause the release of some essential nutritional elements. Although there does exist the possibility of some ion exchange as the result of the application of nematocides, such claims have not been substantiated.

The so-called "*increased growth response*" of plants grown on soil treated to control nematodes is now recognized to be due largely to the control of nematodes and the subsequent development of normal functional roots by the plant.

The effect of soil fumigation with D-D mixture and chloropicrin on nitrification and growth of pineapple has been studied by Tam (1945). He found that these nematocides suppress nitrification, that ammonia accumulates in the soil, and that pineapple plants are able to obtain nitrogen from the ammonia. He indicated also that chloropicrin suppresses nitrification for a longer period of time than D-D mixture because of its greater toxicity to nitrifying bacteria. Increased amounts of nitrogen are also present in the leaves of plants grown on treated soil.

Tarjan (1950) reported that boxwood infested with *Pratylenchus spp.* is deficient in several elements and there was some indication of an increase in the amount of sodium in the leaves. Oteifa (1952) found that lima beans infested with root knot nematode have lower amounts of nitrogen, phosphorus, calcium, magnesium, and potassium.

He also indicated that there is differential uptake of these elements in the presence of nematodes. Sher (1958) found that the leaves of roses infested with the root lesion nematode, *Pratylenchus vulnus* Allen and Jensen, 1951, contain lower amounts of iron, copper, and magnesium. The foliage of the infested roses exhibits symptoms of deficiency disease.

Rose plants not inoculated with the root lesion nematode and growing in the same soil as inoculated rosese do not show symptoms of deficiency.

It might be anticipated that one of the side effects of controlling parasitic nematodes would be restoration of normal nutrition of plants if they are growing in soil with sufficient available amounts of required elements. This seems to be so in the field since plants grown on treated soil are usually normal in appearance and make vigorous growth.

Water Relationships

That nematode infested plants suffer from water deficiency was observed many years ago in sugar beets infested with sugar beet nematode. Infested plants frequently exhibit severe wilting during the daytime and recover at night.

In cases of heavy infestations, this condition of wilting becomes permanent and the plants do not recover regardless of the application of large amounts-of irrigation water.

This is an extreme example and does not occur to the same extent in other crops.

In conducting trials in California with nematocides to control root knot nematode infestations of cotton we have observed that cotton plants growing on untreated plots show evidence of the need for irrigation in advance of ..plants on treated plots.

In these experiments, if irrigations were applied on the basis of the need of the plants on the untreated plots, then plants on treated plots were irrigated too frequently.

This results in a lowered yield on the treated plots due to the increased vegetative growth induced by overirrigation. It has been the experience of growers that the use of nematocides on root knot nematode infested soils frequently allows a reduction in the number of irrigations required when the same soils were not treated for nematode control.

It is sometimes stated by growers that nematodes not only reduce yields, but they also increase the ;production costs because of the excessive amounts of fertilizers and water that are required to grow susceptible crops on infested land.

Disease Complexes

The associations of nematodes with certain fungal and bacterial diseases of plants have been suggested by a number of early authors. Gilbert (1914) suggested that *Fusarium* wilt of cotton causes greater crop losses when root knot nematode is present. Hastings and Bosher (1938) found that meadow nematode and *Cylindrocarpon radicicola* Wr. cause greater damage in combination than is caused by either organism alone.

Young (1939) presented evidence indicating that root knot nematode decreases resistance of many tomato varieties *to Fusarium. To* the present time there have been numerous contributions to the subject of disease complexes involving—nematodes and other organisms.

Some of the best known of these associations are as

follows: meadow nematode and brown root rot of tobacco, meadow nematode and root rot disease of small grains *Aphelenchoides ritzema-bosi* and *Corynebacterium fascians* in cauliflower disease of strawberry sting nematode, *Belonolaimus gracilis,* and *Fusarium* wilt of cotton reniform nematode, *Rotylenchulus reniformis,* and *Fusarium wilt* of cotton root knot nematodes, *Meloidogyne spp.,* and black shank of tobacco root knot nematode and Granville wilt of cotton nematodes and bacterial wilt of carnations tobacco stunt nematode and *Fusarium* wilt of tobacco root knot nematodes, *Pratylenchus spp., Tylenchorhynchus claytoni* and black shank of tobacco root knot nematode and *Rhizoctonla* disease of cotton.

One of the most significant developments in these disease complexes involving nematodes is the discovery that certain disease-resistant varieties lose their resistance when nematodes are present along with the fungus or bacteria.

Equally important is the fact that if nematodes are controlled by nematocides the plants do not lose their resistance. It is also of interest that some of these relationships between nematodes, pathogenic fungi, and bacteria, have been discovered through the use of nematocides.

Certain of these diseases have been controlled by the use of nematocides before there was evidence of the cause of the disease.

These instances have sometimes resulted in the discovery that nematodes are the primary cause of the disease and that other associated organisms are secondary, e.g., brown root rot of tobacco.

Perhaps the most farreaching of the developments in this field is the discovery that nematodes are sometimes responsible for breaking of resistance and that resistance can be preserved by the use of soil treatments that reduce or control nematode populations.

FOLIAR AND SEED-BORNE NEMATODES

Most pathogenic nematodes live in the soil and invade

the roots of plants. On that account, most nematocides are soil treatments.

Still, there are a few foliar and seed-borne nematodes and they will be treated briefly before going into the main topic of soil-borne nematodes, and soil nematocides.

Foliar Nematodes

Several species in the genus *Aphelencholdes* are pathogens on the foliage of plants. They are ordinarily not present in large numbers in the soil, even in soil around infested plants. Control of these species with nematocides involves treatment of the foliage with chemicals that have relatively low phyto- toxicity.

A unique characteristic of several of these species is their ability to be ecto or endoparasitic depending on the host plant. *A. ritzema-bosi is* endoparasitic in chrysanthemum, but if transferred to strawberry it becomes an ectoparasite. It has been observed to be both endoparasitic and ectoparasitic on, gooseberry.

A. fragariae is ectoparasitic on strawberry but becomes an endoparasite in Croft lily and ferns. As ectoparasites these nematodes ordinarily are located in tightly folded leaf and flower buds. When the leaves unfold and are exposed to drying, the nematodes soon disappear from the exposed surfaces.

Practical control of foliar nematodes with chemicals has been obtained with relatively few materials. Chemicals are mot ordinarily used to control any of the *Anguina* spp. that attack. cultivated plants.

The use of sodium selenate as a systemic nematocide to control foliar nematode infestations in chrysanthemums has been reported by Dimock (1944). Tarjan (1950) investigated the use of this material as a soil treatment to control *Pratylenchus* spp. infesting boxwoods and indicated that root populations are significantly reduced.

Practical control of foliar type nematodes by the use of chemical sprays became possible with the development of the organic phosphates as insecticides. Raski and Allen (1948) used parathion as a foliar spray on strawberries infested with *Aphelenchoides fragariae.* Populations were reduced to a low level, but satisfactory control was rot obtained in tightly folded leaf buds.

Dimock and Ford (1950) obtained "*spectacular*" control of the foliar nematode of *chrysanthemum. Aphelenchoides ritzema-bosi,* with parathion sprays. Systox sprays have been found to be effective in experiments on the stem and bulb nematode in daffodils by Feder (1952) and in alfalfa by Bergeson (1955).

Seed-Borne Nematodes

Nematodes carried as seed contaminants, particularly stem and bulb nematode on onion, teazle, and clover seed can be successfully controlled by fumigation with methyl bromide, T. Goodey (1945) and J. B. Goodey (1949).

However, methyl bromide fumigation is mot effective against nematodes imhedded in plant tissues or within seeds or galls. This is undoubtedly due to poor penetration and to the fact that nematodes within galls (wheat nema) are usually very inactive at the time of treatment.

3-p-chlorophenyl-5-methyl rhodanine has been reported to control *A. besseyi* infestations of rice seed. Hot water treatments have been much more satisfactory for the treatment of bulbs and corms infested with nematodes.

SOIL-BORNE NEMATODES

Since most plant pathogenic nematodes live in the soil and attack the plants from that position, our best information -deals with soil-borne nematodes.

As a basis for understanding how nematocides act and how nematocides are used, we must first discuss the biology of the nematodes themselves. Plant nematodes, with few exceptions, are unable to complete their life cycle except in the presence of higher plants.

"Their life cycles are relatively simple and consist of egg, larval, and adult stages. All species, that have been thoroughly studied, have been found to undergo one larval molt in the egg, so that the youngest active stage found in the soil or within plant tissue is usually the second stage larva.

There are ordinarily three larval stages outside the egg. These larval stages and the adults are found in the soil in some species of plant parasites while in other species only the second stage larvae are found in the soil.

Because of differences in parasitic habit and certain specializations exhibited by some groups of plant pathogenic nematodes it is desirable to classify them into .a number of groups and consider each group separately.

Ectoparasites of Roots and Underground parts of Plants

The ectoparasitic nematodes are characterized by having all stages present in the soil around the roots of host plants. These nemas feed upon plant cells by means of the stomatostyle orodontostyle depending on the particular parasite concerned. Ordinarily, the ectoparasites of the underground parts of plants do not enter the roots.

They are able to move from one feeding site to another and they are active nematodes in the larval and adult stages. These nemas are also characterized by the fact that they lay their eggs singly in the soil and the eggs are not known to be protected by any specialized structures other than the egg shell.

In considering control of ectoparasites of underground plant parts we can conclude that it is unlikely that these will be present, in the soil, in the absence of a host, large numbers of eggs. The majority of the soil population will be adults and larvae.

So far as is known these stages show no particular resistance to the action of nematocides. The ectoparasites are regarded as easily killed by present-day nematocides. An exception is the stubby root nematode according to Perry (1953).

It has been reported by Todd and Furgeson (1956) that ethylene dibromide is superior to D-D for control of tobacco stunt nematode and by Good and Parham (1957) that ethylene dibromide is more effective against sting nematode.

Ectoparasitic nemas should theoretically be easier to control than endoparasites with postplanting applications of nematocides because they are not protected by plant tissues and because eggs deposited in the soil are without specialized protective structures.

Included in this group are nemas in the following genera: *Trichodorus*, *Tylenchorhynchus*, *Rotylenchus*, *Helicotylenchus*, *Belonolaimus*, *Doltchodorus*, *Xiphinema*, *Longidorus*, *Criconemoldes*, *Paratylenchus*, *Hemfcycliophora*, and *Criconema*.

Vagrant Endoparasites

Nematodes in this group are characterized by their endoparasitic habit as well as by the fact that larval and adult stages retain their ability to move actively in soil and roots. The females and males do not, at any time, become sessile or saccate.

In some respects the vagrant endoparasites are similar to the ectoparasitic group in that they are able to leave the feeding site. In addition, eggs are deposited singly.

Unlike the ectoparasites the vagrant endoparasitic species deposit the majority of their eggs within the host tissue. Thus, it is possible for the individual nematode to spend its entire life span within the host and never be exposed to the soil environment outside the host tissues.

The presence of endoparasitic nematodes within host tissues has an important implication with respect to the application of nematocides to soil. It is well established that nematodes in undecomposed root, bulb, corm, or tuber tissues are protected from the toxic action of the various nematocides.

In order to 1kill the nematodes and their eggs satisfactorily within the plant tissues, greater volumes of fumigant are usually required. It is, therefore, extremely important to recognize the type of nematode involved and to undertake preplanting treatments only after the infested roots of previous crops have decomposed or to use the higher dosage rate.

Species in the genera *Pratylenchus* and *Radopholus* are the most commonly encountered vagrant endoparasites. The nemas in these genera are frequently more difficult to control in ordinary field preplanting treatments than the infective larvae of the root knot nematodes.

There is a marked difference in ectoparasitic and vagrant endoparasitic nematodes with respect to their control with postplanting applications of nematocides.

The protection afforded the endoparasites by the host tissues adds materially to the difficulty of securing adequate population reductions. It has been observed that the vagrant endoparasitic forms that are outside root tissues are readily killed by postplanting treatments but those individuals inside plant tissues ordinarily survive treatment unless the root tissues are also killed by the nematocide.

It is thought that nematocides with relatively low phytotoxicity and long residual action are more effective because they remain in the soil and are toxic to nemas that leave plant tissues.

Experimental results to the present time indicate that postplanting treatments are generally of little value when applied to heavily infected mature plants.

Exposed Endoparasites (Noncyst-Forming)

The placement of several forms in this classification is questionable, but they do differ in their parasitic habit from those nemas previously discussed as well as those discussed in the following sections.

These nemas undergo rather extreme morphological changes in their development. The females become saccate and are unable to move from the site of feeding after they have penetrated into host plant tissues. The exposed sessile endoparasites never completely penetrate into the hust tissue.

The infective stage penetrates only partly into the host with the posterior portion of the body remaining outside the root. Males of these species do not penetrate plant tissues.

In addition to their sessile habit these nemas deposit their eggs into a gelatinous matrix which serves as a protective device against drying and possibly affords some protection from parasitic and predaceous soil organisms.

It is also known that the gelatinous matrix affords some protection from the toxic action of nematocides. However, unlike the nemas in the previous group the exposed sessile endoparasites are not at any time completely protected by plant tissues, and are exposed to the toxic action of nematocides regardless of whether they are present on roots at the time of treatment.

They are generally regarded as more susceptible to the action of nematocides than those nematodes that are completely protected by root tissues. The major characteristic of this group is the presence of the gelatinous matrix and the production of a relatively large number of eggs.

At certain times most of the population of nemas in this group occur as eggs. Unsatisfactory results may be obtained under such conditions unless the nematocide used has high ovicidal activity. The two best known species in this group are the citrus nematode, *Tylenchulus semipenetrans* Cobb, 1913, and the reniform nematode, *Rotylenchus reniformis* Linford and Oliveira, 1940.

Some reports indicate that postplanting treatments of crops infested with these nematodes have been more successful than of crops infested with endoparasites that are completely embedded in root tissues. Experimental results with such treatments on citrus infested with citrus nematode have been promising using 1, 2-dibromo-3-chloropropane.

This material and ethylene dibromide have been used successfully as side dressing treatments on pineapple infested with reniform nematode In the latter case the side dressing treatments are made at intervals following planting of the crop on beds receiving preplanting treatments with D—D— mixture or ethylene dibromide.

Nonexposed Sessile Parasites

In this group are included the root knot nematodes, *Nacobbus* species, and *Ditylenchus radicicola*, a pathogen on grasses. These nematodes are characterized by complete penetration of the infective stage into the host plant. In many instances the nematodes mature and produce eggs that are wholly or partly embedded in plant tissue.

In other cases, e.g., root knot nematodes, the female is inside the plant tissue and the eggs are deposited in a gelatinous matrix that is wholly or partly outside the tissue.

Additionally, species in these genera cause the formation of galls which completely or partially enclose the nematode. Under ordinary circumstances control of these nematodes is directed against the infective stage or stages in the soil.

The second stage larva is the infectivestage of root knot nematode and this probably is also the case with *Nacobbus*. Abundant experimental evidence in the literature indicates that when eggs and larvae occur in the roots, satisfactory control is difficult to obtain.

McClintock (1915) subjected egg masses of root knot nematode to mercuric chloride, formaldehyde, nicotine sulphate, lime sulphur, and sulfuric acid: and concluded that nematodes in egg masses are exceedingly difficult to kill.

It has been shown by Taylor (1943) and Stark (1948) that the presence of undecomposed roots containing egg masses presents one of the most difficult problems in controlling root knot nematode. The difficulties of killing nematodes in tissue and eggs protected by the gelatinous matrix apply when control of root knot nematodes is attempted around the roots of living plants.

The infective larvae in the soil are readily killed by the nematocide. In most cases the soil populations build up to a high level within a short time following treatment because of the numbers of nematodes escaping the action of the nematocide.

Satisfactory control under such conditions has not been obtained with regularity in experimental plots. The nematocidal chemicals that are presently available for use around the roots of living plants are not satisfactory in all respects.

In order to control nematodes adequately by treatment of living perennial plants, it would be desirable to have a nonphytotoxic systemic nematocide or a nonphytotoxic nematocide having long persistence in the soil.

Cyst-Forming Nematodes

The nematodes in this group belong to the genus *Heterodera*. They differ markedly from the preceding groups in their biology because of the presence of the cyst stage.

The infective larvae completely penetrate into host roots, but as the body of The immature female enlarges, it bursts from the root tissue, but remains attached to the feeding site by the head and neck.

The female body becomes saclike and completely filled with eggs at maturity. The nematode then gradually changes colour from thickening and tanning of the body wall, ceases to feed, and. may become detached from the root. The female body filled with eggs is referred to as the cyst. There are actually two types of biologies within this genus.

Some *Heterodera* spp. produce a gelatinous matrix into which the female deposits some eggs immediately upon reaching maturity. However, the majority of eggs are retained within the body.

This type of biology is characteristic of *H. schachit* Schmidt, *1871, H. cruciferae* Franklin, *1945, H. trifolii* Goffart, 1932, and *H. glycines* Ichinohe, 1952.

The eggs that are deposited in the matrix hatch within

a short time and the larvae are infective. In all of these species there may be several generations during the season.

This is the result, in part, of the hatching of eggs deposited in the gelatinous matrix and of eggs that hatch from the cyst during the same season they are produced.

In some species of *Heterodera* the females do not produce a *gelatinous matrix*. All of the eggs are retained within the body. These eggs ordinarily do not hatch except in the presence of a hatching factor produced by the roots of certain plants.

This means that the major portion of the soil population remains as eggs within the cyst except in the presence of plants producing the hatching factor. *H. rostochiensis Woll* 1923, the golden nematode of potato, is the best known example of this type of biology.

Allen and Raski (1950) have reported that eggs within the cysts of *H. schachili* are about as susceptible to D—D mixture as the infective larval stages of root knot nematodes.

Mai and Lautz (1953) found the larvae of *H. rostochiensis* to be slightly more susceptible than eggs in cysts. However, satisfactory control of field populations of *Heterodera spp.* are much more difficult to obtain than is the case with *Meloldogyne spp.*

Thorne and Jensen (1946) indicate that in Utah and Idaho satisfactory control of *H. schachtli* can be obtained in most instances with 25 gallons of D-D mixture per acre.

In other areas, due possibly to other soil factors, satisfactory controls are not regularly obtained. The cyst-forming nematodes present a difficult control problem with nematocides because each cyst represents a discrete colony of nematodes.

An important reservoir of infection remains if the nematocide fails to kill the eggs within a single cyst since each cyst may contain several hundred eggs. Most large-scale field treatments are designed to reduce nematode populations to levels that enable the production of satisfactory yields.

It appears that the cyst colonies are to some extent responsible for the failure of nematocides to reduce soil populations except when dosage rates are increased, sometimes beyond economic levels.

Nematode Distribution in the Soil

One of the main obstacles preventing complete eradication of nematodes is their distribution in the soil. It is now generally recognized that most nematode infestations occur throughout the root zone of the particular crop.

To kill all the nematodes present in the soil requires treatment with nematocides that will diffuse or he carried by water to depths of several feet. Root knot populations are greater at depths of 3 to 4 feet than at I to 2 feet in many California fields.

Under such circumstances commercial control is obtained by killing most of the nematodes in the top 3 feet of. soil. However, with perennial crops, e.g., citrus, grapes, and deciduous trees it is frequently necessary to treat with dosage rates that kill nematodes to a depth of at least 8 feet.

Kills at such depth can be obtained only by using large amounts of toxicant under proper conditions for the best nematocidal action. The upper 2 or 3 inches of soil frequently contain living nematodes following fumigation with volatile liquid nematocides such as D—D mixture and ethylene dibromide. This is primarily due to the rapid diffusion of these nematocides into the atmosphere from the surface layer.

This rapid loss prevents the attaining of lethal concentrations in the surface layers. The presence of a few nematodes at the surface after treatment is not important with most annual crops.

However, they are a problem in nursery crops subject to quarintine regulations and in treatments designed to give the long protection required with the tree and vine crops. Gas-tight covers, water seals, high dosage rates, and split applications can be used if maximum kills are required.

Vapam has been reported by Baines *et al.* (1957) to be very efficient in killing all nematodes to depths of 5 or 6 feet when applied in water drenches.

The presence of compaction layers, plow soles, and large -clods can protect nematodes under some circumstances. Thorne (1939) has shown that a plow sole restricts the downward dispersion of calcium cyanide applied for sugar beet nematode control.

METHODS OF APPLYING SOIL NEMATODES

The fact that most successful nematocides are volatile liquids with relatively low boiling points, and with few exceptions rather high vapor pressures, has necessitated the development of special types of application equipment.

For the treatment of relatively small areas a number of kinds of hand applicators have been devised.

Pressure Applicators

Many applicators operate on the principle of a displacement pump and are designed to deliver accurate dosage rates as well as different dosage rates depending on the length of the stroke. Taylor (1939) developed and was granted a public patent for such an applicator.

All subsequent applicators employ the same principle although numerous improvements have been devised. Hand applicators are designed to deliver a measured amount of nematocide into the soil at the injection site.

The depth of the injection is governed by the use of probes of varying length. The spacing of the injection sites may be varied depending on soil type, dosage rate, volatility of the nematocide, etc. In using hand applicators it is customary to mark the soil surface so as to properly space the injections.

Taylor (1939) and Chitwood (1939) have described methods of determining the most efficient spacings for the injection of nematocides in single injection sites. The method depends upon a knowledge of the effective lateral diffusion of the nematocide in a particular soil type.

This is determined by a bioassay method involving nematode kills obtained at varying distances from the injection point. The entire procedure is aimed at securing the most economical dosage rate and spacing for satisfactory nematode control.

In the treatment of large areas the principle of continuous flow is employed rather than injection of the nematocide at a single point.

Virtually all of such equipment in use at the present time employs the principle of continuous flow through a tube mounted on a chisel or shank that is drawn through the soil by power equipment.

Essentially the same principle is employed when carbon bisulphide is applied to the furrow in front of a plow share. The applicator devised by Neller and Allison (1935) for introducing chloropicrin and carbon bisulphide into the soil has been modified by growers, equipment manufacturers, and commercial companies. However, nearly all presently used applicators are based on the same principle.

Neller and Allison (1935) applied constant pressure to the tank containing the famigant and regulated the flow of the toxicant by the use of spray orifices and the speed of the ma chine.

Recent modifications include multiple shanks, constant pressure supplied by gear pumps operating from a power take off, or a ground wheel.

Dosage rates are regulated by pressure, size of orifice, and speed of the machine. Such equipment is usually mounted on a tractor capable of pulling as many as twelve or more shanks through the soil.

Various refinements have been devised until it is now possible to accurately apply dosage rates as low as 4 to 6 gallons per acre when the chisels points are spaced at 12 inches so that every square foot receive the desired dosage rate.

Gravity' Flow Applicators

Numerous types of gravity flow applicators have been devised. They are ordinarily employed to treat small acreages since they are relatively trouble free and are obtained at relatively low cost. Gravity flow combined with a constant head in the fumigant container allows for accurate metering of the fumigant.

This principle is frequently employed when nematocides are applied with a plow applicator. In this case the nematocide is allowed to flow into the furrow immediately in front of the plow share. Such equipment can be used on both single and multiple bottom plows.

A modification of the gravity flow applicator in which capillary tubing is used in place of the ordinary valve or orifice has made it possible to apply dosage rates as low as 0.5 gallons of liquid nematocide per acre.

In this case the rate of flow is governed by the bore of the capillary tube, its length, and the height of the liquid column. The use of this type of applicator depends on a constant speed in order to apply accurate dosages.

Solid Carriers

The effectiveness of modern nematocides when impregnate & upon solid carriers has been reported by Taylor and Golden > (1954) and Sasser and Nusbaum (1954). The latter authors applied ethylene dibromide with vermiculite as a carrier and employed a fertilizer rig for applying the impregnated vermiculite.

The principle involved is essentially that used in the conventional liquid applicators, that of applying continuous lines of the nematocide to the required depth in the soil.

This method has no advantage for field scale applications other than the possibility of using equipment designed to make fertilizer applications. Field tests conducted in California in 1955, 1956, and 1957 indicate that applications of dibromo-chloropropane impregnated on Attaclay were as effective as similar dosage rates of the liquid fumigant.

Greater cost per unit volume of nematocide and the difficulty of obtaining accurate dosage rates compare unfavorably with the liquid applications. Equipment designed especially for distributing desired dosage rates of nematocides on solid carriers is not presently available for large-scale treatments.

The packaging of volatile fumigants impregnated on solid carriers also adds to the expense of such treatments. Moreover, the nematocide is rapidly lost if the containers are left open for any length of time.

Drenches

The chemical and physical properties of several nematocides preclude their being injected into the soil. These chemicals are characterized by having extremely low vapour pressures and by not diffusing readily through the soil.

Some are relatively insoluble in water and must be applied as emulsions. One currently used material, sodium-N-methyl dithiocarbamate (Vapam) is very soluble in water and is ordinarily applied as a water solution drenched into the soil.

Drenches containing ethylene dibromide, D—D mixture, allyl alcohol, and similar materials in emulsified form have been used under special circumstances to control nematodes in the surface, 2 to 3 inches of soil.

The use of nematocides whose movement in the soil is dependent upon water has been generally restricted to special uses such as preplanting treatments for trees, vines, and nursery beds. Their use may depend on the presence of pathogenic organisms such as fungi, although nematodes may also be present and controlled by the treatment.

Over-all and Strip Treatments

Soil treatments may be applied over the whole of the area or in narrow strips where the row of crops will be. Area, over-all, or broadcast treatments involve treating the entire area to be planted.

The nematocide is usually applied in continuous lines

at the desired depth and spacing so as to effectively treat as much of the soil as possible. Such applications may also be made by hand injections.

Conventional treatments are usually made by applying the volatile liquid nematocides to a depth of 8 inches with 12 inch spacing of the chisel shanks. For special problems the depth of application .and the spacing may be varied.

Baines *et al.* (1957) recommend a spacing of 18 to 20 inches and a depth of 10 to 14 inches for preplanting treatment of old citrus soil. If, however, the soil contains large amounts of clay these authors . recommend a. spacing of 12 to 15 inches.

These treatments involve the application of 50 to 240 gallons of D-D mixture per acre, the amount used depending upon soil type and the depth of the soil. Row or strip treatments. are designed to reduce or eliminate nematode populations in the immediate planting area.

Row treatments have been developed over a long period of time and for a variety of situations. The treating of planting sites with carbon bisulphide for the control of *Armillaria mellea* embodies the same principles.

Among the first and most widely used of the row or strip treatments is that used in pineapple fields in Hawaii. Chloropicrin was used in this manner prior to the discovery of D—D mixture. The procedure in this case involved the injection of chloropicrin into the immediate soil area upon which plants were to be grown.

The planting area was covered subsequent to injection of the chemical by specially treated paper to aid in retaining the fumigant in the soil. The area between beds was left untreated. D—D mixture has been used in the same manner since it became available.

The basic idea is to provide protection for young plants for a period of time that will allow them to become well established before they are subjected to attack by large populations of nematodes. The protection afforded by row or bed treatments is not equal to that obtained by area treatments, but row or bed treatments are frequently more economical in terms of net profit.

It is common practice to employ row or bed treatments to control nematodes on cotton, tomato, bean, melons, and similar crops. Dosage rates are dependent upon row or bed spacing, soil type, the nematocide used, and the susceptibility of the particular crop to nematode damage.

Generally row treatments are not employed when the marketable portion of the crop is subject to nematode attack, e.g., carrots, Irish potato. Row treatments are not employed to treat land that is to be used to grow perennial crops.

Special Procedures

There has been limited use of nematocides to control *Ditylenchus spp.* Adults and larvae are usually found in the upper layer of the soil. This is the area where most volatile nematocides are least effective and high dosage rates in addition to special procedures are required to secure adequate control which involves covering the soil with gas-impervious covers or using split treatments.

The latter procedure is carried out by applying one-half the dosage rate and then plowing after a 2 or 3 day interval and injecting the other half. Dallimore (1955) has reported that a scraper attachment mounted in front of the plow provides a successful means of adequately treating the upper 3 or 4 inches of the spit.

The nematocide is injected and after an interval of 4 to 5 days the soil is plowed, at which time the scraper pushes the top soil into the furrow.

The plow then covers the soil in the furrow where it is exposed to the action of the nematocide. This method is expressly for the purpose of treating the upper layers of the soil and seems to be effective only against such nematodes as *Ditylenchous displace* and *D. destructor* that are found in upper soil layers.

The method has no appreciable advantage for use

against species that are distributed to considerable depths in the soil, e.g., root knot nematodes, cyst nematodes, burrowing nematode, and root lesion nematodes.

METHODS OF CONFINING SOIL FUMIGANTS

The effectiveness of volatile nematocides as a means of controlling nematodes in the soil is to a large extent dependent upon the retention of toxic concentrations of the vapors in the soil.

Certain of the physical properties of the soil, e.g., porosity, clay content, water content, compaction, and organic content, influence retention of the vapours.

If gas-impervious covers or water seals are not used to insure the retention of toxic concentrations of the toxicant, then the actual manipulations of the soil and its condition at and subsequent to treatment are extremely important.

Various devices have been used to smooth the surface of the soil following the injection of nematocides with chisel-type applicators. Harrowing, draging a chain, heavy iron bar, or wooden drag behind the -applicator tends to seal the soil surface resulting in better retention of toxic vapours.

In most situations, more effective retention seems to result if a ring-roller or similar implement is .pulled immediately after the applicator. In addition to smoothing the surface, the ring-roller has the added-advantage of compacting the surface layer.

Consistently good results have been obtained in California using this method on experimental plots. Water seals and gas-impervious covers have been mentioned previously and their main effect is to prevent rapid loss of the nematocide from the soil.

Polyethylene covers are regularly employed when soil is treated with methyl bromide, They may also be used with chloropicrin when a high degree of control is desirable. Similarly, water seals increase the effectiveness of chloropicrin.

It has been observed in the field that rain immediately following injection of such materials as D—D mixture and ethylene dibromide results in longer retention of the gases with attendant increased control of nematodes.

Phytotoxicity to subsequent plantings has also been observed when the interval between treating the planting was not increased to allow more time for the diffusion of the toxicant from the soil.

TREATMENT OF LIVING PLANTS (POSTPLANTING)

The injection of volatile liquids into soil around the roots of living plants has been attempted with a variety of materials. D—D mixture and ethylene dibromide are not satisfactory because they are phytotoxic.

Of the presently used volatile liquid nematocides only 1,2; dibromo-3-chloropropane seems to possess low enough phytotoxicity to enable its use around the roots of living plants at dosage rates that are nematocidal, Lownsbery and Sher (1958) have reported significant increase in growth of young walnut trees side-dressed with this material when the trees were planted in soil previously treated with a nematocide.

They indicate that growth rates were not satisfactor; for trees growing on preplanting fumigated soils, but that subsequent side-dressing treatment increased growth and reduced nematode populations.

The use of this material for the purpose of side-dressing established plantings is still in the experimental stage. It is probable that some of the unsatisfactory results that have been obtained are associated with attempts to rejuvenate older plants that had extremely poor root systems.

Satisfactory results have been reported from some experiments using dibromochloropropane to side-dress such crops as cotton and beans for the control of root knot nematode.

However, about an equal number of failures have also

been encountered in the field. In situations where increased yields have resulted, the increases do not compare favourably with those obtained with preplanting treatments with equal amounts of the same material.

In some instances cotton has been severely injured by side-dressing treatments, the treatments also resulted in lower yields than were obtained from untreated areas.

The organic phosphate, o-2,4-dichlorophenyl-o,o-diethylphospho-rothioate, (V-C 13) has been reported to be a satisfactory chemical for treatment of living plants. It is used primarily as an emulsion and drenched into the soil.

It is reported to be chemically stable in the soil, has a very low vapor pressure, and its movement in the soil depends on the movement of the water emulsion.

Christie and Perry (1958) have discussed various aspects of its use and indicate that it is an extremely promising material for use around living plants. V- C 13 applied as a drench is reported to improve the growth of turf by controlling associated pathogenic nematodes.

Tarjan (1955) has reported that aqueous emulsions of 3-pchlorophenyl-5-methyl rhodanine completely control root knot nematode infections when applied to potted tomato plants. He reported that the chemical reduces nematode populations in the soil around the roots of strawberry plants when it is mixed in the dry form with the soil.

PHYSICAL FACTORS INFLUENCING THE EFFICIENCY OF NEMATOCIDES

The soil is the greatest barrier to the successful use of nematocides. Over a period of years, a large body of evidence accumulated indicates that the success of conventional fumigation treatments is largely governed by the soil to which they are applied.

It is also recognized that little can be done to change those characteri-stics of soils that are unfavourable to the effective use of nematocides. The amount of clay and/or the amount of organic matter are the limiting factors that are fairly well fixed and the difficulties inherent in their presence respond only slightly to any practice that can be reasonably carried out in the field.

It is unfortunate from the practical aspects of killing. nematodes, under field conditions, that most of the precise studies on the characteristics of soils that inhibit the diffusion of gases have been made on dry soil.

However, there can be no doubt that some of the soil factors discussed in the following sections are operative, although in several instances experimental evidence is lacking or incomplete concerning the mechanisms that influence or restrict diffusion.

Sandy Soils

Sandy soils and sandy loam soils have relatively low organic and clay contents and are representative of soils in which volatile nematocides as well as other types of nematocides are most effective in controlling nematodes.

The effectiveness of volatile nematocides in these soils is directly attributable to the relatively unrestricted diffusion of the toxic vapors. It is known from the work of Hagan (1941), Call (1957), Wade (1955), and Stark (1948) that carbon bisulphide, ethylene dibromidge and chloropicrin are highly sorbed when they are in contact with dry soil.

Hagan (1941) has indicated that soil moisture is the most important factor limiting diffusion. Call' (1957) and Wade (1955) have shown that ethylene dibromide sorbed by dry soil can be released by the addition of moisture.

It, therefore, follows that moisture must be present in order to prevent the excessive sorption that takes place in dry soil. Lear (1956) has shown that Vapam applied as a concentrate -solution to surface soil is retained in the surface of wet soil .and is carried out of the surface of dry soil by addition of water.

Most consistent results are obtained by applying the complete treatment as a drench. In the field, volatile nematocides are applied to moist soils. It has been observed that these nematocides are most effective when they are applied to sandy loam soils that are at or near their moisture-holding capacity.

We must, therefore, assume that effective treatment of such soils requires a balance between water content and pore space that enables the gaseous phase of the nematocide to diffuse and reach toxic concentrations throughout the soil. It is further assumed that the toxic vapours go into solution in the water phase and nematodes are killed by contact with water solutions.

Clay Soils and Organic Soils

There are no precise data to indicate the exact clay or organic content of the soil that will restrict diffusion to the point where effective control is not obtained. If we assume as Call (1954) and Wade (1955) have indicated for ethylene dibromide that water inhibits adsorption of this material on soil particles, we must look for other causes for poor diffusion of the gaseous phase of volatile nematocides.

As indicated in Table elsewhere in this chapter, the volatile nematocides are slightly soluble in water, varying from 0.09 gm. per 100 ml. of water for methyl bromide to 0.43 gm. per 100 ml. of water for ethylene dibromide.

If a conventional dosage rate of 20 gallons per acre of D—D mixture is applied as a broadcast or area treatment, each cubic .foot of soil receives a dosage rate of 1.87 ml. of the nematocide.

Under field conditions there is sufficient water in each cubic foot of soil to dissolve the entire amount of D—D mixture (sol. 0.27 gm. per 100 ml. of water) applied.

It seems 'likely that in clay and organic soils, having field capacities exceeding *25%,* large amounts of the gaseous phase of the fumigant are dissolved in the water surrounding soil particles at the point of injection, thus restricting the degree and speed of diffusion.

In addition, the presence of smaller pore spaces .in clay soils and the fact that adsorbed water further decreases the size of the pores leads on to the conclusion that clay soils are not successfully treated with volatile nematocides because of the restrictions on movement imposed by water present in these soils.

It is highly probable that other factors are operative in the different types of clays and in organic soils where the situation is complicated by factors that are not well underst-ood at present. Goring and Youngson (1957) have shown that diffusion of ethylene dibromide is restricted by the addition of organic material to sandy soil and that different ,materials have different effects.

In treating clay and organic soils, poor or limited diffusion can be overcome to some extent by the application of higher dosage rates. However, there are economic limitations that sometimes make it impractical to apply dosage rates that are effective.

This is clearly the case with sugar beet nematode in - clay soils (moisture-holding capacity 20% or above) and in highly organic soils as shown by Allen and Raski (1950).

Similarly, the change in dosage rate that is required for various types of soil is indicated by the recommendation of Baines *et al.* (1957) of 60 gallons per acre of D-D mixture as a pre-planting treatment to control citrus nematode on sandy soil and 250 gallons per acre to achieve comparable kills in clay soils.

Moisture

As indicated in the preceding section, it is impossible to discuss soil type without reference to moisture unless dry soils are being considered.

However, the practical use of volatile nematocides never involves completely dry soils. We must, therefore, consider the conditions of moisture that are generally thought to be most advantageous for the use of volatile nematocides.

It is obviously not possible to have .precise data for every soil type encountered in the field. In sandy and sandy loam soils (moisture equivalent 5 to 12%), best results are obtained when treatments are made at or near field capacity.

Soils with high clay content cannot be cultivated when at field capacity and it is necessary that these soils be treated at a time when they are below their field capacity.

It is recommended that these soils should be treated when they are in suitable condition for cultural operations and in seed-bed condition so far as tilth is concerned. Van den Brande *et al.* (1954) have indicated that adequate soil moisture must be present in order to effectively reduce *Heterodera rostochiensis* populations.

Practically no data are available to make possible a comparison between dry and wet soils. There can be no doubt that reasonable soil moisture is desirable but it is not known whether soils with high clay content could be treated successfully if moisture content is near the wilting point. It is likely that the phenomenon of adsorption by soil particles becomes operative if the moisture content is reduced& below this level.

Temperature

The proper temperature for the application of nematocides is a controversial subject probably because no single investigation has been undertaken that includes factors that are operative under field conditions. McClellan *et al.* (1949) have shown that such materials as chloropicrin, D—D mixture, and ethylene dibromide are more effective at 85 to 95° F. than at lower temperatures.

However, these experiments do not have application to field situations since the containers prevented, escape of the nematocide. Furthermore, the length of the exposure period was very short so that at lower temperature not only would one expect slower diffusion, but also the activity of the nematodes would be reduced.

Although laboratory data may indicate greater nematocidal activity at higher temperatures, there is also more rapid diffusion from the soil into the atmosphere.

Successful nematode control has been obtained by the application of some nematocides to field soils at temperatures as low as 37°F. at the 8 inch depth.

It appears that if all other conditions are favorable, there is considerable latitude in the temperature requirements of nematocides. This is a fortunate circumstance since treatments must sometimes of necessity be applied in spring and fall at temperatures that are sometimes lower than those recommended on the basis of laboratory experiments.

Van den Brande *et al.* (1954) have shown that "treatments made at 36.5° F. are as effective as those made at 59° F. Although diffusion may be restricted at low temperatures, escape from the soil is likewise restricted so that satisfactory control is obtained but the period of time to achieve such control is necessarily longer.

Goring and Youngson (1957) have shown that ethylene dibromide does not diffuse in soil at 50°F. but they indicate that the nematocide remains in the soil and kills as the temperature rises.

Preparation of the Soil

Aside from adjusting soil moisture to the optimum level and waiting for favorable temperatures, it is possible to improve the conditions of the soil by cultural operations. Diffusion and resultant kill of nematodes is enhanced when the soil is in a friable condition.

Absence of large clods, compaction, and rough surface tend to provide conditions ,conductive to obtaining maximum efficiency of volatile soil fumigants. Undecomposed crop residues regardless of whether or not they contain nematodes or nematode eggs are detrimental.

These residues tend to collect upon the chisels and to make the surface of the soil rough, which in turn exposes more soil surface and increases diffusion into the atmosphere.

Stems or roots that protrude from the surface of the soil act as chimneys for the escape of the gaseous phase of the fumigant : Excellent results with the volatile soil fumigants are usually obtained when the soil is properly prepared and is free of crop residues, large clods, the surface smooth, and the moisture content is at a favorable level.

Posttreatment Conditions

Atmospheric conditions at, during, and following the - application of volatile soil fumigants are very important is determining the ultimate effectiveness of a nematocidal treatment. Immediately following treatment the soil surface should, be smoothed to fill any channels that maybe left by the chisels as they are pulled through the soil.

It is preferable to pull a ring-roller behind the fumigant applicator. Although. wind and temperatures following treatment cannot be controlled, it is important that the soil mass should remain undisturbed for a period of time following fumigation.

Any disturbance of the soil surface is apt to increase diffusion from the soil. If rain immediately follows treatment it will tend to seal the soil surface and increase the efficiency of the treatment.

If highly phytotoxic materials such as D—D mixture and similar materials are used, and rain follows the treatment, there is a possibility that retention of the toxicant may result in phytotoxicity if planting follows at the recommended interval.

Under such conditions the interval between treatment and planting. should be extended. This is extremely important where recommended intervals are based on minimum times under optimum conditions.

THE MODE OF ACTION OF NEMATOCIDES

Practically no information is available concerning the mode of action of any nematocide. Nearly all of these chemicals, are biocides and do not show enough specificity to indicate a mode of action that would be peculiar to nematodes.

It is assumed that since the phosphate insecticides are toxic to nematodes, these materials act upon the nervous system and the enzyme cholinesterase. It has been suggested by Chitwood and Chitwood (1950) that effective zematocides must be materials that change the permeability of the cuticle and should also be soluble in or dissolved by fat solvents.

However, there are little or no data available to support the necessity of penetration through the cuticle. It is easily observed when nematodes are exposed to water solutions of vital stains that penetration is most rapid through the oral opening, phasmids, vulva, and anus.

There is no reason to assume that most nomatocidal chemicals do not enter the body of the nematode through these avenues as well as through the cuticle. It is reasonable to assume that chemicals that are ovicidal must penetrate through the egg shell in order to be effective.

Ethylene dibromide which is not as ovicidal as D—D mixture or chloropicrin does not kill as rapidly as the latter materials. This might indicate that penetration through the cuticle or the egg shell is not as rapid with ethylene dibromide as with the other materials. Data are not available concerning the ovicidal properties of 1,2,-dibromo-3-chloropropane but since it does not kill larvae of root knot nematode as rapidly as ethylene dibromide it can be assumed that this nematocide might also have rather poor ovicidal properties.

The gelatinous matrix produced by root knot nematodes,. citrus nematode, reniform nematode, and some cyst nematodes protects eggs from nematocidal action. This has been shown when treatments of living roots are attempted.

It has been mentioned previously that the cyst wall does not afford an effective barrier to some nematocides and failure to control *Heterodera spp.* is probably not due to this factor.

Chapter 11 ELECTRICITY IN PLANTS

The processes of life have been found to *generate electric* fields in every organism that has been examined with suitable and sufficiently sensitive measuring *techniques*. In some organisms bioelectricity serves well-*recognized* functions.

The electrical disturbance of the nerve *impulse*, for example, carries information down the length of the nerve *fiber*. The central nervous system as a whole can be compared with a *telegraphic* exchange with electrical pathways linking the nerve cells in networks of almost unimaginable *complexity*.

When measuring techniques similar to those used by the nerve physiologist are applied to plants, it is found that they too generate electric fields and currents. Whether electricity plays any part in the growth or other metabolic activity of the plant, or is merely a by product of these processes, is not yet known.

Recent experiments have pointed, however, to possible ways in which the bioelectric fields and currents *generated* by a plant may serve in the co-ordination and control of its development.

It has been found, for example, that large *individual* plant cells respond to electrical, chemical or even *mechanical* stimulation in just the same way as a nerve cell does with an electrical impulse that sweeps along the surface of the cell. The delicately balanced *distribution* of *inorganic* salts in and around a living cell, whether plant or animal, accounts for its electrical properties.

Living tissues are largely liquid; they consist of watery *solutions* of salts separated into compartments by *membranes*. In solution the salt molecules -dissociate into electrically charged ions, some of which can pass more freely through the *membranes* than others.

Where there are concentration differences across a membrane, positive and negative charges become separated and an electric field is set up. These differences in concentration are maintained by pumps, driven by the *metabolism* of the cell, that push ions through the *membrane* in one direction or the other.

In order to explain potential difference in a given cell, therefore, one must take a complete *inventory* of the ions on each side of the membrane, determine how easily each ion can pass through the membrane and establish whether the ion is moving by diffusion or under an electric force across the membrane or is being *pumped*.

In seeking clues to the working of this cell, investigators have adopted various stratagems. They have extruded the vacuolar sap from the cell and compared its chemical content with that of the pond water.

Thanks to ingenious techniques developed by Nobuo Kamiya of Osaka University, even the cytoplasm that envelops the vacuole can be extracted and analyzed, although the results are uncertain because there is so little cytoplasm and one cannot be sure that its ionic content remains unaltered during extraction.

By the use of radio-active isotopes information has been gained about the movement of ions between the pond water and the cytoplasm and between the cytoplasm and the vacuolar sap. Finally, investigators . have inserted, glass micropipettes, filled with conducting salt solutions, into the cell and used them for measuring membrane potential differences and resistances.

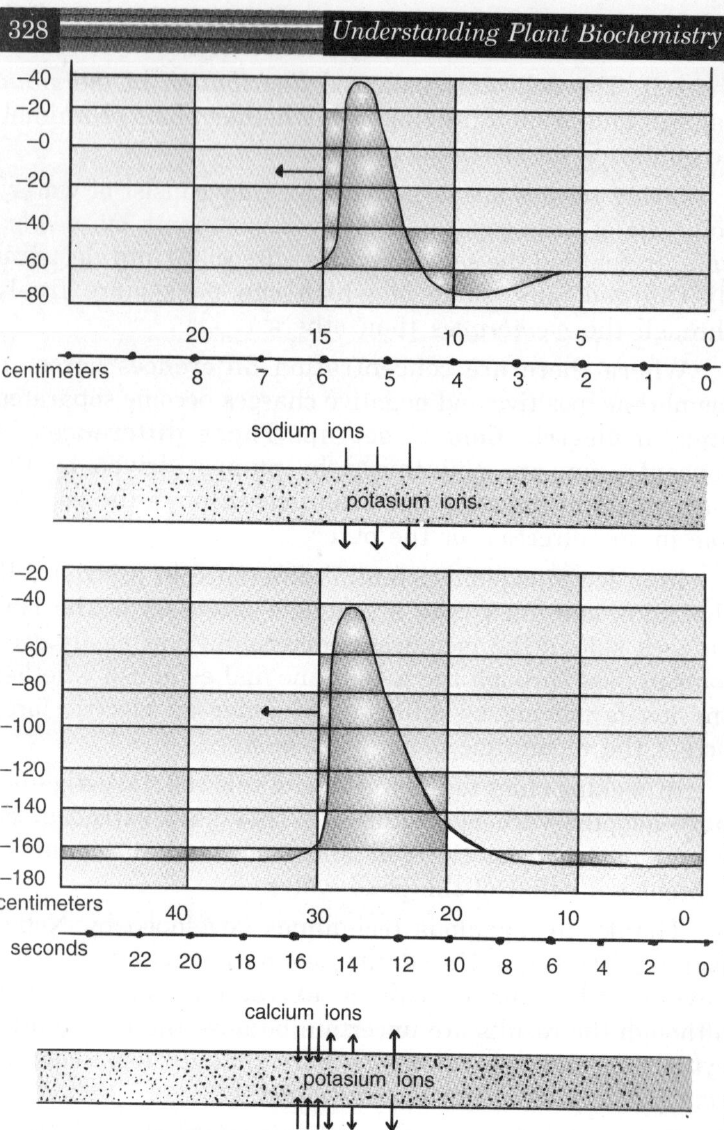

Figure 11.1: Effects of Stanulation on squid axon (top) and the Chara cell (bottom) are compared. In both case stimulation, makes the inside of the cell less negative. At a threshold' the membrane potential spikes into an action potential· wave (colored curves) that moves along the cell. The spike is triggered by a change in membrane permeability: sodium ions flow into the nerve cell, calcium ions into the Chara cell. Potassium then flows out to restore the resting. Potential the marked difference in wave velocity in the two calls.

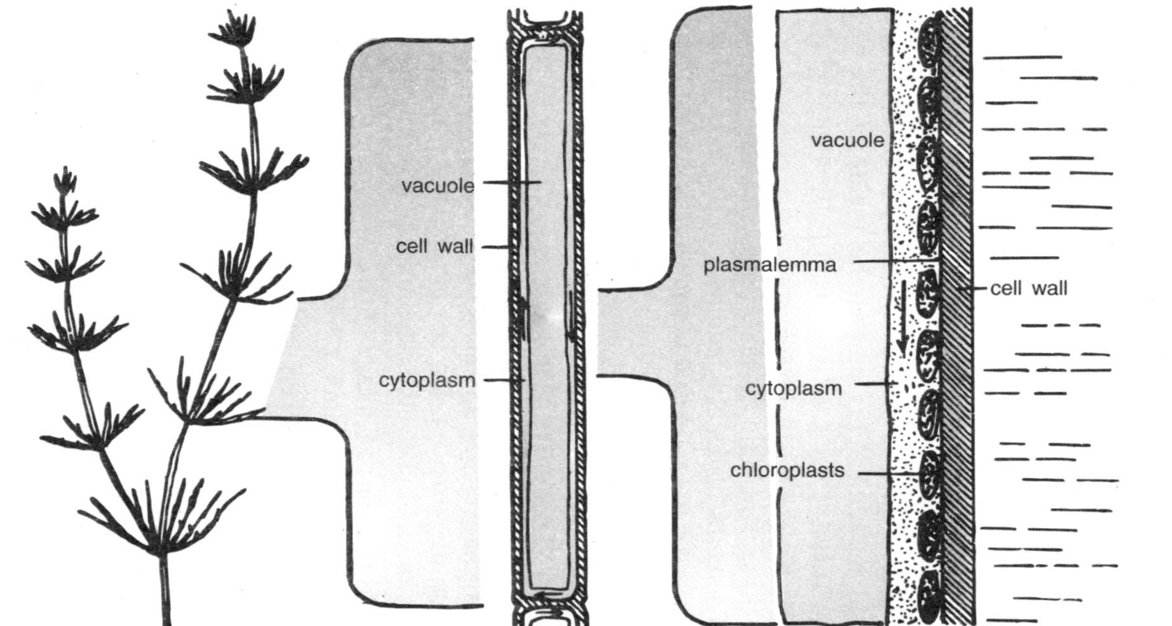

Figure 11.2: Chars Cell used in experiments on plant electricity is from Chara australis, a large fresh-water alga. The Plant. illustrated at left, has a long stem composed of a succession of single giant cells, one of which is indicated by the bracket and is enlarged in the drawing at center. A small segment of the cell wall is in turn enlarged in the drawing at the right. The cytoplasm is the living tissue of the cell and chloroplasts art the organs of photosynthesis. Plasmalemma is the controlling membrane. Vacuole is filled with sap.

Essentially the same methods and tools were employed by the nerve physiologists in their work on the giant axon. The present picture of the electro-chemistry of the *Chara* cell is most notably the product of investigations by J. Dainty at the University of Edinburgh and by A.B. Hope and N.A. Walker of the Commonwealth Scientific and Industrial Research Organisation in Australia.

It appears that the high salt concentration in the fluids of the cell is principally maintained by a chloride pump that pushes the negative chloride ion into the vacuole from the external medium. This makes the inside of the cell negative. As a result the positive ions of potassium, sodium and calcium are pulled in passively.

All of these ions-tend to leak back into the external medium. The cell's books are balanced in the case of each ion only when the net gain due to the electric force and the active pump, if these is one, offsets the loss through leakage. A weak outward pumping of sodium and calcium thus seems to supplement the inward chloride pump in maintaining the interior negative charge.

Because potassium can most easily pass in and out of the cell, it is this ion that has most control over the steady-state, or resting, potential. On the other hand, the resting membrane appears to be relatively impermeable to calcium.

The main barrier to leakage of the ions from the cell is apparently the plasmalemma, on the outer surface of the cytoplasm inside the cellulose wall.

This understanding of how the cell behaves when it is undisturbed sets the stage for consideration of the remarkable way in which it reacts to stimulation. One can stimulate the cell by passing a pulse of electric current through it by treating it chemically in various ways or simply by poking it gently with a fine probe.

The effect is to make the inside of the cell momentarily less negative. If the stimulus exceeds a certain threshold, the membrane potential in the stimulated region does not recover immediately; instead it continues to rise rapidly

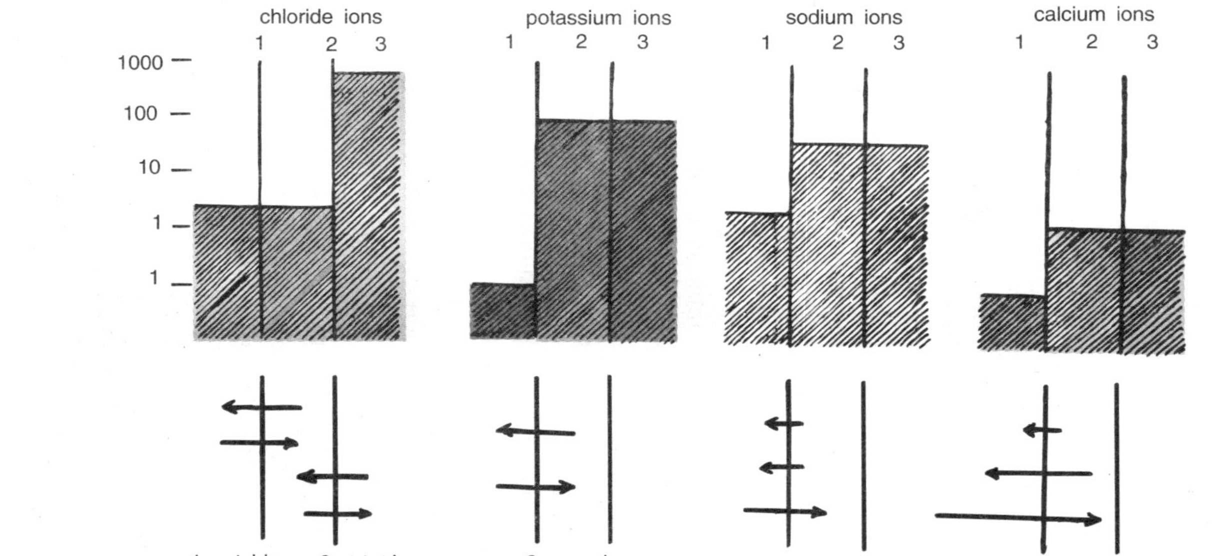

Figure 11.3: Concentrations of four ions inside Chara cells and in the pond water are maintained by three processes. The bars show the concentrations of each ion outside the cell (1), in the cytoplasm (2) and in the vacuole (3) Cytoplasmic concentrations are act well established. The gray arrows represent movement of ions us to concentration differences. The potential difference across the plasmalemma causes positive ions to move in and negative ions to move out (black arrows). Except in the case of potassium, an active pump (colored arrows) is required to balance ion movements. The arrow for pumping is broken in the case of calcium, since these ions may news reach equilibrium across the membrane. The high chloride concentration makes inside of the cell negative.

toward zero and then returns more slowly to its resting value.

Examination of the ion flow at this moment shows that the membrane in the stimulated region has become permeable to calcium; it is the inward rush of this positive ion that depolarizes the membrane.

The local flow of electric current raises the potential above the threshold in a neighboring region of membrane, triggering the same electrochemical changes there.

The disturbance thereby travels over the surface of the cell as a wave. This is almost exactly what happens when a nerve cell is stimulated, and the wave that sweeps over the plant cell fully merits description as an action potential wave, in the same class of phenomena as the nerve impulse.

The shapes of the -waves-are similar, and both waves are initiated by a stimulus ,that must reach, in each case, a threshold value. Of course there are differences also.

The plant cell is relatively sluggish. A complete action "spike" for *Chara* takes about 20 seconds, compared with a few milliseconds for a nerve, and it moves only a few centimeters per second along the cell (even more slowly when the cell is bathed in a weakly conducting solution) instead of many meters per second.

In the nerve cell it is a sudden inward movement of sodium, rather than calcium, that depolarizes the membrane. An outward movement of potassium ions subsequently restores the membrane potential to its resting value in the nerve and probably does so in the plant cell as well.

The most remarkable aspect of this comparison is not that there are differences but that two cells so far removed from each other on the biological scale should have active membrane properties with so many features in common.

One wonders if the action potential wave may not be a characteristic of all cells that has merely been adapted in the nerve cell to the function of communication.

If the relative slowness of the process in *Chara* is a

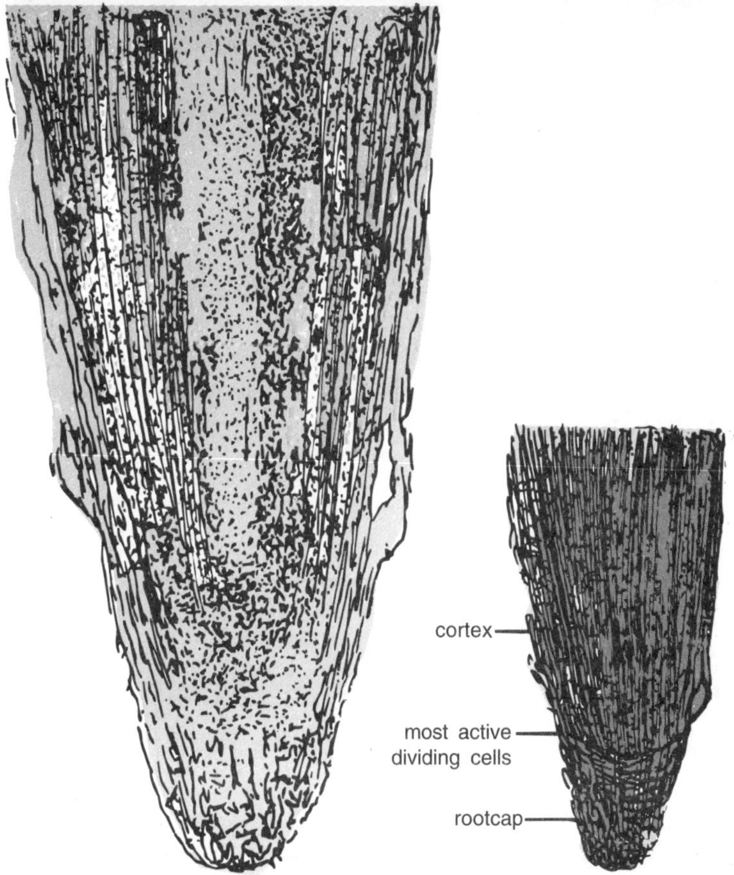

Figure 11.4: Bean-root tip is enlarged about 50 times in the photomicrograph at left. It is composed of a great number of individual cells in various stages of growth, division and development. The root cap protects the tip; call division is concentrated above the cap; cellular elorsation occurs primarily higher in the root, above the three-millimeter section depicted.

feature of plant,cells, this could be related to the general quiescence of plants compared with animals.

Anyone who has seen a speeded up movie of a growing plant, however, must have been impressed by the animal-like character of its movement and responses. In the case of the *Chara* cell no biological function for the action potential wave has yet been established.

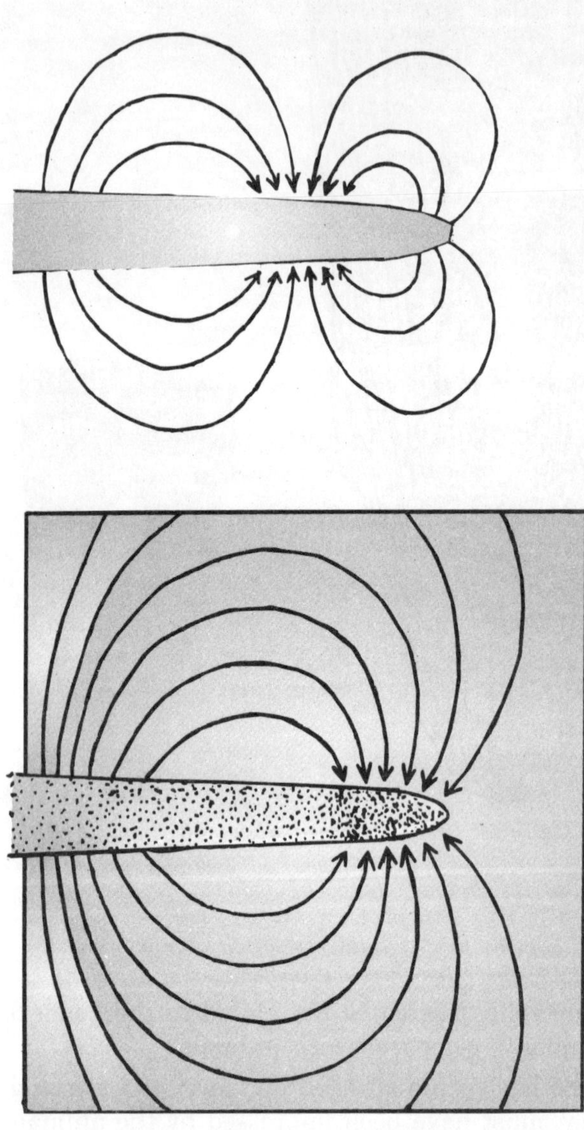

Figure 11.5: Electric Currents are found around bean roots glowing in salt solutions and are related to the concentration of specific ions in the roots. The root at left is growing in a'solution of potassium chloride, the one at right in a sodium chloride solution. Concentrations ,of potassium (fray) and sodium (color) are indicated by density of shading. Apparently each of the two positive ions is concentrated where it is most needed: potassium in the region of actively dividing cells and sodium in a region of maturing cells.

It is rarely seen to stimulate neighboring cells, but this may be because these cells are in contact only at their ends In another plant, with cells in more intimate contact, a stimulus from the environment might be transmitted from cell to cell.

It is interesting to note that the passage of the wave is closely linked to the streaming of the cytoplasm in the cell. Streaming in a stimulated cell does not cease everywhere at the instant of stimulation but stops progressively along the cell as the action wave moves along it.

Although it-is-not possible to follow in detail the electrical activity in the tiny individual cells of higher plants, the plant as a whole and its various organs produce fields and currents that can be measured and plotted.

The root of a beam plantgrowing in a weakly conducting medium, for example is found to act as an electric generator sending tiny currents into the medium and back through the root. This is probably because the growing plant is actively absorbing ions through its roots.

The flow of ions into the root and their movement to other locations in the plant produce a macroscopic electric field that: can be mapped by exploration with a voltage-measuring probe connected to a sensitive electromater.

The instrumentation„ must be highly sensitive, because only about a hundredth of a microampere flows across a square millimeter of root surface. The electric output of 100 billion roots would be needed to light a 100-watt lamp.

Observation of the flow of current tells some interesting things about what is going on in the plant. In a medium containing potassium, for instance, a root sends out a current from its upper part and back into itself near the tip.

Because the cells at the tip are actively dividing and the creation of newcytoplasm sets up a high demand for potassium, one may deduce that the in-flow of positively charged potassium ions is associated with the in flow of current at the tip. On the other hand, if the growth medium

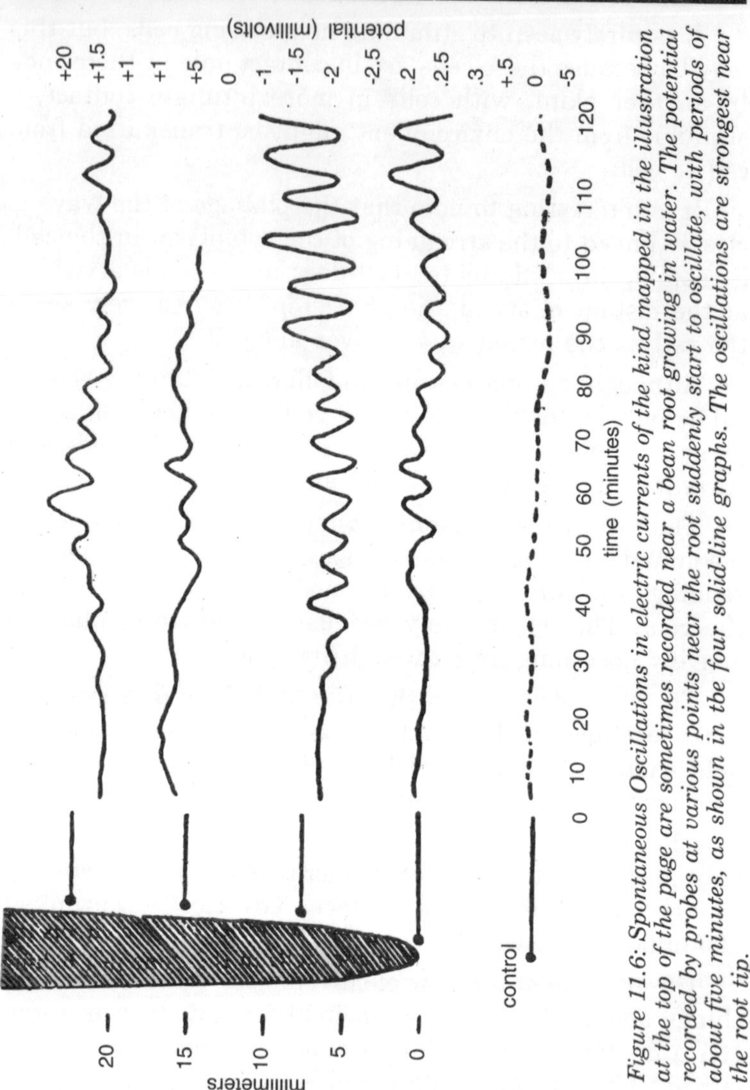

Figure 11.6: Spontaneous Oscillations in electric currents of the kind mapped in the illustration at the top of the page are sometimes recorded near a bean root growing in water. The potential recorded by probes at various points near the root suddenly start to oscillate, with periods of about five minutes, as shown in tbe four solid-line graphs. The oscillations are strongest near the root tip.

is rich in sodium, the root sends a current outward from both the tip and the base of the root and inward most strongly where the cells have almost reached their maximum length.

This suggests that these cells . are now Illing their vacuoles with the sodium, contributing . to the build-up of

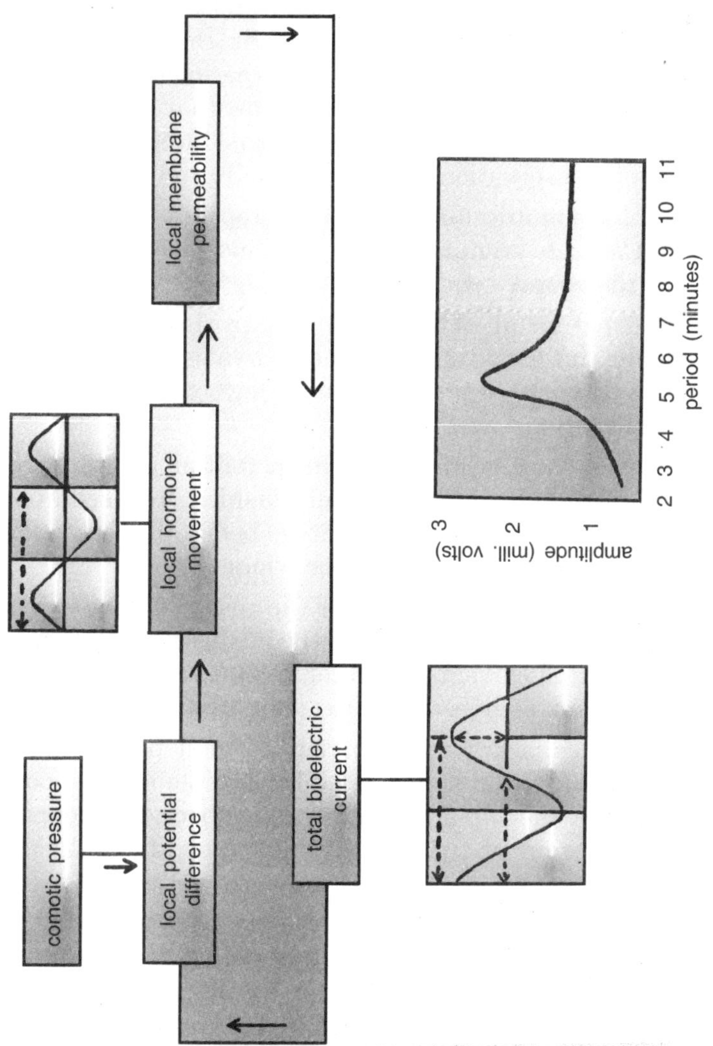

Figure 11.7: Feedback Loop is proposed to explain oscillations in the bean root's field. Rhythmic variation of the indo-leacetic acid (IAA) content of the medium induces oscillations of the same period (T) in the bioelectric current near the root. But these oscillations lag behind the input, oscillations.

osmotic pressure that gives the root its turgor. Analysis of the ion content of successive small cross sections of root tissue from the tip upward confirms these deductions. Further confirmation is supplied by experiments with radioactive sodium and potassium that show that their paths of entry into the root follow the paths indicated by our bioelectric observations.

That the multicellular root tissue reponds like the single cell of *Chara* to stimulation can be demonstrated by simply giving the root a gentle poke.

The potential at any point near the root changes suddenly and usually makes one or two oscillations before settling down to a steady state. A few roots behave in a more mysterious way.

Without any stimulation the potential near the root starts of oscillate in a rhythmic fashion, the scillations continuing for perhaps several hours before the root reverts to its normal steady electric behaviour.

The periods of oscillation for the roots we have studied are about five minutes. Evidently in these cases there is an alternating-current generator in the root as well as a direct-current source.

In **a** feedback control system a small portion of the energy of the output signal is fed back to the input opposite in phase to the input signal. The feedback thus opposes the coscillation of the signal and, when the linkage is properly adjusted, damps the response of the system.

In the case of our recorder, the feedback made the pen move quickly to a new position without—overshooting and stay there without oscillating, or "bunting."

By increasing the amount of the feedback we could cause the pea to make a few rapid oscillations before it settled down, and with a further increase we could make it oscillate wildly 'back and forth across the scale.

The reason for this is that there is always some delay in the feedback path and too much feedback too late can cause overshooting and oscillation instead of control. It

Figure 11.8: Apparatus for studying the electric field generated by a bean root is shown in this photograph. The bean plant is held by a clamp at center. The glass tubes are probes to measure bicelectric potentials. The lens at left foreground projects a magnified image of the root.

occurred to us that we had a modern recording device and an old-fashioned bean root behaving in the same way. The behaviour could be regarded as being perfectly natural in each case, because the feedback loop that is the genius of the automatic-control revolution in contemporary technology is really an adaptation of a universal principle that makes living.

Systems self-regulating. If the electrical oscillations of the bean root were indeed a symptom that some feedback loop had become over-corrected, what was the nature of the linkage?

We considered various sequences of processes that might form a loop with the characteristics required to fit the observed oscillations. The most promising is a scheme that involves the plant hormone called indoleacetic acid.

This hormone, it is believed, controls the elongation of the maturing plant cells in the zone just behind the growing point of a root or shoot. In very small concentrations it appears to soften the cell wall; this would allow osmotic pressure in the vacuole to lengthen the cell.

At higher concentrations it seems to inhibit elongation. According to our scheme electric forces set up in the root by the action of indoleacetic acid may provide the feed-back Iinkage that in turn controls the distribution of the hormone. As a weak acid if forms negative ions in solution.

The amount of indoleacetic acid reacting sites in the cell where it is active therefore likely to depend on local electric forces, particularly voltage changes across cellular membranes.

Since it appears to modify the permeability of the membrane to variousinorganic ions, the movement of indoleacetic acid in the plant tissue may affect the pattern of current flow around the root.

These current changes would in turn influencelocal potential' differences in the root tissue through which the negative ions of indoleacetic acid pass.

In this way the bioelectric current observed in the vicinity of the root may serve to close thefeedback loop between events- in the individual cell and; processes in the root as a whole. It is one thing to suggest such a cycle of feedback interactions and quite another to test it in a living plant in which the individual reactions cannot be isolated.

In one test we have used we subjected a root that was not itself producing oscillations to deliberately timed oscillation it the concentration of indoleacetic acid in the fluid medium bathing the root. The root responded by producing, electric oscillations all of the same period.

We found that we could elicit maximum oscillation from

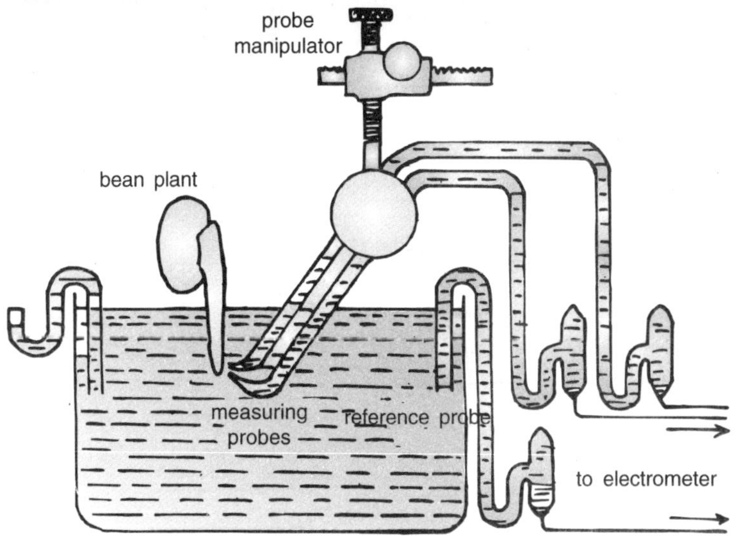

Figure 11.9: Potentials are measured as shown in this diagram of the apparatus in the photograph at the top. Two glass probes explore the vicinity of the root and another probe is used as a reference. Probes are connected to an electrometer through mercury-calomel cells.

the root at a period of about five minutes. This resonance identified the natural period of the loop, because it marked the time required for the imposed disturbance to travel around the loop and return, just one cycle later, to reinforce the next oscillation.

The hormone oscillation and the resulting electric oscillation are out of step with each other. This is, another expected characteristic of a feedback loop, in which there are always time lags. It gives further clues to the way the components may be linked up in the loop.

We have subjected the root to a similar "frequency response" test by varying the sugar content and thereby the osmotic pressure of the culture medium. This variable does not directly form part of the proposed feedback loop, although variation in osmotic pressure intimately affects the system.

It quickly alters the membrane potential in the root's

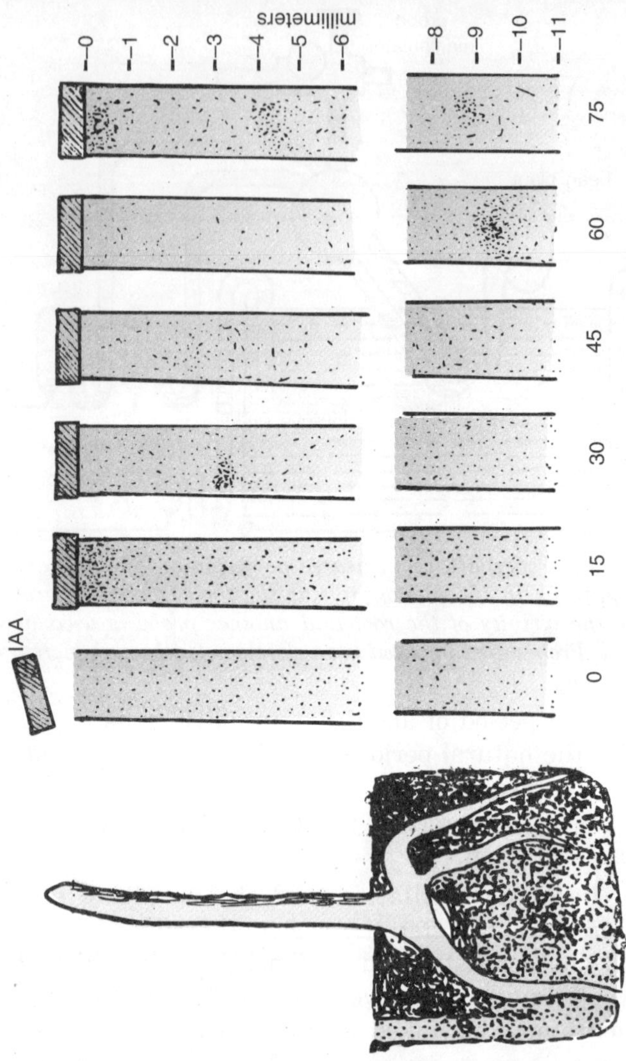

Figure 11.10: IAA manufactured by the tip of theoleoptile that sheathes a young oat shoot moves down the coleoptile to its growing region. When a block of agar containing I AA is placed on a decapitated coleopt the IAA's progress down the sheet is accompanied by an electric wave. The density of the gray shoding indicates the strength of the downward potential gradient that is recorded A small upward gradent (colour) precedes the initial downward pulse. The downward gradient may influence ;AA movement.

outer cells, probably by rapid water movement and change in the salt concentration in these cells. Resonance again occurs at periods of about five minutes. This, we expect, is close to the period of any spontaneous oscillatory behaviour of the root.

We are confident that there is a feed-back system in the root in which the interactions appear to be as described. It may even be that the over-all growth of the root is co-ordinated by the indicated interaction of hormone and electric field.

We have not, however, been able to observe any departure from normal growth in roots that have been subjected to sustained overcorrection and oscillation of the postulated. feedback system. The demonstration in a lower organism of a feedback system with characteristic periods of oscillation is of interest in still another connection.

This is the time sense, or "biological clock," of such organisms. It is now well known that all living systems from higher animals down to single-celled organisms behave in ways that vary rhythmically even when there is no apparent periodic change in their environment.

A built-in electrochemical oscillator governed by a feedback loop nicely fits the specifications for a biological clock. No less than the roots, the above ground portions of the plant generate electric fields that may have significance in growth processes.

As long ago as 1932, Frits W. Went, now director of the Missouri Botanical Carden, suggested that indoleacetic acid moves down in the coleoptile of the grasslike plants under the influence of electric forces.

The coleoptile is a hollow sheath that groves upward in the seedlings of these plants and serves as protection for the developing shoot; it is a favorite subject for study of the effects of light, gravity and various hormones on the plant bending.

Like the root tip, the tip of the coleoptile manufactures indoleacetic acid, which moves down the coleoptile to the growing region, where it controls the rate at which the cells elongate.

Winslow R. Briggs and his co-workers at Stanford University showed in 1957 that light shining on one side of the tip of a corn coleoptile makes some of the indoleacetic acid that would have traveled down the lighted side move down the darkened side instead.

The extra amount of hormone on the darkened side makes the cells there elongate more than those on the lighted side and the coleoptile bends toward the light. Recently, in partial confirmation of Went's prediction.

A.R. Schrank at the University of Texas has found lateral differences in potential around a coleoptile corresponding to the distribution of indoleacetic acid when the coleoptile is illuminated from one side. C.H. Hertz at the University of Lund in Sweden has found a similar distribution of potential in coleoptiles placed horizontally and in process of bending upward against the force of gravity. We have addressed our experimental effort in this connection to the question of how the indoleacetic acid moves down the coleoptile as fast as it does.

It moves at the relatively high speed of 15 millimeters per hour through tissue that does not appear to contain any long pipelike cells that might carry it downward ii a flowing solution.

Our observations show that a change in indoleacetic acid concentration in the coleoptile is accompanied by a change in electric field along the colcoptile surface. As the hormone moves down the plant, the electric change moves with it as an electric wave.

We can initiate these waves either by lighting the coleoptile from one side or by cutting off the tip aid placing some of the hormone on the cut end. The association of the hormone aid the electric field suggests a possible explanation for the rapid movement of the hormone.

Through a feedback interaction, such as that postulated for the root, the advancing front of indoleacetie acid sets up an electric field that in turn may push the hormone farther down the coleoptile.

Conservation and speculation so far have not answered the question of whether or not the electric fields set up by a growing plait influence its development. There are encouraging indications that they do play such a role. The discovery of more conclusive evidence awals further refinement ii techniques for the detection and perhaps the markulation of these fields.

INDEX

A

B

D

E

F

G

H

I

J

K

L

M

N

O

Q

R

S

T

U

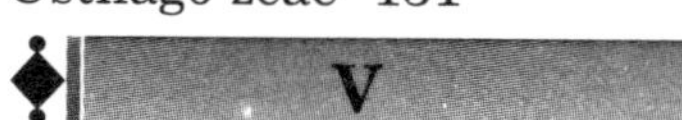

V

W

X

Y

Z